THE BOOK OF
WHO?

AN ONOMASTICON OF PEOPLE AND CHARACTERS REAL AND IMAGINARY

Compiled and edited by
Rodney Dale

COLLECTOR'S
REFERENCE
LIBRARY

To my wife, family and friends

This edition first published in 2004 by CRW Publishing Limited,
69 Gloucester Crescent, London NW1 7EG

ISBN 1 904919 22 7

Typeset and designed in Bliss by Bookcraft Limited, Stroud, Gloucestershire
Printed and bound in China by Imago

Contents

Introduction

I keep six honest serving men
(They taught me all I knew);
Their names are What and Why and When
And How and Where and Who.

Rudyard Kipling

The Book of Who? is the third in the series, following as it does *When?* and *Where?*, and preceding *What?* All gradually came into being when I was in that delightful garden at Probus in Cornwall, contemplating the raised Cornwall-shaped bed on whose surface are laid geological specimens from various parts of the Duchy. I envisaged an account of the materials from which matter, and hence the universe, is made; then the universe itself, then the earth, then its peoples, and so on and so on, until *The Book of Who?* emerged as part of the Grand Scheme.

The book is in two Parts. Part 1 is the A to Z, listing people (in the widest sense) in alphabetical order. This section also directs the seeker to Part 2, the groups, where people information is arranged in categories. By this arrangement, I intend to guide the seeker towards the information sought. The scope of such a work is enormous, but one purpose to inform my selection has been to help those solving crosswords and other types of quiz (again in the widest sense) which may explain some of the emphases.

No doubt the book will be used in many different ways for many different purposes, and I will welcome comments and feedback – preferably by e-mail.

Rodney Dale
Haddenham, Cambridgeshire 2004
info@fernhouse.com

Acknowledgements

Many people have helped to bring this book into being, and I would particularly like to thank Nick and Sue Webb whose research has been all important in providing the groups for Part 2.

I am also deeply indebted to Charlotte Edwards in my office for her crucial part in marshalling the computer files and keeping everything in order as the project developed.

Others have provided and confirmed information, made comments, and generally facilitated the work: Stephen Adamson, Anne Challis, Christopher Dunn, Lindsay Goddard, Richard Gregory, Mark Hatcher, Gina Keene, Meredith MacArdle, Michael and Valerie Grosvenor Myer, Georgia Parkes, Roger Pratt, Steve Puttick and Mike Waggett.

A book such as this stands or falls by its design, and I would like to thank John Button of Bookcraft Ltd, and typesetter Matt Gavan, for an especially creative relationship. Proofreader Graham Frankland's contribution to the reader's wellbeing has been more than helpful – having said which my shoulders accept the usual author's burden as the place where the buck stops.

And for their faith, patience, and ever-cheerful encouragement, Marcus Clapham, Clive Reynard and Ken Webb – in other words, CRW.

Abbreviations used in this book

=	generally indicates a translation
ACT	Australian Capital Territory (Australia)
aet	aged
aka	also known as
AS	Australian slang
b	born
C	century
c	about
d	died
et al	and others
HK	Hong Kong
inter alia	among others
nr	no relation
NSW	New South Wales (Australia)
NT	Northern Territory (Australia)
NZ	New Zealand
OE	Old English
PH	public holiday
PNG	Papua New Guinea
pron	pronounced
pt	part
Qld	Queensland (Australia)
qv	which see
RS	rhyming slang
SA	South Australia (Australia)
Tas	Tasmania (Australia)
UK	United Kingdom of Great Britain and Northern Ireland
US	United States of America
vi	see below
Vic	Victoria (Australia)
vs	see above
WA	Western Australia (Australia)
WW1	World War 1
WW2	World War 2

Abdals

In Moslem lore, it is through Abdals that the world continues to exist; their identity is known only to God. When an Abdal dies, God secretly appoints another.

Abdul

Generic soldiers' term (WW1) for a Turk (especially in uniform), or an Arab.

Abe, Old; Old Honest

Abraham Lincoln (1809–65), Republican president of the US 1861–5; assassinated by John Wilkes Booth.

Abelard, Peter

(1079–1142), scholar, philosopher and theologian, who founded schools of theology in Paris, and in Nogent-sur-Seine (Paraclete).

Abelites

A C4 CE North African Christian sect whose members were allowed to marry, but not to have sexual relations; they kept the sect going by adopting children.

Abo

Australian colloquialism short for Aboriginal; PC version = Native Australian.

Abominable Snowman

The elusive yeti of the Himalaya, of whom there have been no authenticated sightings, only questionable footprints.

Abra

Solomon's most beloved concubine.

Abraham

Hebrew patriarch (Gen 11–25), married to Sarah, had eight sons; God commanded Abraham to sacrifice one of them – Isaac – to test his obedience; having passed the test, Abraham was allowed to substitute a ram at the last minute; see Who's who in major religions of the world.

Abrahams, Ivor

See Royal Academicians.

Abu Bakr

See Who's who in major religions of the world.

Abu Talib

See Who's who in major religions of the world.

Ace

Someone of great skill, or worthy of admiration.

Part 1   A–Z

A.L.O.E.
A Lady Of England; pseudonym of the children's evangelical author Miss Charlotte Maria Tucker (1821–93) from 1854.

Aalto, Alvar
See Architects.

Aaron
The elder brother of Moses and first high priest of the Israelites.

Aaron, Hank
(Henry Louis Aaron *b* 1934) baseball outfielder for the Milwaukee (later Atlanta) Braves (1954–74), and the Milwaukee Brewers (1975–76). Member of the Baseball Hall of Fame 1982.

Abaddon
(Rev 9:11) The angel of the bottomless pit.

Abbasid(e)s
A powerful dynasty of caliphs that ruled Islam from 750 to 1258CE descended from Muhammad's uncle al-Abbas 652CE.

Abbott and Costello
Abbott, Bud (William) (1898–1974), US comedian. Born in Asbury Park, New Jersey, the son of a circus bareback rider. In 1931 he teamed up with Lou Costello, originally Louis Francis Cristillo (1908–50), born in Paterson, New Jersey. They began performing as a double act comedy team in Vaudeville, tall thin Abbott as the sour-tempered straight man and Costello short and chubby as the bumbling clown. They later brought their routines to film, television and radio. Their films include *Buck Privates* (1941), *Lost in a Harem* (1944), and *The Naughty Nineties* (1945), in which they performed their famous 'Who's on First' routine.

Abbot of Savigny, the
Granted a concession to build windmills in Bayeux, Coutances, and Evreux.

Abdallah
The father of Muhammad was so beautiful that 200 virgins were heartbroken when he married Amina.

Acheron
One of the Rivers of the Underworld.

Acheson, Dean Gooderham
(1873–1971), US lawyer and statesman, and shaper of foreign policy, particularly how to handle Soviet communism.

Achilles
Son of Pileus (King of the Myrmidons in Thessaly), grandson of Æacus; hero of Homer's *Iliad*. Slew Hector at Troy; slain by Paris, who wounded him in his vulnerable heel.

Acid freak; acid head
A user of LSD.

Ackroyd, Norman
See Royal Academicians.

Acres, Bob
A coward, named after a character in Sheridan's *The Rivals*.

Actæon
Huntsman in Greek mythology who, having seen Diana bathing naked, was changed into a stag, whereupon he was torn to pieces by his own hounds.

Acting jack
A (military) acting sergeant; he has the authority, but not the substantive rank.

Acton, Eliza
See Classical cooks.

Adam
According to Jewish history, the first male member of the human race, whose name in Greek is an acronym of arctos, dusis, anatole, mesembria = north, west, east, south; clay from which God created Adam was gathered from the four quarters of the earth by the angel Azarael, whom God then appointed the angel of death. See Who's who in major religions of the world.

Adam and Eve
See Who's who in cockney rhyming slang.

Adam, Robert
(1728–92), neo-classical architect particularly of the Adelphi, a district of London between the Strand and the River Thames.

Adams, Abigail
(1744–1818), wife of John Adams (2nd US President) and mother of John Quincy Adams (6th US President).

Adams, Charles Francis
(1807–86), son of John Quincy Adams, who dissuaded England from interfering in the US Civil War.

Adams, Frances (Fanny)
A young English girl murdered in 1867, whose name was ghoulishly used by British sailors as an epithet for tinned meat, and later meat stew. As Sweet Fanny Adams, whose initials (FA) stand also for 'f*ck-all', she metamorphosed into a synonym for 'nothing'.

Adams, John
(1735–1826), US statesman, 1st vice-president and 2nd president of the US, a key figure in the move toward independence.

Adams, John Quincy
(1767–1848), US statesman and 6th president of the US; son of John.

Adams, Norman
See Royal Academicians.

Adams, Richard
(b1920), British author of the international oryctolagian best-seller *Watership Down* (1972).

Addams, Jane
(1860–1935), US social worker and reformer; co-founder of Hull House in Chicago (1889), campaigner for better living conditions for the poor, and a beneficiary of the Nobel Peace Prize (1931).

Addison, Joseph
(1672–1719), British commentator and co-founder (with Richard Steele) of *The Spectator* (1711).

Addison, Thomas
(1793–1860), British physician; 'the father of modern endocrinology'; he described Addison's disease (of the adrenal glands) and is buried at Lanercost Priory.

Adenauer, Konrad
(1876–1967), German statesman suppressed by the Nazis, who rose again to become the first chancellor of the Federal Republic of Germany (1949–63).

Adept
Originally, one who has reached proficiency in alchemy; nowadays one who is good at anything.

Aditi
In Hindu mythology, the great earth mother; variously mother, wife and daughter of Vishnu. See **Who's who in major religions of the world**.

Adler, Alfred
(1870–1937), Austrian psychiatrist who broke away from his association with Freud, seeing everyone as an individual seeking to compensate for his inferiority, and sex as a means of demonstrating dominance.

Admetus
King of Thessaly; his wife, Alcestis, offered to die in his place.

Admirable Crichton
(1560–85); James Crichton, Scottish traveller personified in Sir Thomas Urquhart's play *The Exquisite Jewel*, on which was based Harrison Ainsworth's novel *The Admirable Crichton* (1837), a title used also by Sir James Barrie for his play (1902) wherein a hyper-resourceful butler takes charge by making life comfortable for his employers when they are all shipwrecked on a desert island, only to see the relationship revert when they are rescued.

Admirable Doctor, The
Roger Bacon, *Doctor mirabilis* (c1214–94), English philosopher.

Adonai
A Hebrew title for the Deity; see **IHVH**.

Adonais
Shelley's name for Keats in his elegy on the latter's death *Adonais* (1821).

Adonis
The beautiful son of Myrrha; beloved of Aphrodite; killed by a boar while hunting.

Adonis, 'a corpulent A of fifty'
The Prince Regent (later George IV) so described by Leigh Hunt, for which libel Hunt was imprisoned in 1813.

Adrammelech
A Babylonian deity to whom infants were sacrificed (2Kings 17:31).

Adrian IV
Nicholas Breakspear (c1100–59), the only English pope (1154–59).

Adventists
Those Protestants that expect the Second Coming at any minute. The movement was founded in the US (1831) by William Miller, and in

England in the following year. The present-day followers are the Seventh-Day Adventists.

Æacus

King of Œnopia, of such piety and integrity that on his death he was made one of the three judges of hell, along with Minos and Rhadamanthus; a son of Zeus.

Æëtes

King of Colchis; father of Medea; keeper of the Golden Fleece.

Ægeus

Father of Theseus; believing Theseus killed in Crete, he drowned himself; Aegean Sea named for him.

Ægisthus

Son of Thyestes; slew Atreus; with Clytemnestra, his paramour, slew Agamemnon; slain by Orestes.

Ægyptus

Brother of Danaus; his sons, except Lynceus, slain by Danaides.

AEIOU

Albert II and his successor Frederick III, C15 Emperors of Austria, used AEIOU to stand for Albert Electus Imperator Optimus Vivat (Long live Albert, the best elected emperor) and Archidux Electus Imperator Optime Vivat (Long live the Archduke [Albert's previous title] elected emperor for the best).

Ælfric

(c955–c1020), Anglo-Saxon author of *Homilies* and *Lives of the Saints*, also known as *Grammaticus* for his Latin grammar.

Æneas

Legendary Trojan leader, son of Anchises and Aphrodite, and hero of Virgil's *Aeneid*. Fell in love with, but abandoned, Dido:

> When Dido found Aeneas would not come
> She mourned in silence, and was Di-Do-Dum.
>
> Richard Porson,
> a Note on the Latin Gerund

Æolus

Keeper of the winds, which he gave to Odysseus in a bag; O's curious colleagues opened the bag and released a great storm.

Æschylus

(c525–456BCE), Greek dramatist whose innovations included supplementing the chorus with actors who spoke dialogue, and developing the costumes and scenery.

Æsculapius
See Asclepius.

Æson
King of loclus; father of Jason; overthrown by his brother Pelias; restored to youth by Medea.

Æsop
C6 BCE collector of Greek fables, who may himself be fabulous.

Æther
Personification of sky.

Æthra
Mother of Theseus.

Agamemnon
King of Mycenae; son of Atreus; brother of Menelaus; leader of Greeks against Troy; slain on his return home by Clytemnestra and Aegisthus.

Aggerawayter
Jerry Cruncher's name for his wife in Dickens's *A Tale of Two Cities*.

Aglaia
Brilliance; with Euphrosyne and Thalia one of the three Graces; daughters of Zeus and Eurynome.

Agni
See Who's who in major religions of the world.

Agrippina
See Some famous mistresses.

Aintree Iron
Brian Epstein, 'the fifth Beatle', from the double rhyming slang Iron = Brian and iron hoof = poof (from Aintree, a district of Liverpool).

Airbrain, Airhead
A nincompoop.

Aisha
See Who's who in major religions of the world.

Aitchison, Craigie
See Royal Academicians.

Ajax
Greek warrior; killed himself at Troy because Achilles's armour was awarded to Odysseus.

Akershem, Sophronia
A fast young society lady in Dickens's *Our Mutual Friend*.

Al Borak
Muhammad's 'horse', said to have been able to speak with a human voice.

Alastor
A house demon; the skeleton in the cupboard that torments a family so burdened.

Albert
See Fashion Eponyms.

Alberti, Leon Battista
See Gardeners and gardening writers.

Alcestis
Wife of Admetus; offered to die in his place but saved from death by Hercules.

Alcmaeon
Greek physician; see Medical pioneers.

Alcmene
Wife of Amphitryon; mother by Zeus of Hercules.

Alcyone
One of the Pleiades, and one of seven daughters of Atlas, transformed into heavenly constellation, of which six stars are visible.

Alecto
One of the Furies, also known as Erinyes or Eumenides.

Alectryon
Youth changed by Ares into a cockerel.

Alethia
Greek name meaning Wisdom.

Ali
See Who's who in major religions of the world.

Alibi Ike
One who always has an explanation – however implausible – for his dubious actions. *Alibi* (L) = elsewhere; but has shifted from geographical impossibility to embrace any old excuse.

Allbutt, Thomas Clifford
English physician after whom was named Clifford Allbutt ward, part of the larger Musgrave ward at the very top of old Addenbrooke's Hospital, Cambridge; see Medical pioneers.

Al-Sadat, Mohamed Anwar
See Nobel Peace Prizewinners.

Alsop, Will
See Royal Academicians.

Althæa
Wife of Oeneus; mother of Meleager.

Alvin
Conmen's generic codename for a sucker, mark or patsy.

Amazons
Female warriors in Asia Minor; supported Troy against Greeks.

Ambrosian monks
See Who's who in major religions of the world.

Ambulance chaser
A less-than-ethical lawyer who persuades accident victims to sue for damages (sometimes for an exorbitant cut of any award). The result of the 'compensation culture' has been a huge increase in insurance premiums (or sometimes a dearth of insurers), and people afraid to do anything which might result in their being sued – and, worse, employers who prevent their employees from exercising common-sense and humanity lest they should be sued.

Amis, Kingsley
See Booker Prizewinners.

Amor
The Roman equivalent of Eros.

Ampère
See Scientific eponyms.

Amphion
Musician; husband of Niobe; charmed stones to build fortifications for Thebes.

Amphitrite
Sea goddess; wife of Poseidon.

Amphitryon
Husband of Alcmene.

Anaximander of Miletus
Invented the first sundial; see Technologists who made the modern world.

Anchises
Father of Æneas.

Ancient of Days
Thought to be an epithet for God; see Daniel 7:9 'I beheld that the thrones were cast down, and the Ancient of Days did sit ...' and Sir Robert Grant's hymn 'O worship the King'. The *Zohar*, however, takes a different view.

Ancile
Sacred shield that fell from heavens; palladium of Rome.

Andra
A Greek name meaning Strong and Courageous.

Andræmon
Husband of Dryope.

Andreasen, Marta
See Political scandals.

Andrew
See Who's who in major religions of the world.

Andromache
Wife of Hector.

Andromeda
Daughter of Cepheus; chained to cliff for monster to devour; rescued by Perseus.

Ångström
See Scientific eponyms.

Annan, Kofi
See Nobel Peace Prizewinners.

Anteia
Wife of Proetus; tried to induce Bellerophon to elope with her.

Anteros
God who avenged unrequited love.

Antigone
Daughter of Oedipus; accompanied him to Colonus; performed burial rite for Polynices and hanged herself.

Antinoüs
Leader of suitors of Penelope; slain by Odysseus.

Aphrodite (Venus)
Goddess of love and beauty; daughter of Zeus and Dione; mother of Eros; loved Adonis.

Apicius, Marcus Gabius
See Classical cooks.

Apollo
God of beauty, poetry, music; later identified with Helios as Phoebus Apollo; son of Zeus and Leto.

Apollo knot
See Fashion Eponyms.

Apple-polisher
Deriving from 'an apple for the teacher', extended to one who sucks up to another.

Aquilo
One of the Winds. See Boreas.

Arachne
Maiden who challenged Athena to weaving contest; changed to spider.

Arafat, Yasser
See Nobel Peace Prizewinners.

Archimedes
Formalised the principle of leverage; see Technologists who made the modern world.

Ares (Mars)
God of war; son of Zeus and Hera.

Argo
Ship in which Jason and followers sailed to Colchis for Golden Fleece.

Argus
Monster with one hundred eyes; slain by Hermes; his eyes placed by Hera into the peacock's tail.

Ariadne
Daughter of Minos; aided Theseus in slaying Minotaur; deserted by him on island of Naxos and married Dionysus.

Arion
Adrastos's horse, said to have been able to speak with a human voice.

Arion
Musician; thrown overboard by pirates but saved by dolphin.

Armfield, Diana
See Royal Academicians.

Armin, Robert
See Shakespeare's players.

ar-Rumi, Jalal ad-Din
Established Mawlawi order; see Occult leaders.

Artemis (Diana)
Goddess of moon; huntress; twin sister of Apollo.

Artful Dodger, The
See Who's who in cockney rhyming slang.

Arup, Ove
See Architects.

Asclepius (Æsculapius)
Mortal son of Apollo; slain by Zeus for raising dead; later deified as god of medicine. Also known as Asklepios.

Asher
See Who's who in major religions of the world.

Ashoka
See Who's who in major religions of the world.

Astarte
Phoenician goddess of love; variously identified with Aphrodite, Selene, and Artemis.

Asterope
The Roman equivalent of Sterope, and one of seven daughters of Atlas, transformed into heavenly constellation, of which six stars are visible.

Astraea
Goddess of Justice; daughter of Zeus and Themis.

Astrologer
One who purports to be able to guide a subject by an interpretation of the positions of the heavenly bodies at the time of that subject's birth, and their movements during the subject's life. It is difficult to provide a plausible mechanism whereby such an effect might work, other than the possibility of the subject's view of the world being shaped by the conditions obtaining when his or her consciousness developed. If this were to happen at, say, six months after one's birth, then it would be expected that those born in the winter would have a generally sunny view of life, and those born in the summer would have a generally cold and muffled view. But the way the perceived environment (not to mention interpersonal relationships) affects one's general interpretation of the way things are must depend on many factors. It must be said, however, that astrologers tend to agree on their readings, even though the way they might affect an individual may be so ambiguous as to be only in the eye of the beholder.

Atalanta
Princess who challenged her suitors to a foot race; Hippomenes won race and married her.

Athena (Minerva)
Goddess of wisdom; known poetically as Pallas Athene; sprang fully armed from head of Zeus.

Atlas
A Titan; held world on his shoulders as punishment for warring against Zeus; son of Iapetus; father of the Pleiades.

Atreus
King of Mycenae; father of Menelaus and Agamemnon; bro of Thyestes, three of whose sons he slew and served to him at banquet; slain by Aegisthus.

Atropos
Goddess of destiny, see Fates.

Atwood, Margaret
See Booker Prizewinners.

Aurora
Roman equivalent of Eos.

Auster
One of the Winds. See Notus.

Austin, Alfred
See Poets laureate.

Austin, J L
See Some important twentieth-century philosophers who analysed the subtleties of ordinary language.

Avernus
Infernal regions; name derived from small vaporous lake near Vesuvius which was fabled to kill birds and vegetation.

Ayer, A J
British philosopher, studied with the Vienna Circle; see Some important twentieth-century philosophers who analysed the subtleties of ordinary language.

Ayres, Gillian
See Royal Academicians.

Bacchus
Roman equivalent of Dionysus.

Bach family
See Famous families.

Bailey, David
'Who do you think you are – David Bailey?' catch-phrase resulting from the iconic sixties photographer's appearance in an advertisement for Olympus cameras.

Balaam's ass
Said to have been able to speak with a human voice.

Banana bender
Queenslander (AS).

Banting, Frederick Grant
See Medical pioneers.

Barker, Pat
See Booker Prizewinners.

Barker, Ronnie
British comedian, who wrote as Bob Ferris or Gerald Wiley so that his work would be judged on its own merits.

Barkla, Charles Glover
See Medical pioneers.

Barleycorn, John
Personification of the Demon Drink.

Barnabas
See Who's who in major religions of the world.

Barnaby Rudge
See Who's who in cockney rhyming slang.

Bartholinus, Thomas
See Medical pioneers.

Bartholomew
See Who's who in major religions of the world.

Baudrillard, Jean
French; see Some important twentieth-century philosophers who analysed the subtleties of ordinary language.

Beaufort scale
See Scientific eponyms.

Becquerel
See Scientific eponyms.

Beethoven, Ludwig van
(1770–1827) German composer who greatly extended the form and scope of symphonic and chamber music, bridging the classical and romantic traditions. His works include nine symphonies, 16 string quartets, 32 piano sonatas, five piano concertos, a violin concerto, two masses, the opera *Fidelio* (1805), and choral music.

Beeton, Isabella
See Classical cooks.

Begin, Menachem
See Nobel Peace Prizewinners.

Behring, Emil von
See Medical pioneers.

Bell; Acton, Currer and Ellis
See Famous families.

Bellany, John
See Royal Academicians.

Bellerophon
Corinthian hero; killed Chimera with aid of Pegasus; tried to reach Olympus on Pegasus and was thrown to his death.

Bellona
Roman goddess of war.

Belo, Carlos Felipe Ximenes
See Nobel Peace Prizewinners.

Benfield, Robert
See Shakespeare's players.

Benjamin
See Who's who in major religions of the world.

Benson, Gordon
See Royal Academicians.

Berg, Adrian
See Royal Academicians.

Berger, John
See Booker Prizewinners.

Berners, Gerald Hugh Tyrhitt-Wilson, 14th Baron
(1883–1950) composer and eccentric who dyed his doves various colours and installed a spinet in the back of his Rolls-Royce.

Bernhardt, Sarah

Originally Sarah-Marie-Henriette Rosine Bernhardt (1844–1923), French actress. Born in Paris, made her debut as Iphigénie at the Comédie-Française in 1862, yet attracted little notice and so moved to the Odéon and played minor parts. She later won fame as Zanetto in François Coppée's *Le Passant* (1869) and as the Queen of Spain in Victor Hugo's *Ruy Blas* (1872). Her most famous roles include *Phèdre* (1877) and Marguerite in *La Dame aux camélias* (1884). Considered the greatest *tragédienne* of her day. She founded the Théâtre Sarah Bernhardt in 1899. She had to have a leg amputated in 1915, but continued to appear on stage to the end.

Betjeman, Sir John

See Poets laureate.

Biedermeier, Gottlieb

A fictional character, master of bourgeois bad taste, created by the German poet Ludwig Eichrocht (1827–92). Biedermeier gave his name to a style of furniture and interior decoration popular among the middle classes in Austria, Germany and Scandinavia in the 19th century (*fl* 1816–1848). Biedermeier painting aimed at naturalism, apparently reflected by the English Pre-Raphaelite Brotherhood who – wittingly or no – took over when Biedermeier ended.

Bier, August

See Medical pioneers.

Big Brother

An all-encompassing, seemingly benevolent but in fact oppressive and authoritarian government which is constantly monitoring its citizens. Invented by George Orwell (1903–1950) in his novel *Nineteen Eighty-Four* (1949). Also an inexplicably phenomenally successful television show placing a group of strangers in a house where their interactions are continuously televised.

Black Hand

Forerunner of the US Mafia.

Black pigeons of Dodona and Annon

Said to have been able to speak with a human voice.

Blackadder, Elizabeth

See Royal Academicians.

Blake, Peter
See Royal Academicians.

Blavatsky, Helena Petrovna
See Occult leaders.

Blessed Virgin Mary, Sisters of the Institute of the
See Who's who in major religions of the world.

Bloch, Konrad Emil
See Medical pioneers.

Bloomers
See Fashion Eponyms.

Blow, Sandra
See Royal Academicians.

Boleyn, Mary
See Some famous mistresses.

Bonaparte
Family name of Napoleon I, Jérome, Joseph, Louis and Lucien (*qqv*).

Bono
Paul David Hewson, a singer *b* Dublin 10 May 1960.

Boothby, Robert
See Political scandals.

Borden, Lizzie Andrew
(1860–1927) American woman accused of murdering her wealthy father and hated stepmother with an axe at Fall River, MA, in August 1892; who the murderer actually was has never been established with certainty. The case is immortalised in a children's playground rhyme:

> Lizzie Borden took an axe
>   And gave her mother forty whacks;
> When she saw what she had done
>   She gave her father forty-one.

Boreas
One of the Winds – the north wind.

Boulliau, Ismael
See Medical pioneers.

Bowey, Olwyn
See Royal Academicians.

Bowyer, William
See Royal Academicians.

Boy bishop

St Nicholas of Bari was reckoned to be pious from his earliest days, and was so named; a custom arose as a result that on his day (6 December) a boy should be chosen from a local or cathedral choir to act as a mock Bishop for three weeks, until Holy Innocents' Day (28 December); this practice was followed also at some public schools. Henry VIII abolished the custom in 1541, revived under Edward VI in 1552, and abolished for ever by Elizabeth I (she thought). The custom has been revived; at St Nicholas's Church, Tuxford, Nottinghamshire; on 6 December 2002, retired Bishop John Finney 'enthroned' nine-year-old Louis Maybe as boy bishop 'to help young people feel more included'. Louis Maybe handed his regalia on to eleven-year-old Amanda Brewer the following year, making her the first girl bishop.

Brady, Ian

See Hindley, Myra.

Brahma

See Who's who in major religions of the world.

Brahman

See Who's who in major religions of the world.

Brahmins

See Who's who in major religions of the world.

Brahms and Liszt

See Who's who in cockney rhyming slang.

Breakspear, Nicholas

See Adrian IV.

Brewer, Amanda

See Boy bishop.

Briareus

Monster of hundred hands; son of Uranus and Gaea.

Bridgeman, Charles

See Gardeners and gardening writers.

Bridges, Robert

See Poets laureate.

Brillat-Savarin, Jean-Anthelme de

See Classical cooks.

Briseis

Captive maiden given to Achilles; taken by Agamemnon in exch for loss of Chryseis, which caused Achilles to cease fighting, until death of Patroclus.

Brontë, Charlotte, Emily and Anne
See Famous families.

Brookner, Anita
A winner of the Booker Prize for Fiction; see Booker Prizewinners.

Brown Noser
See Apple-polisher.

Brown, Lancelot 'Capability'
See Gardeners and gardening writers.

Brown, Ralph
See Royal Academicians.

Bruce, David
British physician; see Medical pioneers.

Brun, Christopher Le
See Royal Academicians.

Bryan, George
See Shakespeare's players.

Bubble and Squeak
See Who's who in cockney rhyming slang.

Buddha, The
See Who's who in major religions of the world.

Buddhism
See Who's who in major religions of the world.

Bulbul-Bezar
Talking bird, said to have been able to speak with a human voice.

Burbage, Richard
See Shakespeare's players.

Burgess, Thomas
See The first Channel swimmers.

Burney, Fanny
(Frances, Mme d'Arblay – 1752–1840), daughter of the musician Dr Charles Burney and anonymous author of the epistolary best-selling novel *Evelina* (1778).

Butler, James
See Royal Academicians.

Byatt, A S
See Booker Prizewinners.

Cadbury-Brown, Professor H T
See Royal Academicians.

Cadmus
Brother of Europa; planter of dragon seeds from which first Thebans sprang.

Calliope
One of the Muses and goddesses presiding over arts and sciences (epic poetry) and daughter of Zeus and Mnemosyne.

Calmette, Albert
See Medical pioneers.

Calvi, Roberto
See Political scandals.

Calypso
Sea nymph; kept Odysseus on her island Ogygia for seven years.

Camp, Jeffery
See Royal Academicians.

Cardigan
See Fashion eponyms.

Careme, Antoine
See Classical cooks.

Carey, Peter
See Booker Prizewinners.

Carnap, Rudolf
See Some important twentieth-century philosophers who analysed the subtleties of ordinary language.

Carrel, Alexis
See Medical pioneers.

Carroll, James
See Medical pioneers.

Carter, Jimmy Jr
See Nobel Peace Prizewinners.

Cassandra
Daughter of Priam; prophetess who was never believed; slain with Agamemnon.

Castalia
In Greek Mythology the most powerful Oracle was the oracle of Delphi. People would come from all around with question, seeking answers. The oracle's source of inspiration sprang forth from a fountain called Castalia.

Castor and Pollux
The Twin sons of Jupiter and Leda, also known as the Dioscuri.

Caulfield, Patrick
See Royal Academicians.

Caventou, Joseph Bienaimé
See Medical pioneers.

Celaeno
One of the Pleiades, and one of seven daughters of Atlas, transformed into heavenly constellation, of which six stars are visible.

Celsius
See Scientific eponyms.

Ceng Gong-Liang
Publisher of three recipes for gunpowder.

Centaurs
Beings half man and half horse; lived in the mountains of Thessaly.

Cephalus
Hunter; accidentally killed his wife Procris with his spear.

Cepheus
King of Ethiopia; father of Andromeda.

Cerberus
Three-headed dog guarding entrance to Hades.

Ceres
Roman equivalent of Demeter. Goddess of Harvest.

Chain, Ernst Boris
See Medical pioneers.

Chambers, Sir William
See Gardeners and gardening writers.

Chaos
Formless void; personified as first of gods.

Chaplin, Sir Charles Spencer; Charlie Chaplin
(1889–1977) English film comedian and director, creator of the 'Little Fellow' with baggy trousers, toothbrush moustache, and cane.

Charon
Boatman on Styx who carried souls of dead to Hades; son of Erebus.

Charybdis
Female monster; personification of whirlpool.

Cheshire Cat
Character in Lewis Carroll's *Alice's Adventures in Wonderland*, who has the ability to appear and disappear. After being reprimanded by Alice, the Cat vanished slowly, starting with the tail and ending with the grin. The saying 'to grin like a Cheshire Cat' was in use in Cheshire long before Carroll published the story. Several local families used cats or lions within their coats of arms, many of whom seemed to be grinning.

Chesterfield
See Fashion eponyms.

Childe Harold
A man sated with the world, who roams from place to place, to kill time and escape from himself. From Byron's poem *Childe Harold's Pilgrimage*, which took seven years to write.

Chimera
Female monster with head of lion, body of goat, tail of serpent; killed by Bellerophon.

China Plate
See Who's who in cockney rhyming slang.

Chiron
Most famous of centaurs.

Christianity
See Who's who in major religions of the world.

Christie, John Reginald Halliday
(1898–1953) English murderer. Was born in Yorkshire and was hanged for the murder of his wife and confessed to strangling five other women. This case played an important part in altering legislation affecting the death penalty, as his lodger Timothy Evans had already been hanged for one of Christie's murders.

Christopher, Ann
See Royal Academicians.

Chronos
Personification of time.

Chronotype
Factor in one's make-up that determines whether one is a lark (early to bed, early to rise) or an owl (late to rise, late to bed), or somewhere in between.

Chryseis
Captive maiden given to Agamemnon; his refusal to accept ransom from her father Chryses caused Apollo to send plague on Greeks besieging Troy.

Church of England
See Who's who in major religions of the world.

Cibber, Colley
See Poets laureate.

Circe
Sorceress; daughter of Helios; changed Odysseus's men into swine.

Circuit Judge
A member of the judiciary who travels round a 'circuit' of courts administering justice locally.

Circuit Rider
A preacher, often non-conformist, who travelled from town to town, setting up temporary churches in areas where it was easier for him to travel than for farmers or ranchers to be away from their work for however long it took to get married or whatever.

Clarke, Geoffrey
See Royal Academicians.

Clatworthy, Robert
See Royal Academicians.

Cleopatra
See Some famous mistresses.

Clifford, Rosamond
See Some famous mistresses.

Clio
One of the Muses and goddesses presiding over arts and sciences (history) and daughter of Zeus and Mnemosyne.

Clotho
Goddess of destiny, see Fates.

Clytemnestra
Wife of Agamemnon, whom she slew with aid of her paramour, Aegisthus; slain by her son Orestes.

Cockrill, Maurice
See Royal Academicians.

Cocytus
One of the Rivers of Underworld.

Coetzee, J M
See Booker Prizewinners.

Coke (pron Cook)
On 17 December 1849, William Coke of Holkham (pron hokum) in Norfolk took delivery of a felt hat from Lock & Co of St James's (London), designed and manufactured by Thomas and William Bowler. Coke stamped on it twice, pronounced it acceptable and paid 12/- for it. Lock's still call the bowler hat a 'coke'.

Coker, Peter
See Royal Academicians.

Cole, Sir Henry
(1808–82) organiser of the Great Exhibition of 1851 under the patronage of Prince Albert, and first director (1853–71) of the Museum of Manufactures at Marlborough House set up after the Great Exhibition, which later became part of the South Kensington Museum, renamed the Victoria and Albert museum in 1899.

Colton, Gardner Quincy
See Medical pioneers.

Comical Ali
Mohammed al-Sharif, the starry-eyed Iraqi spin-doctor.

Compton, Arthur Holly
See Medical pioneers.

Comrade
Fortunio's horse, said to have been able to speak with a human voice.

Condell, Henry
See Shakespeare's players.

Confucianism
See Who's who in major religions of the world.

Confucius
See Who's who in major religions of the world.

Cook, Peter
See Royal Academicians.

Cooke, Alexander
See Shakespeare's players.

Cooke, Jean
See Royal Academicians.

Cooper, Eileen
See Royal Academicians.

Corbusier, Le
See Architects.

Corson, Millie
See The first Channel swimmers.

Council of Ten
A secret tribunal exercising unlimited powers in the old Venetian republic. It was instituted in 1310 with ten members. The number was then increased to 17 and it continued in active existence until the fall of the republic in 1797.

Cowly, Richard
See Shakespeare's players.

Cragg, Tony
See Royal Academicians.

Craxton, John
See Royal Academicians.

Creon
Father of Jocasta; forbade burial of Polynices; ordered burial alive of Antigone.

Creüsa
Princess of Corinth, for whom Jason deserted Medea; slain by Medea, who sent her poisoned robe; also known as Glaüke.

Creusa
Wife of Æneas; died fleeing Troy.

Crichton, Admirable
See Admirable Crichton.

Crippen, Hawley Harvey
(1862–1910) US murderer. Executed at Pentonville for poisoning his wife, Cora Turner (stage name Belle Elmore), dissecting the body, burning the bones and burying the rest in the cellar. He fled to the US with his secretary Ethel Le Neve (she dressed as a boy), but their ship was overtaken by another carrying the Scotland Yard detective Inspector Dew, who was waiting to arrest them on their arrival in New York. He had ascertained their identity by the use of the new wireless telegraphy; its first use in criminal detection.

Cronus (Saturn)
Titan; god of harvests; son of Uranus and Gaea; dethroned by his son Zeus.

Cross-connections
Nicholas Parsons's father delivered Margaret Thatcher; Steve Coogan's father was Peter Kay's metalwork teacher.

Crosse, Samuell
See Shakespeare's players.

Crowley, Aleister
See Occult leaders.

Cullinan, Edward
See Royal Academicians.

Cuming, Frederick
See Royal Academicians.

Cummins, Gus
See Royal Academicians.

Cupid
Roman equivalent of Eros.

Curie, Marie and Pierre
See Medical pioneers; Scientific eponyms.

Cybele
Anatolian nature goddess; adopted by Greeks and identified with Rhea.

Cyclopes
Race of single-eyed giants (singular – Cyclops).

Cyril Lord
See Who's who in cockney rhyming slang.

Daedalus
Athenian artificer; father of Icarus; builder of Labyrinth in Crete; devised wings attached with wax for him and Icarus to escape Crete.

Dakin, Henry Drysdale
See Medical pioneers.

Dalai Lama
See Who's who in major religions of the world.

Dalton, John
See Medical pioneers.

Dan
See Who's who in major religions of the world.

Danaë
Princess of Argos; mother of Perseus by Zeus, who appeared to her in form of a golden shower.

Danaïdes
Daughters of Danaüs; at his command, all except Hypermnestra slew their husbands, the sons of Aegyptus.

Danaüs
Brother of Aegyptus; father of Danaïdes; slain by Lynceus.

Dannatt, Professor Trevor
See Royal Academicians.

Daphne
Nymph; pursued by Apollo; changed to laurel tree.

Dark Lady
See Some famous mistresses.

David
See Who's who in major religions of the world.

Davidson, Revd Harold Francis
(1875–1937) Better remembered as the Rector of Stiffkey, Davidson purported to have saved the lives of more than 1,000 fallen women. Eventually he was unfrocked, and took to exhibiting himself in a barrel in Blackpool, protesting his innocence. He then moved into a cage in Skegness with a lion called Freddy, from whose claws he died.

Davies, W(illiam) H(enry)
(1871–1940) Welsh poet and 'supertramp' widely known for his poem beginning:

> What is this life if, full of care,
> We have no time to stop and stare ...

Day-Lewis, Cecil
See Poets laureate.

Deacon, Richard
See Royal Academicians.

Dean, The Gloomy
(of St Paul's) W R Inge (1860–1954); also a journalist of some notoriety, described as 'not so much a pillar of the church as a column in the *Evening Standard*.'

Deborah
See Who's who in major religions of the world.

Decuma
Roman goddess of fate; see Fates.

Deino
One of the Old Women, or Graeae; daughters of Phorcys and Ceto; shared a tooth and an eye with Enyo and Pephredo, which they passed from one to another.

Demeter (Ceres)
Goddess of agriculture; mother of Persephone.

Dennett, Daniel
See Some important twentieth-century philosophers who analysed the subtleties of ordinary language.

Derby
See Fashion eponyms.

Derrida, Jacques
See Some important twentieth-century philosophers who analysed the subtleties of ordinary language.

Devil, The Tasmanian
Errol Flynn.

Dewey, John
American; see Some important twentieth-century philosophers who analysed the subtleties of ordinary language.

Diana
Roman equivalent of Artemis.

Dick-Read, Grantly
See Medical pioneers.

Dickson, Jennifer
See Royal Academicians.

Dido
Founder and queen of Carthage; stabbed herself when deserted by Æneas (qv).

Diomedes
Greek hero; with Odysseus, entered Troy and carried off Palladium, sacred statue of Athena.

Diomedes
Owner of man-eating horses, which Hercules, as ninth labour, carried off.

Dione
Titan goddess; mother by Zeus of Aphrodite.

Dionysus (Bacchus)
God of wine; son of Zeus and Semele.

Dioscuri
Twins Castor and Pollux; sons of Leda by Zeus.

Dis
Roman equivalent of Pluto.

Discalced Carmelite friars
See Who's who in major religions of the world.

Doctor, the Invincible
William of Ockham.

Dodd, (Dr) William
(1729–77) English preacher and forger. Born in Lincolnshire, graduated from Clare Hall, Cambridge, in 1750, took orders and became a popular preacher. Was made a king's chaplain in 1763 and was tutor to Philip Stanhope, Lord Chesterfield's nephew. He fell into debt despite his large income, and his attempt to buy the rich living of St George's, Hanover Square, led to his name being struck off the list of chaplains in 1774. He went to Geneva where he was welcomed by his pupil, now Lord Chesterfield, yet despite being granted the living of Wing in Buckinghamshire, he was still in debt and so offered a stockbroker a bond for £4,200 signed by Chesterfield – this turned out to be a forgery. He refunded a great part of the money, but was tried, sentenced to death, and hanged.

Doe, John
1   (formerly) the plaintiff in a fictitious legal action, Doe – v – Roe, to test a point of law.
2   John or Jane, in US, an unknown or unidentified male or female.

Dolby, Richard
See Classical cooks.

Dolly Varden
See Fashion eponyms.

Domagk, Gerhard
See Medical pioneers.

Dowson, Sir Philip
See Royal Academicians.

Doyle, Roddy
See Booker Prizewinners.

Dracula

Vlad IV of Wallachia (1430–76) is thought by some to be the model for the Dracula story written by Bram Stoker. Known as Vlad the Impaler, he impaled his enemies on wooden stakes and left them to die slowly in agony. The name *Dracula* derives from the Order of the Dragon, of which Vlad was a member (although *dracul* in Romanian means 'devil'). The blood-sucking element of the vampire story is thought to be inspired by the Countess Báthori (*d*1614), who murdered 650 young women and girls. In order to remain youthful, she bathed in, and drank, their blood.

Draper, Ken

See Royal Academicians.

Dryads

Wood nymphs.

Dryden, John

See Poets laureate.

Dryope

Maiden changed to Hamadryad.

Dunstan, Bernard

See Royal Academicians.

Durrant, Jennifer

See Royal Academicians.

Eames, Charles and Ray

See Architects.

Ebadi, Shirin

See Nobel Peace Prizewinners.

Ecclestone, William

See Shakespeare's players.

Echo

Nymph who fell hopelessly in love with Narcissus; faded away except for her voice.

Ederle, Gertrude

See The first Channel swimmers.

Eichrocht, Ludwig

See Biedermeier.

Electra

Daughter of Agamemnon and Clytemnestra; sister of Orestes; urged Orestes to slay Clytemnestra and Aegisthus.

Electra
One of the Pleiades, and one of seven daughters of Atlas, transformed into heavenly constellation, of which six stars are visible.

Elephant, The
See Some famous mistresses.

Elephant Man
Joseph Carey Merrick (1862–90), who suffered from the Proteus syndrome and was shut away because of his strange appearance.

Elijah Muhammad
See Who's who in major religions of the world.

Eliot, George
Pseudonym of Marian (or Mary-Ann) Evans (1819–80), English writer.

Elysium
Abode of blessed dead.

Emerson and Jayne
Jack Emerson Skinner (1915–95) and his wife Joy (née Bolton-Carter) who devised and flew their magic carpet for over forty years.

Emma, Lady Hamilton
See Some famous mistresses.

Emperor Ming
See Who's who in major religions of the world.

Emperor Wu Ti
See Who's who in major religions of the world.

Endymion
Mortal loved by Selene.

Enlightened, The
See Who's who in major religions of the world.

Enyo
One of the Old Women, or Graeae; daughters of Phorcys and Ceto; shared a tooth and an eye with Deino and Pephredo, which they passed from one to another.

Eos (Aurora)
Goddess of dawn.

Epimetheus
Titan; Brother of Prometheus; husband of Pandora.

Episcopal Church
See Who's who in major religions of the world.

Erasistratus
See Medical pioneers.

Erato
One of the Muses and goddesses presiding over arts and sciences (lyric and love poetry) and daughter of Zeus and Mnemosyne.

Erebus
Spirit of darkness; son of Chaos.

Eris
Goddess of discord.

Erlang, A K
(1879–1924) Danish mathematician who gave his name to the unit of telephonic traffic density.

Eros (Amor or Cupid)
God of love; son of Aphrodite.

Escoffier, Auguste
See Classical cooks.

Esquivel, Adolfo Perez
See Nobel Peace Prizewinners.

Esther
See Who's who in major religions of the world.

Eteocles
Son of Oedipus, whom he succeeded to rule alternately with Polynices; refused to give up throne at end of year; he and Polynices slew each other.

Eulenspiegel, Till
Mischievous German practical-joking folk hero based on a C14 inhabitant of Brunswick; the mythical Till is hanged for going too far; the real one died of the plague.

Euphrosyne
Joy; with Aglaia and Thalia one of the three Graces; daughters of Zeus and Eurynome.

Europa
Mortal loved by Zeus, who, in form of white bull, carried her off to Crete.

Eurus
One of the Winds – the east wind.

Euryale
One of the Gorgons.

Eurydice
Nymph; wife of Orpheus.

Eurystheus
King of Argos; imposed twelve labours on Hercules.

Eusden, Laurence
See Poets laureate.

Euterpe
One of the Muses and goddesses presiding over arts and sciences (music) and daughter of Zeus and Mnemosyne.

Evans, Mary-Ann
See Eliot, George.

Eve
See Who's who in major religions of the world.

Evelina
Or, *a Young Lady's Entrance into the World*, epistolary novel published anonymously in 1778 that brought its author (Fanny Burney (*qv*)) great fame.

Evelyn, John
See Gardeners and gardening writers.

Everest
The world's highest mountain, in the Himalaya (pron him-aal-year), was named in 1865 after Sir George Everest (1790–1866), Surveyor General of India from 1830, knighted in 1861; properly pronounced Eve-Rest; it has now reverted to its PC name: in Nepal Sagarmatha (means mother goddess of the sky) and in Tibet Chomolungma (means mother goddess of the universe).

Eyton, Anthony
See Royal Academicians.

Fabius, Laurent
See Political scandals.

Factotum
One who does everything.

Fahrenheit
See Scientific eponyms; Medical pioneers; and Technologists who made the modern world.

Faraday
See Scientific eponyms.

Farley, John
See Classical cooks.

Farrell, J G
See Booker Prizewinners.

Farthing, Stephen
See Royal Academicians.

Fat and Wide
See Who's who in cockney rhyming slang.

Fates
Moirae (Parcae); determine the length of human life; Clotho spins the thread, Lachesis determines its length, and Atropos cuts it; Roman equivalents Decuma, Morta and Nuna.

Father Time
Personification of time, often shown carrying a scythe with which to determine our lives (in some unspecified way) when we reach our allotted span. Alternatively, he may at midnight on 31 December hand over the old year to a babe-in-arms who personifies the new year; in this case, his rate of aging is remarkable. The conventional figure is represented by the engraver William Hogarth (1697–1764) in *Time Smoking a Picture* – to make it look old, a satire on the connoisseurs of the day who, it appears, would buy anything as long as it looked old. Hence Hogarth's picture bears the gnomic phrase: 'As statues moulder into worth', and the contemporary poet James Bramston (*d*1744) wrote in *The Man of Taste*:

> In curious paintings I'm exceeding nice,
>> And know their several beauties by their price ...
> Originals and copies much the same,
>> The picture's value is the painter's name.

Fatima
See Who's who in major religions of the world.

Fauns
Roman deities of woods and groves.

Faunus
Roman equivalent of Pan.

Favonius
One of the Winds. See Zephyrus.

Fedden, Mary
See Royal Academicians.

Ferris, Bob
See Barker, Ronnie.

Field, Nathan
See Shakespeare's players.

First Foot
The first visitor at a house after midnight has ushered in New Year's Day, especially in Scotland; it is considered lucky if the first footer is carrying symbols of warmth, wealth and food (a handsel), usually a piece of coal, some salt (once more valuable than today) and cake; he or she is rewarded with refreshment such as the Het Pint (a mixture of beer, whisky, eggs and sugar). There are local names for first footing, such as the Yorkshire Lucky Bird, and the Manx Quaaltagh.

Fitzgerald, Penelope
See Booker Prizewinners.

Fitzherbert, Mrs
See Some famous mistresses.

Flanagan, Barry
See Royal Academicians.

Fleming, Alexander
See Medical pioneers.

Flittersnoop, Mrs
Professor Branestawm's housekeeper.

Flora
Roman goddess of flowers.

Florey, Howard Walter
See Medical pioneers.

Fluffer
A tunnel cleaner on the London Underground.

Flywheel, Rufus T
Name of character played by Groucho Marx (*qv*) in the US radio sitcom *Shyster & Shyster*, and in certain of his films.

Fortuna
Roman equivalent of Tyche.

Foster, Norman
See Architects.

Foster of Thames Bank, Lord
See Royal Academicians.

Four-minute Men
Those who run a mile in under four minutes, the first of whom was Dr (now also Sir) Roger Bannister (*b*1929) at an athletics meeting at Iffley Road, Oxford, in 1954; his time was 3m 59.4s.

Fraser, Donald Hamilton
See Royal Academicians.

Freeth, Peter
See Royal Academicians.

Fuller, Buckminster
See Architects.

Fundi
1   Slang for Fundamentalist.
2   A skilled mechanic (from Swahili).

Furniss, Harry
(1854–1925) Popular Irish artist whose work appeared widely in the *Illustrated London News* and *Punch*.

Gad
See Who's who in major religions of the world.

Gaea
Goddess of earth; daughter of Chaos; mother of Titans; known also as Ge, Gea, Gaia, etc.

Galatea
Sea nymph; loved by Polyphemus.

Galatea
Statue of maiden carved from ivory by Pygmalion; given life by Aphrodite.

Galen
See Medical pioneers.

Galton, Francis
See Medical pioneers.

Galvanize
(verb) See Scientific eponyms.

Ganesha
See Who's who in major religions of the world.

Ganymede
Beautiful boy; successor to Hebe as cupbearer of gods.

Garbo
Australian binman/dustman/garbage man.

Garbo, Greta
(1905–90) née Greta Louisa Gustafsson, glamorous Swedish born film actress who is remembered for (not) saying 'I want to be alone'.

Gardner, Gerald
See Occult leaders.

Garibaldi
See Fashion eponyms.

Gaudi, Antonio
See Architects.

Gauss
See Scientific eponyms.

Gehry, Frank
See Architects.

Geiger counter
See Scientific eponyms.

Gentleman
Originally a man of noble birth, ranking above a yeoman; now in the true sense (and somewhat begging the question) someone with qualities of refinement associated with a good family; general polite (refeened) word for a man as in: 'I think this gentleman was before me'. G of the Road = a tramp; however, when Capt Mark Phillips stopped to help at a traffic accident, the person involved described him as: 'a true gentlemen of the road'. G's G = a manservant or valet; however, when the disc-jockey Mike Read was ousted from *I'm a Celebrity, get me out of here* (2004), a remaining contestant described him as 'a gentleman's gentleman'.

Gentleman of the Road
See Gentleman.

George Raft
See Who's who in cockney rhyming slang.

George, St
St George is the patron saint of England, and his day is 23 April. Although the feast is rarely celebrated nationally, football supporters have breathed new life into St George's Cross, a red plus on a white background. William Shakespeare died, and is supposed to have been born, on 23 April, though the birthday may be but a patriotic assump-

tion supported by the known day of death and a spurious love of coincidence.

Gideon
See Who's who in major religions of the world.

Gielgud, Sir (Arthur) John
(1904–2000) English actor and producer. Born in London, he made his debut at the Old Vic Theatre in 1921, became a leading Shakespearean actor and was involved in directing many of the Shakespeare Memorial Theatre productions. He also appeared in many films, notably as Disraeli in *The Prime Minister* (1940) and as Cassius in *Julius Caesar* (1952). He played Othello at Stratford in 1961, and Prospero at the National Theatre in 1974. He was knighted in 1953 and appointed to the Order of Merit in 1996.

Gilbert
See Scientific eponyms.

Gilbert of Sempringham, Order of St
See Who's who in major religions of the world.

Gilbreth, Frank Bunker
(1868–1924) American engineer and pioneer of work study who gave his name (more or less) to the Therblig, any of the analysed actions needed to perform a task such as Assemble, Disassemble, Find, Grasp &c.

Gilburne, Samuel
See Shakespeare's players.

Gillies, Harold Delf
See Medical pioneers.

Gimbert, Benjamin
Driver of ammunition train preparing for D-Day, that caught fire in Soham station (2 June 1944) who, with his fireman James Nightall, managed to run the blazing wagon away from the town before it blew up, killing Nightall and damaging some 700 houses.

Gladstone
See Fashion eponyms.

Gladstone, William Ewart
(1809–98) Leader of the Liberal Party and British Prime Minister (1868–74, 1880–85, 1886, 1892–94) of whom Queen Victoria complained that he addressed her like a public meeting (unlike that nice Mr Disraeli); see Political scandals; Prime Ministers of Britain

Glasse, Hannah
See Classical cooks.

Glauber, Johann Rudoph
See Medical pioneers.

Glaucus
Mortal who became a sea divinity by eating magic grass.

Gleitze, Mercedes
See The first Channel swimmers.

Gödel, Kurt
See Some important twentieth-century philosophers who analysed the subtleties of ordinary language.

Godiva, Lady
In 1040 Leofric, Earl of Mercia, demanded heavy taxes from his tenants but, after being petitioned by his wife, agreed to waive them if she rode naked through the town. To his surprise, Lady Godiva did, preserving her modesty with her hair, and the earl removed the taxes. Lady Godiva is patroness of the city of Coventry.

Gog and Magog
The offspring of demons and the 33 daughters of the Emperor Diocletian were giant monsters. Gog and Magog were the only survivors of a killing spree by Brute and were taken as prisoners to London, where they were forced to stand guard in front of the royal palace. Effigies of Gog and Magog have stood on this site, now the Guildhall, since the time of Henry V. Hills to the south of Cambridge are known locally as 'The Gogs', short for the Gogmagog Hills.

Golden Afternoon
4 July 1862 when Revd Robin Duckworth (then a fellow of Trinity College, Oxford) and Revd Charles Lutwidge Dodgson (1832–98; *alias* Lewis Carroll), the Oxford mathematician, rowed a boat in company with the ten-year-old Alice Pleasance Liddell and her sisters Lorina Charlotte (13) and Edith (8) up the River Thames from Folly Bridge (near Oxford) to the village of Godstow, upon which trip the foundations for the classic that emerged as *Alice's Adventures in Wonderland* (1865) were laid.

Golden Fleece
Fleece from ram that flew Phrixos to Colchis; Aeëtes placed it under guard of dragon; carried off by Jason.

Golding, William
See Booker Prizewinners.

Gorbachev, Mikhail Sergeyvich
See Nobel Peace Prizewinners.

Gordimer, Nadine
See Booker Prizewinners.

Gore, Frederick
See Royal Academicians.

Gorgas, William Crawford
See Medical pioneers.

Gorgons
Female monsters; Euryale, Medusa, and Stheno; had snakes for hair; their glances turned mortals to stone; Medusa was slain by Perseus.

Gormley, Antony
See Royal Academicians.

Gough, Piers
See Royal Academicians.

Goughe, Robert
See Shakespeare's players.

Gram, Hans Christian Joachim
See Medical pioneers.

Grant, Cary
Né Alexander Archibald Leach (1904–86), English-born US film actor whose many fims include *Bringing up Baby* (1938), *The Philadelphia Story* (1940), *Arsenic and Old Lace* (1944), and *Mr Blandings builds his Dream House* (1948).

Green, Anthony
See Royal Academicians.

Gregory Peck
See Who's who in cockney rhyming slang.

Greyfriars Bobby
When Dr John Gray died in 1852, his beloved terrier was so distraught that he watched over the grave of his master for twenty years in Greyfriars Churchyard, Edinburgh. After Bobby's death in 1872, the people of the city were so touched by his devotion they erected a statue to him, which stands on Candlemaker Row. He is buried next to his master.

Grimm
Jacob Ludwig Carl (1785–1863) and Wilhelm Carl (1786–1859) – the famous folkloric and philological brothers.

Grimshaw, Nicholas
See **Royal Academicians**.

Gropius, Walter
See **Architects**.

Grossmith, George and Weedon
Brothers who created the immortal Charles Pooter and his circle in *The Diary of a Nobody* which first appeared in *Punch* in 1888–9, and which was augmented, edited, and published as a book in 1892, since when it has never been out of print.

Guy Fawkes' Night
5 November. In 1605, Guy Fawkes and other Catholic conspirators planned to blow up James I and the Houses of Parliament in London. The plot was discovered, the men were tried for treason and executed. November 5 was set aside as 'a day of thanksgiving to be celebrated with bonfires and fireworks'. Effigies of the conspirators (commonly called Guys) are made and burned on the fire.

Gwynne, Nell
See **Some famous mistresses**.

Hades (Dis)
Name sometimes given to Pluto; also, the abode of the dead, ruled by Pluto.

Hadid, Zaha
See **Architects**.

Haemon
Son of Creon; promised husband of Antigone; killed himself in her tomb.

Hahnemann, Christian Friedrich Samuel
See **Medical pioneers**.

Haigh, John George
(1909–49) English murderer. Convicted of shooting a widow and disposing of her body in sulphuric acid. However, the clue that led to his conviction and execution was a plastic denture which had not been broken down by the acid. It is believed he murdered five others in the same way – the motive being for money – although in an effort to be found insane he had claimed that he drank his victims' blood.

Hall, Marshall
See **Medical pioneers**.

Hall, Nigel
See **Royal Academicians**.

Halsted, William Stewart
  See Medical pioneers.

Hamadryads
  Tree nymphs.

Hanratty, James
  (c1936–1962) English alleged murderer. Reportedly a petty criminal
  of low intelligence was hanged for murdering Michael Gregsten while
  he was in his car with his lover Valerie Storie in a layby on the A6 on
  22 August 1961. Storie, who had been raped and paralysed by several
  bullets, picked out Hanratty from an identity parade. Hanratty would
  not name his alibis claiming that if he did so it would betray his friends'
  trust, which ultimately led to his conviction and hanging 4 April 1962.
  After 30 years of campaigning by his family, a police inquiry in 1997
  found him to be innocent, and wrongly convicted.

Hansen, Armauer
  See Medical pioneers.

Hanuman
  See Who's who in major religions of the world.

Harel, Mme Marie
  See Classical cooks.

Harpies
  Monsters with heads of women and bodies of birds.

Harvey, William
  English physician; see Medical pioneers.

Hashem
  See IHVH.

Havelock
  See Fashion eponyms.

Hawker, Revd R S
  The vicar of Morwenstow, Cornwall, who, on Sunday 1 October 1843,
  held a service to thank God for the harvest, an innovation that the
  Church of England picked up and ran with as the Harvest Festival.

Hayward-Jones, David Robert
  David Bowie (b 8 January 1947).

Hebe (Juventas)
  Goddess of youth; cupbearer of gods before Ganymede; daughter of
  Zeus and Hera.

Hecate
Goddess of sorcery and witchcraft.

Hector
Son of Priam; slayer of Patroclus; slain by Achilles.

Hecuba
Wife of Priam.

Heidegger, Martin
See Some important twentieth-century philosophers who analysed the subtleties of ordinary language.

Helen
Fairest woman in world; daughter of Zeus and Leda; wife of Menelaus; carried to Troy by Paris, causing Trojan War. It was said that the beauty of her face 'launched 1,000 ships'; the measure of beauty is thus the millihelen which will launch one ship.

Heliades
Daughters of Helios; mourned for Phaëthon and were changed to poplar trees.

Helios (Sol)
God of the sun; later identified with Apollo.

Helle
Sister of Phrixos; fell from ram of Golden Fleece; water where she fell named Hellespont.

Helmholtz, Hermann von
See Medical pioneers.

Hemmings, John
See Shakespeare's players.

Hench, Philip Showalter
See Medical pioneers.

Henry
See Scientific eponyms.

Hephaestus (Vulcan)
God of fire; celestial blacksmith; son of Zeus and Hera; husband of Aphrodite.

Hera (Juno)
Queen of heaven; wife of Zeus.

Hercules (Herakles)
Hero and strong man; son of Zeus and Alcmene; performed twelve labours or deeds to be free from bondage under Eurystheus; after

death, his mortal share was destroyed, and he became immortal. Labours – (1) killing Nemean lion; (2) killing Lernaean Hydra; (3) capturing Erymanthian boar; (4) capturing Cerynean hind; (5) killing man-eating Stymphalian birds; (6) procuring girdle of Hippolyte; (7) cleaning Augean stables; (8) capturing Cretan bull; (9) capturing man-eating horses of Diomedes; (10) capturing cattle of Geryon; (11) procuring golden apples of Hesperides; (12) bringing Cerberus up from Hades.

Hermes (Mercury)
God of physicians and thieves; messenger of gods; son of Zeus and Maia.

Hero
Priestess of Aphrodite; Leander swam Hellespont nightly to see her; drowned herself at his death.

Herod
See Who's who in major religions of the world.

Hertz, Heinrich Rudolf
(1857–94) the German physicist who transformed Maxwell's predictions into the reality of Hertzian – or, as we now call them electromagnetic, or radio – waves, and gave his name to the SI unit of frequency, equal to one cycle per second; see Scientific eponyms.

Hesperus
The Evening star.

Hestia (Vesta)
Goddess of hearth; sister of Zeus.

Heymans, Corneille
See Medical pioneers.

Hindley, Myra
(1942–2003) English murderess. She met Ian Brady whilst working as a typist, and the pair began to lure children back to their house in Manchester, torturing them before killing them. It was Hindley's brother-in-law that contacted the police on 7 October 1965 about the murders. The pair were arrested after the body of 17-year-old Edward Evans was found at their house, and the graves and remains of 10-year-old Lesley Ann Downey and 12-year-old John Kilbride were found on Saddleworth Moor – hence the name 'Moors Murderers'. Hindley was convicted on two counts of murder and was given life imprisonment; she died of cancer in prison in 2003.

Hinduism
See Who's who in major religions of the world.

Hippolyte
Queen of Amazons; wife of Theseus.

Hippolytus
Son of Theseus and Hippolyte; falsely accused by Phaedra of trying to kidnap her; slain by Poseidon at request of Theseus.

Hippomenes
Husband of Atalanta, whom he beat in a race by dropping golden apples, which she stopped to pick up.

Hockney, David
See Royal Academicians.

Hodge
C16 condescending name for a rustic; a cat belonging to Dr Samuel Johnson (1709–84) was so named; Johnson went himself to buy oysters for Hodge, for he felt that he could scarcely ask his servant, Francis Barber, to go.

Holmes, Oliver Wendell
American writer and physician; see Medical pioneers.

Hood, Robin
Traditional English outlaw whose redeeming feature in the popular consciousness is that he 'robbed from the rich and gave to the poor'. He and his 'Merrie Men', who first appeared in legend nearly 1,000 years ago, were no doubt included in 'the poor.'

Hood, Thomas
(1799–1845); English poet and humorist; an editor of *Punch*.

Hopkins, Sir Michael
See Royal Academicians.

Hornung, E W
See Raffles.

Hoskins, Cyril Henry
See Rampa, T Lobsang.

Houyhnhnms
[pron Whin-hims] In Swift's *Gulliver's Travels*, the horses possessed of human intelligence who rule men (Yahoos).

Howard, Harriette
See Some famous mistresses.

Howard, Ken
　　See Royal Academicians.

Hoyland, John
　　See Royal Academicians.

Hsun Tzu
　　See Who's who in major religions of the world.

Hubbard, Lafayette Ronald
　　See Occult leaders.

Hughes, Ted
　　See Poets laureate.

Hulme, Keri
　　See Booker Prizewinners.

Hume, Gary
　　See Royal Academicians.

Hume, John
　　See Nobel Peace Prizewinners.

Humpty Dumpty
　　A nursery-rhyme egg who, falling from a wall and disintegrating, cannot be reassembled by all the military and equine members of the Royal Household; in [Alice] *Through the Looking-Glass*, he is noted for making words mean what he wants them to mean.

Husserl, Edmund
　　See Some important twentieth-century philosophers who analysed the subtleties of ordinary language.

Huxley, Andrew Fielding
　　See Medical pioneers.

Huxley, Paul
　　See Royal Academicians.

Hyacinthus
　　Beautiful youth accidentally killed by Apollo, who caused flowers to spring up from his blood.

Hydra
　　Nine-headed monster in the marsh of Lernea; slain by Hercules.

Hygeia
　　Personification of health.

Hymen
　　God of marriage.

Hypatia
    Inventor of the hygrometer.

Hyperion
    Titan; early sun god; father of Helios.

Hypermnestra
    Daughter of Danaüs; refused to kill her husband Lynceus.

Hypnos (Somnus)
    God of sleep.

Iapetus
    Titan; father of Atlas, Epimetheus, and Prometheus.

Ibrahim
    See Who's who in major religions of the world.

Icarus
    Son of Daedalus; flew too near sun with wax-attached wings, fell into
    sea and was drowned.

IHVH
    One of the Hebrew names for God, derived from the earlier Yahweh
    who took Israel as his bride in order to ensure her prosperity; because
    the name was not to be pronounced (except by the High Priest when
    he entered the Holy of Holies), it may appear as Jehovah (same letters,
    different vowels), Adonai (Lord), Hashem (the Name); also as 'the
    Tetragrammaton' (Greek = 'four-letter word'). When the four Hebrew
    characters are written vertically, they look like a stick-figure of a man,
    which may give us a clue to its origin.

Io
    Mortal maiden loved by Zeus; changed by Hera into heifer.

Iobates
    King of Lycia; sent Bellerophon to slay the Chimera.

Iphigenia
    Daughter of Agamemnon; offered as sacrifice to Artemis at Aulis;
    carried by Artemis to Tauris where she became priestess; escaped from
    there with Orestes.

Iris
    Goddess of rainbow; messenger of Zeus and Hera.

Irvin, Albert
    See Royal Academicians.

Irving, Sir Henry

originally John Henry Brodribb (1838–1905) English actor. Born in Keinton-Mandeville, Somerset, and made his first appearance at the Sunderland Theatre in 1856, thereafter acting in Edinburgh, Manchester and Liverpool, before moving to London, and transferring to the Lyceum in 1871. He gained his reputation as the greatest English actor of his time from his *Hamlet* (1874), *Macbeth* (1875) and *Othello* (1876). In 1878 he began his famous theatrical partnership with Ellen Terry at the Lyceum where he became actor-manager-lessee. In 1895 he became the first actor to receive a knighthood. Of his sons, Laurence (1871–1914) was a novelist and playwright who was drowned in the *Empress of Ireland* disaster, and Henry Brodribb (1870–1919) was an actor.

Irwin, Flavia

See **Royal Academicians**.

Isaiah

See **Who's who in major religions of the world**.

Ishiguro, Kazuo

See **Booker Prizewinners**.

Ishmael

In the Bible, the son of Abraham and his concubine Hagar, handmaid of Abraham's wife Sarah who cast out Hagar when she was pregnant; hence the opening of Herman Melville's *Moby-Dick* (1851): 'Call me Ishmael.'

Islam

See **Who's who in major religions of the world**.

Ismail

See **Who's who in major religions of the world**.

Ismene

Daughter of Oedipus; sister of Antigone.

Issachar

See **Who's who in major religions of the world**.

Istra

The Greek Goddess of Psyche.

Iulus

Son of Aeneas.

Ixion

King of Lapithae; for making love to Hera he was bound to endlessly revolving wheel in Tartarus.

J Arthur Rank
See Who's who in cockney rhyming slang.

Jack the Ripper
Unidentified murderer C19. Between August and November 1888, six prostitutes were found murdered and mutilated in the East End of London, yet the murderer was never found. He has been the subject of many novels and films, and speculation on his identity still continues. As a result, a reform of some police methods came about, due to the public alarm and violent press campaign against the CID and the Home Secretary.

Jacklin, William
See Royal Academicians.

Jacobsen, Arne
See Architects.

James
See Who's who in major religions of the world.

Janus
Roman god of gates and doors; represented with two opposite faces.

Jason
Son of Aeson; to gain throne of Ioclus from Pelias, went to Colchis and brought back Golden Fleece; married Medea; deserted her for Creüsa.

Jehovah
See IHVH.

Jekyll, Gertrude
See Gardeners and gardening writers.

Jenner, Edward
See Medical pioneers.

Jeremiah
See Who's who in major religions of the world.

Jesus
See Who's who in major religions of the world.

Jhabvala, Ruth Prawer
See Booker Prizewinners.

Jiricna, Eva
See Royal Academicians.

Joanna
See Who's who in cockney rhyming slang.

Job
See Who's who in major religions of the world.

Jocasta
Wife of Laius; mother of Oedipus; unwittingly became wife of Oedipus; hanged herself when relationship was discovered.

Joe Blake
Australian snake (RS).

John, John of God, Hospitaller friars of St, John the Baptist, John the Divine, Sisterhood of St, John the Evangelist, Society of St
See Who's who in major religions of the world.

Jonah
See Who's who in major religions of the world.

Jones, Allen
See Royal Academicians.

Jooss, Kurt
(1901–79), German dancer, producer, and choreographer, a student of Rudolf von Laban and influenced by Émile Jacques-Dalcroze. His most famous ballet *The Green Table* (1932), was an expressionistic view of the origins of war. He left Hitler's Germany before the war, and continued to run the Ballet Jooss based in Cambridge. His group was disbanded in 1962, but he continued to perform with other Western European companies.

Joseph, Joshua
See Who's who in major religions of the world.

Joule
Named in honour of the English physicist James Prescott Joule; see Scientific eponyms.

Judah, Judaism, Judas Iscariot, Jude, Judith
See Who's who in major religions of the world.

Jung, Kim Dae
See Nobel Peace Prizewinners.

Juno
Roman equivalent of Hera.

Jupiter
Roman equivalent of Zeus.

Juventas
Roman equivalent of Hebe.

Kali
See Who's who in major religions of the world.

Kalki
See Who's who in major religions of the world.

Kapoor, Anish
See Royal Academicians.

Katmir
The dog of the seven sleepers, said to have been able to speak with a human voice.

Kean, Charles John
(1811–68) English actor. Born in Waterford, Ireland, son of Edmund Kean. To support his mother and himself he became an actor. His first appearance was at Drury Lane in 1827 as Young Norval, yet this had little success. He married actress Ellen Tree (1805–80) who played opposite him in many of his major productions. He became joint-lessee of the Princess's Theatre in 1850. He virtually retired from London stage in 1859, yet continued to play in the USA to within seven months of his death.

Keeler, Christine
See Some famous mistresses.

Keiko
Killer whale, the star of *Free Willy* who was captured off Iceland in 1979, released in 2002, and died in 2003 when he was 27 years old, 35 feet long, and weighed seven tons.

Kelman, James
See Booker Prizewinners.

Kelvin
See Scientific eponyms.

Kempe, Will(iam)
(c1550–c1603) an actor in Shakespeare's Company who in 1600 performed a nine-day Morris dance from London to Norwich, and wrote *Nine Daies Wonder* to commemorate it, wherefrom comes the phrase concerning something big at the time but subsequently forgotten. See Shakespeare's players.

Keneally, Thomas
See Booker Prizewinners.

Kent, William
See Gardeners and gardening writers.

Keppel, Alice
See Some famous mistresses.

Keroualle, Louise de
See Some famous mistresses.

Khadja
See Who's who in major religions of the world.

Kingsley, Sir Ben
(1943–) né Krishna Bhanji, actor who achieved wide fame playing Ghandi (1982).

KIPPERS
Kids In Parents' Pockets Eroding Retirement Savings.

Kitaj, R B
See Royal Academicians.

Kitasato, Shibasaburo
See Medical pioneers.

Kneale, Professor Bryan
See Royal Academicians.

Knickerbockers
See Fashion eponyms.

Koch, Robert
See Medical pioneers.

Koralek, Paul
See Royal Academicians.

Krishna
See Who's who in major religions of the world.

Kronus
See Cronus.

Kshatriyas
See Who's who in major religions of the world.

Ku Klux Klan
Founded in 1866 in Pulaski, Tennessee, the American secret society preached white supremacy. Klansmen took part in rituals and wore hooded white robes. Laws were passed against the group in 1870 and 1871 for terrorist activities – although it was disbanded by the Grand Wizard in 1869, local Klansmen continued their activities. A new league of the Ku Klux Klan was set up in 1915, adding to the ritualistic practices and spouting anti-Catholic, anti-Jewish and xenophobic tracts. During the 1930s and 1940s the Klan was known for its Fascist

sympathies and was officially disbanded in 1944; the name is an elaboration of Greek *kuklos* = 'circle'.

Kublai Khan
The grandson (1214–94) of Genghis Khan, as immortalised in the 1816 poem by Samuel Taylor Coleridge. Kublai Khan extended the Mongol Empire to China and founded a dynasty of Chinese Emperors.

Kurma
See Who's who in major religions of the world.

Kuze, Kamitaka
See Political scandals.

Kyi, Aung San Suu
See Nobel Peace Prizewinners.

Lachesis
Goddess of destiny, see Fates.

Laennec, René Théophile Hyacinthe
See Medical pioneers.

Laius
Father of Oedipus, by whom he was slain.

Lakshmi
See Who's who in major religions of the world.

Lama, Mystic
See Rampa, T Lobsang.

Lama, The 14th Dalai
See Nobel Peace Prizewinners.

Lambert
See Scientific eponyms.

Lamington
1   Australian sponge cube dipped in chocolate and coconut, named after Baron Lamington, governor of Queensland 1896–1901.
2   A type of hat otherwise described as a Homburg.

Landammann
Chairman of the governing council in certain Swiss cantons.

Landsteiner, Karl
See Medical pioneers.

Langton, Stephen
Archbishop of Canterbury 1213–28, credited with dividing the Bible into chapters.

Laocoön
Priest of Apollo at Troy; warned against bringing wooden horse into Troy; destroyed with his two sons by serpents sent by Poseidon.

Lao-Tzu
See Who's who in major religions of the world.

LaPierre, Cherilyn Sarkisian
(*b* 20 May 1946) of an Armenian father and part Cherokee mother. Paired with Phil Spector's studio assistant and PR man Sonny Bono to form first Caesar and Cleo, and then Sonny and Cher.

Lardner, Dr Dionysius
(1793–1859) Irish science writer and promoter of the railway principle of 'undulating lines': that an undulating railway 'worked' better than a level one. With steam, no; with regenerating electrical railways and controlled gradients into and out of stations, perhaps.

Lardner, Ring(gold Wilmer)
(1885–1933) US journalist and short-story writer.

Lares
Roman ancestral spirits protecting descendants and homes.

Latona
Roman equivalent of Leto.

Laurel and Hardy
Oliver Hardy, originally Norvell Hardy Junior (1892–1957), Stan Laurel, originally Arthur Stanley Jefferson (1890–1965), were a US comic double-act. Hardy was born near Atlanta, Georgia, and ran away from home at the age of eight to become a boy singer in a travelling minstrel show, but returned home later to enter films in 1913. He played the Tin Man in the 1925 version of *The Wizard of Oz*. Stan Laurel was born in Ulverston, Lancashire, England and was a teenage member of Fred Karno's touring company and understudy to Charlie Chaplin. He first went to the USA in 1910. He gained his first film part in 1917, appearing in many silent comedies. The pair became partners in 1926, and made more than 100 films, several of which were full-length feature films – slap-stick comedy which was made universally popular.

Lavinia
Wife of Aeneas after defeat of Turnus.

Lawson, Sonia
See Royal Academicians.

Leander
Swam Hellespont nightly to see Hero; drowned in storm.

Leda
Mortal loved by Zeus in form of swan; mother of Helen, Clytemnestra, Dioscuri.

Leishman, William Boog
See Medical pioneers.

Lenotre, Andre
See Gardeners and gardening writers.

Leotard
See Fashion eponyms.

Lethe
One of the Rivers of Underworld.

Leto (Latona)
Mother by Zeus of Artemis and Apollo.

Levene, Ben
See Royal Academicians.

Levi
See Who's who in major religions of the world.

Lewinsky, Monica
See Some famous mistresses.

Light of the Age
Rabbi Moses ben Maimon of Cordova (Maimonides) (1135–1204).

Lincoln, Abraham
An important and revered figure in American history, he was born on 12 February 1809, became President on 4 March 1861, was shot at Ford's Theatre, Washington by the 26-year-old actor John Wilkes Booth on Good Friday (14 April) 1865, and died the following day.

Lindemann, Frederick Alexander, 1st Viscount Cherwell
(1886–1957) English physicist born in Baden-Baden, Germany. Educated at the University of Berlin and at the Sorbonne, Paris, at which he worked on the problems of atomic heat. He then became director of the Royal Flying Corps Experimental Physics Station at Farnborough, and was the first to evolve and put into practice the mathematical theory of aircraft spin. During WW2, he was Sir Winston Churchill's advisor and confidant.

Lipmann, Fritz Albert
See Medical pioneers.

Lister, Joseph; Liston, Robert
See Medical pioneers.

Little Green Bird
Of Princess Fairstar, said to have been able to speak with a human voice.

Little Sisters of the Poor
See Who's who in major religions of the world.

Lively, Penelope
See Booker Prizewinners.

Liverpool Poets
Roger McGough, Adrian Henri and Brian Patten.

Lloyd, Marie
(1870–1922) née Matilda Alice Victoria Wood, who made her début as a music-hall artiste (billed as Bella Delamare) in 1885; her hits include *The boy I love sits up in the gallery*, *My old man*, and *Oh, Mr Porter*.

Löffler, Friedrich August Johann
See Medical pioneers.

Lollards
The followers of John Wyclif, who condemned transubstantiation, indulgences, clerical celibacy, and the worldly possessions and hierarchies of the church. The term was first recorded in 1382 when William Courtenay, Archbishop of Canterbury, criticised their teachings, naming them after the Dutch *Lollaerds* who mumbled prayers and hymns.

Long, Crawford Williamson
See Medical pioneers.

Long, Richard
See Royal Academicians.

Loudon, John Claudius
See Gardeners and gardening writers.

Lowine, John
See Shakespeare's players.

Lucina
Roman goddess of childbirth; identified with Juno.

Ludwig, Karl Friedrich Wilhelm
See Medical pioneers.

Luke
See Who's who in major religions of the world.

Luna
Roman equivalent of Selene.

Lutyens, Edwin
See Architects.

Lynceus
Son of Aegyptus; husband of Hypermnestra; slew Danaüs.

Lynen, Feodor
See Medical pioneers.

MacCormac, Richard
See Royal Academicians.

Mach number
See Scientific eponyms.

Mach, David
See Royal Academicians.

MacIndoe, Archibald
See Medical pioneers.

Mackintosh
See Fashion eponyms.

Mackintosh, Charles Rennie
See Architects.

Macleod, John James Rickard
See Medical pioneers.

Maddock, Sir Ieuan
(1917–89) UK DTI Chief Scientist 1971–77.

Mae West
See Fashion eponyms.

Maia
One of the Pleiades, and one of seven daughters of Atlas; mother of Hermes, transformed into heavenly constellation, of which six stars are visible.

Maine, John
See Royal Academicians.

Majûj
See Yajûi.

Malcolm X
See Who's who in major religions of the world.

Man in Black, The

A sinister and anonymous figure used to introduce BBC Home Service tales of mystery and horror, played by Valentine Dyall who had an appropriate voice.

Man in the Iron Mask

A prisoner of Louis XIV who spent 40 years travelling between different prisons before dying in the Bastille on 19 November 1703. Contrary to popular belief, his mask was made of black velvet, not iron, and protected his identity when on the move. He was buried under the name 'M. de Marchiel', and speculation about his real identity is still rife. He could have been an illegitimate son or elder brother of Louis XIV, or a minister of the treacherous Duke of Mantua who was imprisoned in Pignerol.

Manasseh, Leonard

See Royal Academicians.

Mandela, Nelson

See Nobel Peace Prizewinners.

Manes

Souls of dead Romans, particularly of ancestors.

Manser, Michael

See Royal Academicians.

Marcel

See Fashion eponyms.

Marist brothers

See Who's who in major religions of the world.

Mark

See Who's who in major religions of the world.

Markham, Gervase

See Classical cooks.

Mars

Roman equivalent of Ares.

Marsh, James

See Medical pioneers.

Marsyas

Shepherd; challenged Apollo to music contest and lost; flayed alive by Apollo.

Martel, Yann

See Booker Prizewinners.

Marten, Maria

The mole-catcher's daughter who bore farmer's son (often wrongly cited as Squire) Thomas Corder's illegitimate child at Polstead, Suffolk, in the 1820s; she was later murdered by Thomas's younger brother William; he having lured her to the Corders' Red Barn by a promise of marriage, she was never again seen alive. Her body was found in the Barn and William Corder hanged for her murder at Bury St Edmunds on 11 August 1828. A book giving an account of the trial bound in Corder's skin is to be seen in Moyse's Hall Museum at Bury St Edmunds, Suffolk, along with other relics.

Martin's Law

The right to protect one's property, named after the Norfolk farmer Tony Martin who was jailed for shooting an intruder in self-defence.

Marx Brothers

US family of film comedians. Born in New York City, sons of German immigrants, were Julius Henry (Groucho, 1895–1977), Leonard (Chico, 1891–1961), Adolph Arthur (Harpo, 1893–1964) and Herbert (Zeppo, 1901–79). They began their stage career in a team called the Six Musical Mascots, which included their mother Minnie and an aunt, and another brother, Milton (Gummo, 1894–1977), who left the act early on. They later appeared as The Four Nightingales, and eventually as The Marx Brothers chiefly remembered for their films. Each had his own well-defined role; Groucho with his greasepaint moustache and wisecracks, Chico the pianist with his phoney Italian accent, and Harpo the dumb clown and harp maestro.

Mary Magdalene, Mary, Nuns of the Community of St

See Who's who in major religions of the world.

Masefield, John

See Poets laureate.

Mata Hari

Margaretha Gertruida MacLeod, née Zelle (1876–1917). Mata Hari was a Dutch dancer and courtesan shot by the French after being accused of spying for the Germans in the First World War. Her name, meaning 'eye of the day' in Malay, has come to be used as a term for any (attractive) female spy.

Mathers, Samuel Liddell MacGregor

See Occult leaders.

Matsya, Matthew, Matthias

See Who's who in major religions of the world.

Maudling, Reginald

See Political scandals.

Maxwell
See Scientific eponyms.

May, Robert
See Classical cooks.

Maybe, Louis
See Boy bishop.

Maypole
See Some famous mistresses.

McComb, Leonard
See Royal Academicians.

McEwan, Ian
See Booker Prizewinners.

McKeever, Ian
See Royal Academicians.

McNeill, Anna Matilda
James McNeill Whistler's mother, subject of *Study in Black and White* often wrongly described as *Portrait of the Artist's Mother*.

Medea
Sorceress; daughter of Aeëtes; helped Jason obtain Golden Fleece; when deserted by him for Creüsa, killed her children and Creüsa.

Médecins sans Frontières
See Nobel Peace Prizewinners.

Medusa
In Greek mythology, the chief of the Gorgons, terrible women with snakes for hair, whose face would turn anyone who looked at it to stone. Medusa was the mother of Chrysaor and Pegasus and was beheaded by Perseus.

Megaera
One of the Furies, also known as Erinyes or Eumenides.

Meleager
Son of Althaea; his life would last as long as brand burning at his birth; Althaea quenched and saved it but destroyed it when Meleager slew his uncles.

Melpomene
One of the Muses and goddesses presiding over arts and sciences (tragedy) and daughter of Zeus and Mnemosyne.

Memnon
Ethiopian king; made immortal by Zeus; son of Tithonus and Eos.

Mencius
See Who's who in major religions of the world.

Menelaus
King of Sparta; son of Atreus; brother of Agamemnon; husband of Helen.

Mercury
Roman equivalent of Hermes.

Merope
One of the Pleiades, and one of seven daughters of Atlas, transformed into heavenly constellation, of which six stars are visible. Merope is said to have hidden in shame for loving a mortal.

Mezentius
Cruel Etruscan king; ally of Turnus against Aeneas; slain by Aeneas.

Midas
King of Phrygia; given gift of turning all he touched to gold.

Middleton, Stanley
See Booker Prizewinners.

Milko
Australian milkman (AS).

MILT
Mothers in leather trousers.

Minerva
Roman equivalent of Athena.

Minim brothers
See Who's who in major religions of the world.

Minos
King of Crete; after death, one of three judges of dead in Hades; son of Zeus and Europa. See Æacus.

Minotaur
Monster, half man and half beast, kept in the Labyrinth in Crete; slain by Theseus.

Mirza Husaynali
See Who's who in major religions of the world.

Mistry, Dhruva
See Royal Academicians.

Mitterand, President
See Political scandals.

Mnemosyne
Goddess of memory; mother by Zeus of Muses.

Möbius strip
See Scientific eponyms.

Mohammed
See Who's who in major religions of the world.

Moirae
See Fates.

Momus
God of ridicule.

Monroe, Marilyn
See Some famous mistresses.

Moon, Nick
See Royal Academicians.

Moon, Reverend Sun Myung
See Occult leaders.

Moore, G(eorge) E(dward)
See Some important twentieth-century philosophers who analysed the subtleties of ordinary language.

Morpheus
God of dreams.

Mors
Roman equivalent of Thanatos.

Morta
Roman goddess of fate; see Fates.

Moseley, Henry Gwyn Jeffreys
See Medical pioneers.

Moses
See Who's who in major religions of the world.

Motion, Andrew
See Poets laureate.

Muhammad bin' Abd al-Wahhab
See Who's who in major religions of the world.

Mulready, William
(1786–1863) Irish painter who devised the first prepaid postage envelope which, however, attracted such ridicule that it was short lived.

Mummer
A member of a group that visited houses usually at Christmas-time, performing a stock play about St George and the Dragon with other stock characters such as Father Christmas.

Murdoch, Iris
See Booker Prizewinners.

Muses
Goddesses presiding over arts and sciences; daughters of Zeus and Mnemosyne; Calliope, Clio, Erato, Euterpe, Melpomene, Polymnia, Terpsichore, Thalia and Urania.

Myrdal, Alva
See Nobel Peace Prizewinners.

Naiads
Nymphs of waters, streams, and fountains.

Naipaul, V S
See Booker Prizewinners.

Napaeae
Wood nymphs.

Napoleon of Crime
Macavity the Mystery Cat.

Napoleon of Mexico
The emperor Augusto Iturbidê 1784–1824.

Napoleon of Oratory
William Ewart Gladstone.

Napoleon of Peace
Louis Philippe of France (1773–1860; reigned 1830–48).

Napoleon of the Drama
1   Alfred Bunn, lessee of Drury Lane Theatre 1819–26.
2   Robert William Elliston 1774–1826.

Napthali; Narasimha
See Who's who in major religions of the world.

Narcissus
Beautiful youth loved by Echo; in punishment for not returning her love, he was made to fall in love with his image reflected in a pool; he pined away and became a flower.

Nash, David
See Royal Academicians.

Nasier, Alcofribas
A pseudonym (and anagram) of François Rabelais as author of *Gargantua and Pantagruel*.

Neiland, Professor Brendan
See Royal Academicians.

Nemesis
Goddess of retribution.

Neoptolemus
Son of Achilles; slew Priam; also known as Pyrrhus.

Neptune
Roman equivalent of Poseidon.

Nereids
Sea nymphs; attendants on Poseidon.

Nestor
King of Pylos; noted for wise counsel in expedition against Troy.

Newby, P H
See Booker Prizewinners.

Newton
See Scientific eponyms.

Nichiren
See Who's who in major religions of the world.

Nicholas, St
His day is 6 December; he is one of the most popular saints in Christendom, and appears sonically corrupted as Santa Claus, aka Father Christmas, Father Frost, Joulupukki, Kris Kringle, Père Noël, Sabdiklos, Sancte Claus, Sinter Klaas, and Weihnachtsmann.

Nicolle, Charles Jules Henri
See Medical pioneers.

Niemeyer, Oscar
See Architects.

Nightall, James
See Gimbert, Benjamin.

Nike
Goddess of victory.

Nine Days' Wonder

An event on everyone's lips at the time, but then completely forgotten, named for the actor Will(iam) Kempe (c1550–c1603), a member of Shakespeare's Company who in 1600 performed a nine-day Morris dance from London to Norwich, and wrote *Nine Daies Wonder* to commemorate it.

Niobe

Daughter of Tantalus; wife of Amphion; her children slain by Apollo and Artemis; changed to stone but continued to weep her loss.

Nixon, President Richard Milhous

See Political scandals.

Noguchi, Hideyo

See Medical pioneers.

Nona

Roman goddess of fate; see Fates.

Non-humans with speech

Arion, Balaam's Ass, the Black Pigeons of Dodona and Annon, Bulbul-Bezar, Comrade, Katmir, the Little Green Bird, Saleh's camel, Temilha, the White Cat, Xanthos.

North, Colonel Oliver

See Political scandals.

Notus

(Auster) One of the Winds – the south wind.

Nox

Roman equivalent of Nyx.

Nymphs

Beautiful maidens; minor deities of nature.

Nyx (Nox)

Goddess of night.

Oceanids

Ocean nymphs; daughters of Oceanus.

Oceanus

Eldest of Titans; god of waters.

Odysseus (Ulysses)

King of Ithaca; husband of Penelope; wandered ten years after fall of Troy before arriving home.

Oedipus
King of Thebes; son of Laius and Jocasta; unwittingly murdered Laius and married Jocasta; tore his eyes out when relationship was discovered.

Oenone
Nymph of Mount Ida; wife of Paris, who abandoned her; refused to cure him when he was poisoned by arrow of Philoctetes at Troy.

Oersted; Ohm
See Scientific eponyms.

Okri, Ben
See Booker Prizewinners.

Old Foss
Edward Lear's cat; when Lear built a new house, its layout was the same as the previous one, lest Foss should be put out of countenance.

Olivier, Laurence Kerr, Baron Olivier of Brighton
(1907–89) English actor, producer and director. Born in Dorking. First professional appearance was as the Suliot officer in Chapman's *Byron* in 1924, and he joined the Old Vic Company in 1937. He played all the great Shakespearean roles, and after war service he became co-director of the Old Vic Company (1944). He produced, directed and played in many acclaimed films, *Henry V*, *Hamlet* and *Richard III*. He was knighted in 1947. In 1962 he undertoook the directorship of the Chichester Festival, and was appointed director of the National Theatre until 1973, then Associate Director for a year. After 1974 he appeared chiefly in films and television productions, was made a life peer in 1970, and awarded the Order of Merit in 1981.

Olmsted, Frederick Law
See Gardeners and gardening writers.

Omar
See Who's who in major religions of the world.

Ondaatje, Michael
See Booker Prizewinners.

Oprah's Law
Named after the American chat-show hostess Oprah Winfrey who used her influence to support a US child protection Bill.

Ops
Roman equivalent of Rhea.

Oreads
Mountain nymphs.

Orestes
Son of Agamemnon and Clytemnestra; brother of Electra; slew Clytemnestra and Aegisthus; pursued by Furies until his purification by Apollo.

Orion
Hunter; slain by Artemis and made heavenly constellation.

Orpheus
Famed musician; son of Apollo and Muse Calliope; husband of Eurydice.

Orr, Professor Chris
See Royal Academicians.

Orrery
See Scientific eponyms.

Ossian
Third Century Gaelic warrior bard (cf The Minstrel Boy), son of Fionn Mac Cumhail, or Fingal. In 1760, the Scottish poet James Macpherson published books of poems that he claimed were translations of Ossian's work, but were in fact by Macpherson himself with some authentic material (cf The Lord of the Rings). The literary world was taken in, and the poems were widely circulated and translated, but Macpherson was at length exposed not least by the doubts of Dr Johnson.

Ostler, William
See Shakespeare's players.

Pales
Roman goddess of shepherds and herdsmen.

Palinurus
Aeneas' pilot; fell overboard in his sleep and was drowned.

Pam
1   Jack of Clubs (Fr pamphile), hence the name of a card game.
2   Henry John Temple, 3rd Viscount Palmerston (1784–1865), Foreign Secretary, Home Secretary and Prime Minister (1855–65). The people of Rugeley, Staffs, were ashamed of the notoriety brought upon them by Palmer the poisoner, and appealed to the Home Secretary for permission to change the name of their town. 'Certainly,' replied Lord Palmerston, 'you may name it after me.'

Pan (Faunus)
God of woods and fields; part goat; son of Hermes.

Pandion
King of Athens, son of Erichthonius, father of Procne and Philomela.

Pandora
Owner of box containing human ills; mortal wife of Epimetheus.

Paolozzi, Professor Sir Eduardo
See Royal Academicians.

Parashurama
See Who's who in major religions of the world.

Parcae
Roman equivalent of Fates (Moirae), *qv*.

Pariah
See Who's who in major religions of the world.

Paris
Son of Priam; gave apple of discord to Aphrodite, for which she enabled him to carry off Helen; slew Achilles at Troy; slain by Philoctetes.

Park Bench
Telegraphic addresses of Robert Benchley and Dorothy Parker.

Parker-Bowles, Mrs Camilla
See Some famous mistresses.

Parkinson, James
See Medical pioneers.

Partridge, John
See Royal Academicians.

Pasteur, Louis
French chemist; see Medical pioneers.

Pasteurise
See Scientific eponyms.

Patroclus
Great friend of Achilles; wore Achilles' armour and was slain by Hector.

Paul
See Who's who in major religions of the world.

Pauling, Linus Carl
See Medical pioneers.

Pavlov, Ivan Petrovich
See Medical pioneers.

Paxton, Sir Joseph
See Gardeners and gardening writers.

Pegasus
Winged horse that sprang from Medusa's body at her death; ridden by Bellerophon when he slew the Chimera.

Pei, I M
See Architects.

Pelias
King of loclus; seized throne from his brother Aeson; sent Jason for Golden Fleece; slain unwittingly by his daughters at instigation of Medea.

Pelletier, Pierre Joseph
See Medical pioneers.

Pelli, Cesar
See Architects.

Pelops
Son of Tantalus; his father cooked and served him to gods; restored to life; Peloponnesus named for him.

Penates
Roman household gods.

Penelope
Wife of Odysseus; waited faithfully for him for many years while putting off numerous suitors.

Pephredo
One of the Old Women, or Graeae; daughters of Phorcys and Ceto; shared a tooth and an eye with Enyo and Deino, which they passed from one to another.

Peres, Shimon
See Nobel Peace Prizewinners.

Periphetes
Giant; son of Hephaestus; slain by Theseus.

Perret, Auguste
See Architects.

Persephone (Proserpine)
Queen of the infernal regions; daughter of Zeus and Demeter; wife of Pluto.

Perseus
Son of Zeus and Danaë; slew Medusa; rescued Andromeda from monster and married her.

Peru, The Barber in
The voice of reason, or the 'reasonable man' at law; *cf* the Man on the Clapham Omnibus, or, more recently, the Man in the Blue Anorak. The title refers to Peru Indiana, not the South American country.

Peter
See Who's who in major religions of the world.

Peter the Great
The cat Louis Wain was given by his sisters as a wedding present, that spent so many hours on the bed of Wain's dying wife; Wain's endless sketches laid the foundation of his fame when they were published as *A Cats' Christmas Party* in the *Illustrated London News*, Christmas 1886.

Petersham
See Fashion eponyms.

Pfeiffer, Richard Friedrich Johannes
See Medical pioneers.

Phaedra
Daughter of Minos; wife of Theseus; caused the death of her stepson, Hippolytus.

Phaethon
Son of Helios; drove his father's sun chariot and was struck down by Zeus before he set world on fire.

Pharisees
See Who's who in major religions of the world.

Philip
See Who's who in major religions of the world.

Philippa
A Greek name meaning Lover of Horses.

Phillips, Augustine
See Shakespeare's players.

Phillips, Tom
See Royal Academicians.

Philoctetes
Greek warrior who possessed Hercules's bow and arrows; slew Paris at Troy with poisoned arrow.

Philomela

Daughter of King Pandion of Athens; loved by her brother-in-law Tereus (qv); turned into a swallow (or a nightingale).

Phineus

Betrothed of Andromeda; tried to slay Perseus but turned to stone by Medusa's head.

Phiz

Hablot Knight Browne (1815–82), book illustrator remembered especially for his collaboration with Charles Dickens (who wrote as Boz – hence Phiz (short for physiognomy; the face)).

Phlegethon

One of the Rivers of Underworld.

Phosphor

Morning star.

Phrixos

Brother of Helle; carried by ram of Golden Fleece to Colchis.

Piano, Renzo

See Architects.

Pied Piper of Hamelin

There are several stories relating to a mysterious piper who rid a German town of rats or other vermin. One tale names the piper as Bunting, who freed the town of Hamelin, in Brunswick, of rats, and drowned them in the river Weser. But the townsmen refused to pay and Bunting, in revenge, enticed all the children into a cavern on the side of the Koppenberg mountain. 130 children went into the pit alive, and none came out. No music was to be played in the street he led them through from that day onwards (26 June 1284). Other, similar, tales exist of the fiddler of Brandenburg; the town of Lorch which suffered plagues of ants, crickets and rats, and lost its pigs, sheep and children when the townsfolk refused to pay the hermit, charcoal-burner and old man who had cleared the infestations; and a Chinese tale which relates that when the townsfolk rewarded the dwarf Giouf with bad coins after he cleared the city of all its vermin, he summoned his mother, the genie Mergian Banou. The fifty-foot-high old woman strangled fifteen women each day for four days, taking forty others to a magic tower on the fifth, never to be seen again. The expression 'Don't forget to pay the piper' derives from these tales.

Pierre, D B C

See Booker Prizewinners.

Pilate, Pontius

C1 Roman governor; as procurator of Judaea (26–36CE) he was responsible for the first Easter; regarded as a martyr by the Coptic Church, his feast day is 25 June. See Who's who in major religions of the world.

Pilgrim Fathers

In 1608, a Puritan congregation from Scrooby in Nottinghamshire moved to Leiden in Holland, and 12 years later set sail from Plymouth in *The Mayflower* to found the colony of Plymouth (now in Massachusetts) in America.

Pirithous

Son of Ixion; friend of Theseus; tried to carry off Persephone from Hades; bound to enchanted rock by Pluto.

Plagues, Heroes of

Borremo, cardinal and archbishop of Milan (1538–84); Revd William Mompesson (1639–1709) of Eyam, Derbyshire; St Roche (d1327) of Piacenza.

Pleiades

The seven daughters of Atlas – Alcyone, Celaeno, Electra, Maia, Merope, Sterope (Asterope) and Taygeta; became a heavenly constellation, though Merope is invisible, hiding in shame for loving a mortal.

Plimsoll

See Fashion eponyms.

Pluto (Dis)

God of Hades; brother of Zeus.

Plutus

God of wealth.

Pollux

One of the Dioscuri (see Castor).

Polymnia (Polyhymnia)

One of the Muses and goddesses presiding over arts and sciences (sacred poetry) and daughter of Zeus and Mnemosyne.

Polynices

Son of Oedipus; he and his brother Eteocles killed each other; burial rite, forbidden by Creon, performed by his sister Antigone.

Polyphemus

A Cyclops; devoured six of Odysseus's men; then blinded by Odysseus.

Polyxena

Daughter of Priam; betrothed to Achilles, whom Paris slew at their betrothal; sacrificed to shade of Achilles.

Pomona
Roman goddess of fruits.

Pompadour
See Fashion eponyms.

Pompadour, Madame de
See Some famous mistresses.

Pontus
Sea god; son of Gaea.

Poope, Thomas
See Shakespeare's players.

Pooter, Charles
With his wife Carrie and son Lupin, chief characters in *The Diary of a Nobody*; see Grossmith, George and Weedon.

Poseidon (Neptune)
God of the sea; brother of Zeus.

Poulson, John
See Political scandals.

Prabhupada, Swami
See Occult leaders.

Presbyterian Church
See Who's who in major religions of the world.

Priam
King of Troy; husband of Hecuba; ransomed Hector's body from Achilles; slain by Neoptolemus.

Priapus
God of regeneration.

Primrose Day
19 April, the anniversary of the death of Benjamin Disraeli (1804–81), Lord Beaconsfield, to whose funeral HM Queen Victoria sent a wreath of primroses from Osborne: 'His favourite flowers'; not true, but the idea caught on in the name of the Conservative League founded in 1883.

Princess Pushy
Princess Michael of Kent, of whom HM Queen Elizabeth II is said to have remarked to Prince Philip that 'she's more royal than we are'.

Procne
Daughter of King Pandion of Athens; wife of Tereus (*qv*); turned into a nightingale (or a swallow).

Procris
Wife of Cephalus, who accidentally slew her.

Procrustes
Giant; stretched or cut off legs of victims to make them fit iron bed; slain by Theseus.

Proetus
Husband of Anteia; sent Bellerophon to Iobates to be put to death.

Profumo, John
See Political scandals.

Prometheus
Titan; stole fire from heaven for man. Zeus punished him by chaining him to rock in Caucasus where vultures devoured his liver daily.

Proserpine
Roman equivalent of Persephone.

Proteus
Sea god; assumed various shapes when called on to prophesy.

Prout, William
English chemist and physiologist; see Medical pioneers.

Psalmanazar, George
An unknown Frenchman who appeared in London in 1703, saying that he was from Formosa; the following year he published a book about Formosa with an exposition of its language – a complete fabrication. Literary London was completely taken in, until he was exposed by missionaries, whereupon he confessed his fraud and embarked on serious studies, becoming a friend of Dr Johnson. He died in 1763, and the secret of his true history died with him.

Psyche
Beloved of Eros; punished by jealous Aphrodite; made immortal and united with Eros.

Ptolemaic System
Ptolemy's C2 system to account for the apparent motion of the heavenly bodies. He believed in a geocentric universe with 'the heavens' revolving from east to west, in which there were spheres, each with its own period of rotation, bearing the sun, the planets and the fixed stars. The tenth, outer, sphere was the *primum mobile* that carried all the others. The whole thing was somewhat like a geocentric orrery, and made sweet sounds to boot: the 'music of the spheres'. The heliocentric Copernican System, was introduced by Nicholas Copernicus (1473–1543), but was prohibited by the RC church in 1616. Galileo (1564–1642) was no mean astronomer, and affirmed the truth of the

Copernican System in 1632; this brought him before the Inquisition which caused him to recant (but uttering under his breath, it is said, 'Eppur si muove' = 'and yet it [the earth] moves'). It's this sort of man-delivered short-sightedness that brings God into disrepute.

Pugwash Conferences on Science and World Affairs
See Nobel Peace Prizewinners.

Pye, Henry James
See Poets laureate.

Pygmalion
King of Cyprus; carved ivory statue of maiden which Aphrodite gave life as Galatea.

Pyramus
Babylonian youth; made love to Thisbe through hole in wall; thinking Thisbe slain by lion, killed himself.

Pyrrhus
See Neoptolemus.

Python
Serpent born from slime left by Deluge; slain by Apollo.

Q
See Quiller-Couch, Sir Arthur.

Quakers
See Who's who in major religions of the world.

Quiller-Couch, Sir Arthur
(1863–1944), Cornishman who became professor of English Literature at Cambridge (1912) and edited the *Oxford Book of English Verse*; wrote under the pseudonym 'Q'.

Quine, William Van Orman
See Some important twentieth-century philosophers who analysed the subtleties of ordinary language.

Quirinus
Roman war god.

Quraysh
See Who's who in major religions of the world.

Rabin, Yitzhak
See Nobel Peace Prizewinners.

Rae, Barbara
See Royal Academicians.

Rae, Fiona
See Royal Academicians.

Raffles
The Gentleman Thief, hero of *The Amateur Cracksman* (1899) created by the English writer E(rnest) W(illiam) Hornung (1866–1921), whose other claim to fame was being Sir Arthur Conan Doyle's brother-in-law.

Raffles, Sir (Thomas) Stamford
(1781–1826), English colonial administrator, and founder of Singapore, where the famous Raffles Hotel is to be found.

Raglan
See Fashion eponyms.

Rahula
See Who's who in major religions of the world.

Raj, The Hollywood
Pre-WW2 English actors in Hollywood, prized for their Englishness.

Rama
See Who's who in major religions of the world.

Ramos-Horta, Jose
See Nobel Peace Prizewinners.

Rampa, T Lobsang
The self-styled Mystic Lama, who was exposed as Cyril Henry Hoskins, a plumber's son from Devon.

Rankine
See Scientific eponyms.

Réaumur scale
See Scientific eponyms; see Technologists who made the modern world.

Redgrave, Vanessa
(1937–) English actress. Born in London, the eldest daughter of Sir Michael Redgrave and actress Rachel Kempson. She made her professional debut at the Frinton Summer Theatre in 1957 and her London stage debut alongside her father in *A Touch of the Sun* in 1958. She later joined the Royal Shakespeare Company. Her first film, *Behind the Mask* was in 1958, and she received an Academy Award nomination for *Morgan* (1966), *Isadora* (1968), *Mary, Queen of Scots* (1971) and *The Bostonians* (1984). She won Best Supporting Actress for *Julia* (1977) and an Emmy for *Playing for Time* (1980). She is well known for her active support in left-wing and humanitarian causes.

Remus
Brother of Romulus; slain by him.

Repton, Humphrey
See Gardeners and gardening writers.

Reuben
See Who's who in major religions of the world.

Rhadamanthus
One of three judges of dead in Hades; son of Zeus and Europa. See Æacus.

Rhea (Ops)
Daughter of Uranus and Gaea; wife of Cronus; mother of Zeus; identified with Cybele.

Rice, Iohn
See Shakespeare's players.

Richardson, Sir Ralph David
(1902–83) English actor. Born in Cheltenham, Gloucestershire. Established himself with the Birmingham Repertory Company in 1926, then moved to the Old Vic Company in 1930, where he took many leading parts, including the title roles of W Somerset Maugham's *Sheppey* (1930–32) and J B Priestley's *Johnson over Jordan* (1938). He later led its postwar revival, as co-director after his service in World War II. He also played with the Stratford-on-Avon company in 1952, and toured Australia and New Zealand in 1955. He was noted for his love of powerful motorcycles.

Richter scale
See Scientific eponyms.

Rideal, Eric Keightley
See Medical pioneers.

Ritchie, Ian
See Royal Academicians.

Rivers of the Underworld
Acheron (woe), Avernus (poison), Cocytus (wailing), Lethe (forgetfulness), Phlegethon (fire), Styx (across which souls of dead were ferried by Charon).

Roberts, Peter
Maggot Pete; purveyor of meat unfit for human consumption.

Robinson, Jack
If something is done really quickly, it is done before his name can be articulated; according to one source, Robinson was a London tobacco-

nist in a song, but his name was earlier associated with a Jack Robinson who was wont to call on people, but be gone by the time they were ready to receive him.

Robinson, Richard
See Shakespeare's players.

Robinson, William
See Gardeners and gardening writers.

Robles, Alfonso García
See Nobel Peace Prizewinners.

Rochester
John Wilmot, second Earl of Rochester (1647–80), Restoration poet and member of the decadent court of Charles II. He was a leading member of the 'Merry Gang', whose behaviour often landed them in court for debauchery. Returning home one night, they came across the King's Sundial, an arrangement of phallic glass globes which caused them inordinate mirth. 'What?' shouted Rochester, 'Dost thou stand here to f*ck time?' and he laid about it with his stick. The King was far from amused. Rochester died aged 33 from syphilis and poisoning from the mercury administered for its supposed curative effects.

Rogers, of Riverside Lord
See Royal Academicians.

Rogers, Richard
See Architects.

Rohe, Mies van der
See Architects.

Romulus
Founder of Rome; he and Remus suckled in infancy by she-wolf; slew Remus; deified by Romans.

Röntgen
See Scientific eponyms; see Medical pioneers.

Rooney, Michael
See Royal Academicians.

Roscius
Quintus Roscius (*d* 62BCE) Roman actor who excelled in all aspects of thespianism. Hence 'Another Roscius' (Richard Burbage (*d* 1619)), 'The British Roscius' (Thomas Betterton (1635–1710) and David Garrick (1717–79)), 'The Young Roscius' (William Henry West Betty (1791–1874) whose highly successful acting career began when he was 12 years old in 1803; he retired at the age of 33 in 1824).

Rosie Lea
See Who's who in cockney rhyming slang.

Rosoman, Leonard
See Royal Academicians.

Rotblat, Joseph
See Nobel Peace Prizewinners.

Roux, Pierre Émile
See Medical pioneers.

Rowe, Nicholas
See Poets laureate.

Roy, Arundhati
See Booker Prizewinners.

Rubens, Bernice
See Booker Prizewinners.

Ruby Murray
See Who's who in cockney rhyming slang.

Rudbeck, Olof
See Medical pioneers.

Rundle, Mrs A
See Classical cooks.

Rushdie, Salman
See Booker Prizewinners.

Russell, Bertrand
See Some important twentieth-century philosophers who analysed the subtleties of ordinary language.

Rutherford
See Scientific eponyms.

Ryle, Gilbert
See Some important twentieth-century philosophers who analysed the subtleties of ordinary language.

Saarinen, Eero
See Architects.

Sackville-West, Victoria
See Gardeners and gardening writers.

Sacred Heart of Jesus, Society of the
See Who's who in major religions of the world.

Sacred Heart, Priests of the
See Who's who in major religions of the world.

Sadducees
See Who's who in major religions of the world.

Saki
Hector Hugh Munro (1870–1916), novelist and writer of humorous, macabre and generally delightful short stories; another victim of the shameful WW1.

Sakya tribe
See Who's who in major religions of the world.

Saleh's camel
Said to have been able to speak with a human voice.

Salk, Jonas Edward
See Medical pioneers.

Samson
See Who's who in major religions of the world.

Sánchez, Oscar Arias
See Nobel Peace Prizewinners.

Sanctorius
See Medical pioneers.

Sands, Mr
(Theatrical code) Fire.

Sanger, Margaret
See Medical pioneers.

Sangha
See Who's who in major religions of the world.

Saravasti
See Who's who in major religions of the world.

Sarpedon
King of Lycia; son of Zeus and Europa; slain by Patroclus at Troy.

Sartre, Jean-Paul
See Some important twentieth-century philosophers who analysed the subtleties of ordinary language.

Sati
See Who's who in major religions of the world.

Saturn
Roman equivalent of Cronus. See Cronus.

Satyrs
Hoofed demigods of woods and fields; companions of Dionysus.

Scaffold
The 60s Liverpudlian trio comprising Roger McGough, Mike McArtney (Paul's brother), and John Gorman, known for *Lily the Pink* and *Thank you very much for the Aintree Iron*.

Scarlet Pimpernel
The nickname of Sir Percy Blakeney, the hero of several novels by Baroness Orczy. The name came from Blakeney's use of the pimpernel, a plant of the primrose family, as his emblem.

Schaudinn, Fritz Richard
See Medical pioneers.

Sciron
Robber; forced strangers to wash his feet, then hurled them into sea where tortoise devoured them; slain by Theseus.

Scott, Paul
See Booker Prizewinners.

Scribes
See Who's who in major religions of the world.

Scylla
Female monster inhabiting rock opposite Charybdis; menaced passing sailors.

Searle, John
See Some important twentieth-century philosophers who analysed the subtleties of ordinary language.

Selene (Luna)
Goddess of the moon.

Selkirk, (or Selcraig) Alexander
(1676–1721) A Scottish sailor who quarrelled with his captain and asked to be put ashore on Juan Fernández, an uninhabited island, in 1704. He spent nearly four and a half years there before being rescued. He is said to have been the original Robinson Crusoe, a book published in 1720, by Daniel Defoe.

Semele
Daughter of Cadmus; mother by Zeus of Dionysus; demanded Zeus appear before her in all his splendour and was destroyed by his lightning bolts.

Senior citizen
A pseudo-polite or euphemistic term for the even less attractively described 'old-age pensioner'.

Service User
PC term for a resident of an old folks' (or senior citizens') home.

Seuss, Dr
Pseudonym of Theodore (Ted) Seuss Geissel (1904–91) US children's author and illustrator, most famous for *The Cat in the Hat* (1958).

Shadwell, Thomas
See Poets laureate.

Shancke, Iohn
See Shakespeare's players.

Shang, Kings of the
See Who's who in major religions of the world.

Sharpey-Schafer, Edward
See Medical pioneers.

SHAZAM
Egyptian wizard who enables Billy Batson to transform himself into Captain Marvel; the wizard in turn is granted his powers by the deities Solomon for wisdom, Hercules for strength, Atlas for stamina, Zeus for power, Achilles for courage, Mercury for speed ... SHAZAM.

Sherrington, Charles Scott
See Medical pioneers.

Shi'ite
(Of Muslims) Turkish = *master ruler*.

Shi'ites
See Who's who in major religions of the world.

Shipman, Harold Frederick
(1946–2003) English mass-murderer. After a clinical audit commissioned by the Department of Health, it is estimated that he was responsible for the deaths of at least 236 people, although at the time of his trial, he was convicted of only 15 deaths. In 1976 he was dismissed from his post as a GP for illegally obtaining the morphine-like drug pethidine, but re-emerged as a GP in the late 70s at Hyde, Greater Manchester. He was at last arrested in connection with the murder of his patient Kathleen Grundy, and later charged with a series of other apparently motiveless murders of elderly patients by morphine injection. He never explained why, and committed suicide in prison.

Shiva
See Who's who in major religions of the world.

Sibyls
Various prophetesses; most famous, Cumaean sibyl, accompanied Aeneas into Hades.

Siemens
See Scientific eponyms.

Sikes, Bill
A character in Dickens's *Oliver Twist*.

Sileni
Minor woodland deities similar to satyrs (singular – Silenus). Sometimes Silenus refers to eldest of satyrs, son of Hermes or of Pan.

Silvanus
Roman god of woods and fields.

Simeon; Simon
See Who's who in major religions of the world.

Simpson, Mrs
See Some famous mistresses.

Simpson, Sir James Young
See Medical pioneers.

Sinis
Giant; he bent pines, with which he hurled victims against side of mountain; slain by Theseus.

Sirens
Minor deities who lured sailors to destruction with their singing.

Sisters of Mercy
See Who's who in major religions of the world.

Sisyphus
King of Corinth; condemned in Tartarus to roll huge stone to top of hill; it always rolled back down again.

Skidmore Owings and Merrill
See Architects.

Sleipnir
In Norse mythology, Odin's eight-legged horse (the sliding one), which could carry its owner over both land and sea; said to represent the winds which might blow from any of the eight principal points of the compass.

Slye, William
See Shakespeare's players.

Smith, Elisabeth
See Classical cooks.

Smudger
A 'beach photographer' who developed the pictures on site; the title reflects the quality of the pictures. 'On the smudge' – working as a smudger.

Sol
Roman equivalent of Helios.

Somnus
Roman equivalent of Hypnos.

Southey, Robert
See Poets laureate.

Soyer, Alexis
See Classical cooks.

Spallanzani, Lazaro
See Medical pioneers.

Spencer
See Fashion eponyms.

Sphinx
Monster of Thebes; killed those who could not answer her riddle; slain by Oedipus. Name also refers to other monsters having body of lion, wings, and head and bust of woman.

Starling, Ernest Henry
See Medical pioneers.

Sterope (Asterope)
One of the Pleiades, and one of seven daughters of Atlas, transformed into heavenly constellation, of which six stars are visible.

Stetson
See Fashion eponyms.

Stheno
One of the Gorgons.

Stirling, James
See Architects.

Stopes, Marie Carmichael
See Medical pioneers.

Storey, David
See Booker Prizewinners.

Styx
One of the Rivers of Underworld. The souls of the dead were ferried across the Styx by Charon with a coin (obelus) on the tongue.

Suddodhana, Prince
See Who's who in major religions of the world.

Sudras
See Who's who in major religions of the world.

Sufis
See Who's who in major religions of the world.

Sullivan, Henry
See The first Channel swimmers.

Sullivan, Louis Henry
See Architects.

Sung, Dukes of
See Who's who in major religions of the world.

Supertramp
See Davies, WH.

Sutcliffe, Peter
(1946–) English murderer known as the Yorkshire Ripper. He was finally arrested and charged in January 1981, despite having been interviewed on several occasions during the 'Ripper' enquiry by the police but released each time. He was given 20 life sentences for thirteen murders; several of his victims were prostitutes, and most were killed in the same way – beaten over the head with a hammer and stabbed with a screwdriver – and seven attempted murders over five years in northern England and the Midlands.

Sutton, Philip
See Royal Academicians.

Swammerdam, Jan
See Medical pioneers.

Swampy
Daniel Hooper.

Swedenborg, Emanuel
See Occult leaders.

Sweeney Todd
See Who's who in cockney rhyming slang.

Swift, Graham
See Booker Prizewinners.

Symplegades
Clashing rocks at entrance to Black Sea; Argo passed through, causing them to become forever fixed.

Syrinx
Nymph pursued by Pan; changed to reeds, from which he made his pipes.

Tagliacozzi, Gasparo
See Medical pioneers.

Taizé Community, The
See Who's who in major religions of the world.

Tall poppy
(sl) Australian who needs cutting down to size.

Tange, Kenzo
See Architects.

Tantalus
Cruel king; father of Pelops and Niobe; condemned in Tartarus to stand chin-deep in lake surrounded by fruit branches; as he tried to eat or drink, water or fruit always receded.

Tartarus
Underworld below Hades; often refers to Hades.

Tate, Nahum
See Poets laureate.

Tatlin, Vladimir
See Architects.

Taygeta
One of the six visible Pleiades.

Tea-Leaf
See Who's who in cockney rhyming slang.

Teenage
Relating to, denoting, or suitable for teenagers – people in their teens. A teenager comes into being on a thirteenth birthday, and ends as the nineteenth year gives way to the twentieth. As for the word, teenagers appeared in the 1940s, teeners having emerged in the 1890s.

Telemachus
Son of Odysseus; made unsuccessful journey to find his father.

Tellus
Roman goddess of earth.

Temliha
The king of serpents, said to have been able to speak with a human voice.

Temme, Edward
See The first Channel swimmers.

Tennyson, Alfred, Lord
See Poets laureate.

Teresa, Mother
See Nobel Peace Prizewinners.

Tereus
Son of Ares (Mars); King of the Thracians; husband of Procne and father of Itys, slain by Procne and served to Tereus when she found that he was wooing her sister Philomela; turned into a hoopoe (or a hawk).

Terminus
Roman god of boundaries and landmarks.

Terpsichore
One of the Muses and goddesses presiding over arts and sciences (choral dance and song) and daughter of Zeus and Mnemosyne.

Terra
Roman earth goddess.

Terry, Dame (Alice) Ellen
(1848–1928) English actress. Born in Coventry, daughter of a provincial actor and sister of Fred Terry. She first appeared on stage at the age of eight as Mammilius in *The Winter's Tale* at the Prince's Theatre, London. From 1862 she played in Bristol and after a brief marriage to the painter G F Watts in 1864 and a second retirement from the stage during which her two children by E W Godwin were born; Edith and Edward Gordon Craig. She established herself as the leading Shakespearean actress in London, dominating the English and US theatre during 1878 to 1902 with Henry Irving. In 1903 she entered theatre management without Irving and toured and lectured widely. She married Charles Kelly (Wardell) in 1876 and in 1907 the US actor James Carew. She received the DBE in 1925.

Tesla
See Scientific eponyms.

Tetragrammaton
See IHVH.

Thalia
A sea-nymph, attendant upon Poseidon.

Thalia
Bloom; with Aglaia and Euphrosyne one of the three Graces; daughters of Zeus and Eurynome.

Thalia
One of the Muses and goddesses presiding over arts and sciences (comedy and bucolic poetry) and daughter of Zeus and Mnemosyne.

Thanatos (Mors)
God of death.

Themis
Titan goddess of laws of physical phenomena; daughter of Uranus; mother of Prometheus.

Theodore, Constitutions of
See Who's who in major religions of the world.

Therblig
A modified reversal of the surname of the American engineer Frank Bunker Gilbreth (1868–1924) who invented the term (which it must be said has a somewhat Swiftean appearance) in about 1919 to describe any of the types of action involved in carrying out a task, as a means of task analysis – time-and-motion study. Therbligs include: | Assemble | Disassemble | Find | Grasp | Inspect | Load/unload transport |Position | Release load | Rest (take a break) | Search | Select | Use | Wait (avoidable delay) | Wait (unavoidable delay).

Theseus
Son of Aegeus; slew Minotaur; married and deserted Ariadne; later married Phaedra.

Thisbe
Beloved of Pyramus; killed herself at his death.

Thomas
See Who's who in major religions of the world.

Thyestes
Brother of Atreus; Atreus killed three of his sons and served them to him at a banquet.

Tilson, Joe
See Royal Academicians.

Tindle, David
See Royal Academicians.

Tiraboschi, Enrico
See The first Channel swimmers.

Tiresias
Blind soothsayer of Thebes.

Tisiphone
One of the Furies, also known as Erinyes or Eumenides.

Tithonus
Mortal loved by Eos; changed into a grasshopper.

Tizard, Sir Henry Thomas
(1885–1959) English chemist and administrator. Born in Gillingham, Kent, and studied chemistry at Magdalen College, Oxford. His appointment as Fellow and Tutor of Oriel College, was interrupted by WWI, when he was an assistant controller of experiments and research for the RFC. He returned to Oxford and became Reader in Thermodynamics, but left to be secretary of the department of scientific and industrial research. From 1929 to 1942 he was Rector of Imperial College, 1942 to 1946 he was president of Magdalen College, Oxford. His personal scientific work included some electro-chemistry and work on aircraft fuels, and he was involved as an adviser to the British Government in the scientific aspects of air defence. He was also chairman of the Aeronautical Research Committee from 1933 to 1943 and led a mission to the USA in 1940. He received many military honours and was elected FRS in 1926.

Tod Sloan
See Who's who in cockney rhyming slang.

Tompion, Thomas
(1639–1713) English master clockmaker – 'the father of English watchmaking'.

Tooley, Nicholas
See Shakespeare's players.

Tosher
Victorian totting sewerman.

Toth, Charles
See The first Channel swimmers.

Totter
One who sifts rubbish to find items worth savaging.

Treviranus, Ludolf Christian
See Medical pioneers.

Trevor, Sir John
See Political scandals.

Trilby
See Fashion eponyms.

Trimble, David
See Nobel Peace Prizewinners.

Trinitarian order
See Who's who in major religions of the world.

Triton
Demigod of sea; son of Poseidon.

Trouble and Strife
See Who's who in cockney rhyming slang.

Trump
Dog belonging to the English artist William Hogarth (1697–1764).

Tucker, William
See Royal Academicians.

Tum, Rigoberta Menchu
See Nobel Peace Prizewinners.

Turnus
King of Rutuli in Italy; betrothed to Lavinia; slain by Aeneas.

Turpin, Dick
A famous Highwayman, Dick Turpin (1705–1739) was born in Hempstead, Essex, and after his apprenticeship to a butcher in Whitechapel set up a shop of his own in 1728. His criminal career began with the sale of stolen sheep and cattle through his shop, but when he was caught he turned to smuggling near Canvey Island. Housebreaking soon followed and in 1735 he became a highwayman, working in Epping Forest and Hounslow Heath. Turpin's name soon became famous, as did his horse, Black Bess, and he was arrested in Yorkshire. He was hanged at the Mount, outside York, in 1739.

Tutu, Desmond Mpilo
See Nobel Peace Prizewinners.

Twort, Frederick William
See Medical pioneers.

Tyche (Fortuna)
The Goddess of fortune.

Ulysses
Roman equivalent of Odysseus.

Underwood, John
See Shakespeare's players.

Unitarians
See Who's who in major religions of the world.

Unsworth, Barry
See Booker Prizewinners.

Urania
One of the Muses and goddesses presiding over arts and sciences (astronomy) and daughter of Zeus and Mnemosyne.

Uranus
Personification of Heaven; husband of Gaea; father of Titans; dethroned by his son Cronus.

Utzon, Jørn
See Architects.

Vaisnava Bhakti
See Who's who in major religions of the world.

Valentine's Day
St Valentine's Day is 14 February; the C14 writers Chaucer and Gower both cite the day as that upon which birds (of whom Valentine was patron saint) choose their mates. Later, it became the day upon which, with much merrymaking, tokens of affection are sent by members of both sexes to those of the other. Valentine was a Roman who was martyred for becoming a Christian and a priest to boot, on 14 February 269. Some say he left a note for the jailer's daughter, who had befriended him, signed 'From your Valentine'; others add that 14 February was a holiday for the love-goddess Juno, and the day before the beginning of the love-feast of Lupercal.

Valkyries
The handmaidens of Odin, in Norse mythology, who decided which soldiers would die in battle. The seven, nine or twelve mounted Valkyries swept onto the battlefield with swords drawn and took the dead to Valhalla, where they were served mead and ale in the skulls of their vanquished enemy (*valr* = 'slain warriors' + *köri* = 'to choose').

Vallombrosan monks
See Who's who in major religions of the world.

Vamana
See Who's who in major religions of the world.

Vanbrugh, Sir John
See Gardeners and gardening writers.

Vandals
A race of warriors from north-east Germany who attacked Gaul, Spain and North Africa before rampaging through Rome, destroying the city and plundering it of its treasures. The term *vandal* is now used to refer to anyone who wilfully destroys works of art or property.

Varaha
See Who's who in major religions of the world.

Varenne, Francois La
See Classical cooks.

Venus
Roman equivalent of Aphrodite.

Vertumnus
Roman god of fruits and vegetables; husband of Pomona.

Vesta
Roman equivalent of Hestia.

Viasyas
See Who's who in major religions of the world.

Vierkotter, Arnst
See The first Channel swimmers.

Villiers, Barbara
See Some famous mistresses.

Vincent de Paul, Sisters of Charity of
See Who's who in major religions of the world.

Vishnu
See Who's who in major religions of the world.

Volta
See Scientific eponyms.

Voltaire
Pseudonym of François Marie Arouet (1694–1778), French writer and philosopher. A prolific pamphleteer, he used over 50 pseudonyms to conceal his identity. He took the name Voltaire in 1718; it is assumed to be an anagram of Arouet l(e) j(eune) [j = i and u = v].

Vulcan
Roman equivalent of Hephaestus.

Wahhabis
See Who's who in major religions of the world.

Waksman, Selman Abraham
American biologist; see Medical pioneers.

Wallace D Fard
See Who's who in major religions of the world.

Walesa, Lech
See Nobel Peace Prizewinners.

Warburg, Otto Heinrich
See Medical pioneers.

Warton, Thomas
See Poets laureate.

Washington, George
See Political scandals.

Watson, Revd John Selby
(1804–84) He was ordained in 1839, and married in 1845 the wife whom he was to murder in 1871. After his conviction, with a recommendation for mercy, he was sent to Parkhurst Prison where he died at the age of 80.

Watt
See Scientific eponyms; see Technologists who made the modern world.

Wauchope, Capt Robert
Knowing the 'exact' time at sea is necessary for fixing one's position. Armed with a sextant and a chronometer set to the time at the home port, the navigator can work out the position of the vessel. Chronometers of the necessary accuracy were developed from the end of the 18th century, but how to fix the time at one's home port? To avoid ships' timekeepers having to go ashore, a visible time signal was needed, and the first was the 'time ball' which, set on high, drops at a known time each day. This device was proposed by Captain Robert Wauchope of the British Royal Navy in 1824. A manually operated device was first set up at the Royal Observatory, Greenwich in 1833. In due course, time balls were erected in London and in many ports and, in 1862, time balls in The Strand and Cornhill in London, and at the ports of Deal and Liverpool, were dropped by telegraph signals from Greenwich to inaugurate Greenwich Mean Time. In the United States, the Naval Observatory was set up at Washington in 1845; one of its tasks was to provide a national time service, and it first sent out automatic time signals in 1880.

Webb, Matthew
See The first Channel swimmers.

Wellington
See **Fashion eponyms**.

West, Fred(erick) and Rosemary
(1942–95) (1953–) English alleged murderers. Fred was a builder by trade, and in 1972 he married Rosemary, his second wife, and they had seven children. Their daughter Heather went missing in 1987, and it wasn't until 1994 that the remains of her body were found underneath the floor of their home in Gloucester. The remains of eight more bodies of young women were found there, and at three other sites, some of which had been buried in the 1970s. Before he could be tried, Fred hanged himself in prison on 1 January 1995, and so the murder charges against him were dropped. Rosemary was found guilty of 10 murders, one of them being one of her daughters, and was sentenced to life imprisonment.

Whishaw, Anthony
See **Royal Academicians**.

Whitehead, A N
See **Some important twentieth-century philosophers** who analysed the subtleties of ordinary language.

Whitehead, William
See **Poets laureate**.

Whittington, Sir Richard, 'Dick'
The pantomime story invents lowly parentage in order to tell a rags-to-riches story, but Dick was in fact the youngest son of Sir William Whittington of Pauntley in Gloucestershire. He married Alice Fitzwaryn and became the richest merchant in the country. He was mayor of London 1397–98, 1406–07 and 1419–20. He was a great philanthropist and at his death in 1423 left his fortune for charitable works. Dick Whittington's famous cat never existed in the feline sense. *Cats* were a type of sailing vessel, which Whittington used to transport coal to London, from which he made his fortune.

Wiesel, Elie
See **Nobel Peace Prizewinners**.

Wilding, Alison
See **Royal Academicians**.

Wiley, Gerald
See **Barker, Ronnie**.

Wilkes, John
See **Political scandals**.

Williams, Jody
See Nobel Peace Prizewinners.

Williams, Sir Kyffin
See Royal Academicians.

Wilson, Harriette
See Some famous mistresses.

Wilson, Keppel and Betty
Jack Keppel from Liverpool and Joe Wilson from Cork, Ireland, formed a tap-dancing act before being joined by Betty Knox (once Jack Benny's partner) and developing their trademark 'sand dance' to music arranged by Hoagy Carmichael.

Wilson, Professor Sir Colin St John
See Royal Academicians.

Withering, William
See Medical pioneers.

Wittgenstein, Ludwig
See Some important twentieth-century philosophers who analysed the subtleties of ordinary language.

Wood Family
(Theatrical slang) Empty seats.

Wood, Mr
Policeman's truncheon.

Woodgate, Clare
Kim Cattrall (*b* 21 August 1956).

Woodrow, Bill
See Royal Academicians.

Woolworth, Frank Winfield
(1852–1919) Founder (inter alia) of the 5 and 10-cent store chain in the US, and the 3d and 6d stores in Britain, which are still much in evidence in High Streets. The name Winfield lives on as a Woolworth brand.

Worde, Wynkyn de
See Classical cooks.

Wordsworth, William
(1770–1850) British poet who settled in the Lake District with his wife Mary and sister Dorothy; his Dove Cottage remains a tourist attraction; he is chiefly known for his poem *Daffodils*. See **Poets laureate**.

Wragg, John
See **Royal Academicians**.

Wright, Almroth Edward
See **Medical pioneers**.

Wright, Frank Lloyd
See **Architects**.

Xanthos
Achilles' horse, said to have been able to speak with a human voice.

Xantippe
1   Socrates' scolding, nagging, peevish wife.
2   Daughter of Cimonos, who suckled her father in prison to keep him alive. (Euphrasia, d of Evander, is said to have employed the same ruse to fool the prison guard.)

Xavier de Belsunce
Administered to the plague-stricken people of Marseilles (1720–22).

Xenocrates
Greek philosopher tempted unsuccessfully by the courtesan Laïs, who said: 'I thought he had been a living man and not a mere stone.'

Ximena
Count de Gormez insulted El Cid's father, and was slain; four times his daughter X demanded vengeance of the king, but the king perceived that El Cid was in love with her, delayed vengeance and at last she married El Cid.

Xit
Royal dwarf of Edward VI.

Xury
In Defoe's *Robinson Crusoe* a Moresco boy, servant to Crusoe.

Yahoo
In Swift's *Gulliver's Travels*, one of the human brutes subject to the Houyhnhnms.

Yahweh
See **IHVH**.

Yajûi and Majûj
The Arabian form of Gog and Magog. Gog is a tribe of Turks and Magog of the Gilân (the Geli or Gelæ of Ptolemy and Strabo). They were said to be man eaters and, according the *The Holy Koran*, Dhulkarnein made a rampart of red-hot metal to keep them out.

Yama
A Hindu deity in the form of a four-armed man riding a bull.

Yamen
In Hindu mythology, the lord and potentate of Pandalon (Hell).

Yarico
Thomas Inkle fell in love with this young Indian maiden; they lived as man and wife, and he then sold her into slavery in Barbados.

Yasodhara, Princess
See Who's who in major religions of the world.

Yellow Dwarf, The
An ugly malignant imp who carried Princess Allfair off to Steel Castle on his Spanish Cat, on the very day that she was to be married to the King of the Gold Mines. A good siren gave the King a magic sword to rescue the Princess, but he dropped it as he rushed to embrace her and the YD picked it up and slew both the King and the Princess as she rushed to avert the blow. The story is recounted by Comtesse D'Aulnoy in *Contes des Fées* (1682), along with 'The White Cat'.

Yenadizze
According to Longfellow's *Hiawatha*, an idler, gambler and fop.

Yendys, Sydney
Nom de plume of the English poet of the Spasmodic school Sydney Thompson Dobell (1824–74).

Yersin, Alexandre Emile John
See Medical pioneers.

Zebulun
See Who's who in major religions of the world.

Zephaniah
See Who's who in major religions of the world.

Zephyrus
(Favonius) One of several Winds – the west wind.

Zeus (Jupiter)
Chief of Olympian gods; son of Cronus and Rhea; husband of Hera.

Zouave
A French soldier.

Zwingli, Hulderich (or Ulrich)
(1484–1531), Swiss religious philosopher and reformer.

Part 2   The groups

Fine arts

Painting

Royal Academicians

The Royal Academy of Arts was founded in 1768 for the encouragement of the fine arts, with Joshua Reynolds as its first President. Its present membership is limited to eighty in number, all of whom are painters, engravers, sculptors or architects, and an unlimited number of Senior Academicians who are over seventy-five years old. Perhaps the Academicians' most memorable group likeness of any era was *The life school at the Royal Academy* by John (Johann) Zoffany (1733–1810). This work, first exhibited in 1772, appears to represent the members of the day not as craftsmen, but as gentlemen of leisure; almost everyone is surely wearing his best wig.

The two women RAs presented Zoffany with a problem, since his composition centres on a couple of (male) life models, posed in a state of unimpeded nakedness. However, he did manage to save the modesty of the lady members. Firstly he included each of them only as a portrait; furthermore their likenesses are turned towards somewhere decorously out of sight.

The current Academicians are as follows:

A

Ivor Abrahams
Norman Ackroyd
Norman Adams
Craigie Aitchison
Will Alsop
Diana Armfield
Gillian Ayres

B

John Bellany
Gordon Benson

Adrian Berg
Elizabeth Blackadder
Peter Blake
Sandra Blow
Olwyn Bowey
William Bowyer
Ralph Brown
James Butler

C

Professor H T Cadbury-Brown
Jeffery Camp

Patrick Caulfield
Ann Christopher
Geoffrey Clarke
Robert Clatworthy
Maurice Cockrill
Peter Coker
Peter Cook
Jean Cooke
Eileen Cooper
Tony Cragg
John Craxton
Edward Cullinan
Frederick Cuming
Gus Cummins

D
Professor Trevor Dannatt
Richard Deacon
Jennifer Dickson
Ken Draper
Sir Philip Dowson
Bernard Dunstan
Jennifer Durrant

E
Anthony Eyton

F
Stephen Farthing
Mary Fedden
Barry Flanagan
Lord Foster of Thames Bank
Donald Hamilton Fraser
Peter Freeth

G
Frederick Gore
Antony Gormley
Anthony Green
Piers Gough
Nicholas Grimshaw

H
Nigel Hall
David Hockney
Sir Michael Hopkins
Ken Howard
John Hoyland
Gary Hume
Paul Huxley

I
Albert Irvin
Flavia Irwin

J
William Jacklin
Eva Jiricna
Allen Jones

K
Anish Kapoor
Phillip King PRA
R B Kitaj
Professor Bryan Kneale
Paul Koralek

L
Sonia Lawson
Christopher Le Brun
Ben Levene
Richard Long

M
David Mach
Richard MacCormac
Leonard McComb
Ian McKeever
John Maine
Leonard Manasseh
Michael Manser
Dhruva Mistry
Nick Moon

N
David Nash

Professor Brendan Neiland

O

Professor Chris Orr

P

Professor Sir Eduardo Paolozzi
John Partridge
Tom Phillips

R

Barbara Rae
Fiona Rae
Ian Ritchie
Lord Rogers of Riverside
Michael Rooney
Leonard Rosoman

S

Philip Sutton

T

Joe Tilson
David Tindle
William Tucker

W

Sir Kyffin Williams
Professor Sir Colin St John Wilson
Anthony Whishaw
Alison Wilding
Bill Woodrow
John Wragg

Saintly themes in painting

St Agnes, José de Ribera (1588–1652)
As a punishment for refusing to marry the son of the local Roman prefect,
Agnes was made to go naked to a brothel. De Ribera's painting shows how
her hair miraculously grew to cover her on the way. An angel protected
her virginity; but she was later stabbed to death.

Crucifixion of St Andrew, José de Ribera
An Apostle, brother of St Peter; as punishment for his work of conversion
in Greece the local Roman governor had him put to death, on a diagonally
shaped cross. This was consequently known as the cross of St Andrew, as
represented on the Scots flag. He is the patron saint of Scotland and also
seen as a protector against gout. Besides the X-shaped cross of his execution, St Andrew's other attribute is a book.

St Anne teaching the Virgin, Georges de la Tour (1593–1652)
St Anne, wife of Joachim, was the mother of the Virgin Mary. In a strongly
candle-lit scene, she is shown here holding an opened book towards the
Virgin. This subject was used by a number of painters, some of whom
showed St Anne teaching her daughter embroidery.

The Annunciation, Giovanni di Paolo (1403–82)
A frequent theme of Christian art, based on a passage from the Gospel of
St Luke in which Mary is told by the Archangel Gabriel that she is to be the

mother of Jesus. Most versions show a secluded interior where the Virgin kneels in acknowledgement of the angel and his message, or sits reading a book. They also feature the divinely illuminated dove of the Annunciation descending towards Mary, and a white lily, symbol of purity.

The Temptation of St Anthony, Joachim Patinir (early C16)

In C4 Egypt St Anthony gave up the life of a rich young fashionable man in order to live as a hermit in the desert. There he was fed by ravens while resisting a prodigious series of fiendish temptations. These were a popular subject around the date of Patinir's painting, which shows the saint being assailed by three nubile young women while at the edges of the picture lurk a monkey, often symbolising lust, and a repulsive hag. Famously the Temptations were also painted by Bosch and Grünewald, whose works respectively show a black mass conducted by monsters, and a grotesque depiction of disease and deformity.

The saint's help has traditionally been invoked against venereal disease; also St Anthony's fire, or erysipelas. He was patron of an order of Hospitallers whose rights allowed their pigs to scavenge in public places; for this reason he was also the patron of swineherds, and his attributes include a pig, a bell and a crutch.

St Apollonia, Piero della Francesca (c1416–92)

A C3 Alexandrian woman, martyred during the general persecutions of that time. Tradition at first declared that her jaws were broken; in later accounts of her death, her teeth were pulled out. It is this subsequent version to which Piero della Francesca's plain and dignified work refers, via the attributes held up by the saint, ie a pair of pincers, grasping a tooth. St Apollonia, not surprisingly invoked against toothache, is the patroness of dentistry.

St Augustine and the child, Fra Filippo Lippi (c1406–69)

St Augustine (b354, in North Africa) was one of the first to expound Christianity as an organised theology. As described in his Confessions he had been converted by degrees – hence, perhaps, his famous plea: 'Make me continent and chaste, oh Lord ... but not yet.' The picture by Fra Filippo Lippi shows the story of Augustine and the small boy he found trying to empty the sea into a hole on the beach. When the saint told the child he could never succeed, the boy said that Augustine was bound to meet just as much difficulty in explaining the Trinity. St Augustine's attributes are a book, and a heart.

St Bartholomew, Master of St Bartholomew (fl c1500)

An Apostle and evangelist, who suffered martyrdom in Armenia. Since he died by being flayed alive, his attributes, in addition to a book, include a flaying knife. Some technically accomplished likenesses show him wearing his own skin as a form of loincloth; in this portrait he is decorously robed, as are SS Agnes and Cecilia (see below), together with a modestly undersized donor. He is the patron saint of activities including the leather trade and butchery.

St Benedict, from an C11 manuscript

The saint (480–543) was a wealthy native of Umbria who became a hermit. This painting shows him seated, holding a book and raising his hand in blessing. The Benedictine order, founded by him at Monte Cassino, was an influence against the disorder of the times, and an example of monastic organisation that made itself felt for several centuries. Benedict, traditionally invoked against witches, is the patron of coppersmiths; his attributes are a book, a broken sieve and a raven.

The Vision of St Bernard, Fra Filippo Lippi

In 1113 St Bernard joined the Cistercian order. Subsequently his spiritual influence became international; his preaching, at the small French town of Vézelay, initiated the murderous Second Crusade. In this painting, set against a peaceful rural landscape, he sits pen in hand, adoring the Virgin, around whom crowd angels with childlike faces.

St Bonaventura, Francisco de Zurbarán (1598–1664)

Born near Viterbo, in 1221; a Franciscan theologian, and biographer of St Francis (see below). He refused many grand honours, but eventually agreed to become a cardinal. The story goes that when the Pope's representatives brought the saint his cardinal's hat, at a convent where he was performing manual labour, he asked them to hang it on a tree until he had done the washing up. It was rumoured that his death, in 1274 at an Oecumenical Council, was the result of poisoning.

Martyrdom of St Catherine, Lucas Cranach the Elder (1472–1555)

In the C4 this aristocratic Alexandrian convert was noted for her ability in religious debate – so much so that she was condemned to be torn to pieces on a wheel. In the event she was beheaded, the wheel itself having been destroyed by fire from heaven. Cranach's painting shows her richly dressed in the fashion of his time, kneeling in prayer while all around her enemies are struck down by celestial flame. The name of the Catherine wheel has been taken by firework manufacturers from the best-known of her several attributes. She is the patron saint of philosophers.

St Cecilia playing the Organ, Carlo Dolci (1616–86)

A well-born Roman, converted to Christianity in childhood, sometime in C2–4. An early account of her life asserts that she died a virgin despite being given in marriage. Such was her insistence that an angel guarded her virginity, her pagan husband responded by becoming a fellow convert. Having been sentenced to death for her religion, she took three days to expire following an incomplete decapitation. Conventionally, as in Dolci's painting, she is shown playing the organ, and since the C16 she has been the patron saint of church music.

St Christopher, Quentin Massys (1465/6–1530)

The saint, a Palestinian martyred by beheading, is usually described as a benevolent but not very intelligent giant of a man. The central story from his life relates how, in carrying a child across a river, he found himself threatened by drowning, beneath a burden that had somehow grown heavier. On reaching the opposite bank of the river, he discovered that he had been carrying the infant Christ. Massys' painting shows the saint bearing the child on his shoulders and supporting himself, as in other pictures, with a staff.

St Dominic, Lippo di Vanni (fl 1344–75)

In this painting the saint, an aristocratic C13 Spaniard, is shown holding a lily, the emblem most associated with him, and wearing the habit of the Dominican order of mendicants, as its founder. One of his attributes is the rosary, whose popular use he is said to have introduced. Sometimes he is depicted with a dog bearing a fiery torch in its mouth, as a creature to which his mother once dreamed she had given birth.

St Dorothea and the Infant Christ, Francesco di Giorgio (1439–1501/2)

A colourful legend surrounds the martyrdom of this Cappodocian woman, put to death during the reign of the Roman emperor Diocletian. One Theophilus, a member of the court that sentenced her to death, asked her to make him a posthumous present of flowers and fruit from Paradise. Having duly received a basket of roses and apples, delivered to him by a child, Theophilus became a Christian convert. Such a basket is Dorothea's attribute, and she is patron saint of brides, midwives and brewers and, of course, florists.

Martyrdom of St Erasmus, Dieric Bouts (c1415–75)

This painting shows the saint's martyrdom with a frankness typical of the time, notwithstanding the apparent calmness of everyone involved. Erasmus died near Rome during the persecutions of Diocletian and

Maximilian's imperial rule. Various tortures failed to end his life, including battering with mallets, forcing him to drink boiling oil, and cooking him in a giant casserole. Dieric Bouts shows his would-be executioners winding his entrails onto a windlass; eventually, the legend declares, Erasmus achieved a natural death. The windlass is his attribute nonetheless, and as the patron saint of sailors he is invoked against danger at sea as well as colic and the pains of childbirth.

Vision of St Eustace, Antonio Pisanello (c1395–1455)

This mysterious painting, with its scattering of wild creatures against a dark background, shows the moment when Eustace underwent his conversion to Christianity. Allegedly he was a general in the service of the Emperor Trajan who, while out hunting in the Roman countryside, encountered a stag whose antlers framed a crucifix. Subsequently Eustace and his family were martyred, by being roasted in a brazen bull. It follows that his attributes are a stag, a crucifix and an oven.

St Francis receiving the Stigmata, Jan van Eyck (fl 1422–41)

A well-to-do native of Assisi, born c1181. An early turning point in his life followed a bout of illness brought on during imprisonment by the nearby Perugians, after which he was to embrace poverty and the service of lepers, cripples and the poor. He founded the order of Friars Minor (1211), and is credited with introducing the worship of the Christmas Crib. Van Eyck's painting shows him at the moment of receiving the stigmata during a fast, at prayer in a rocky landscape overlooking a distant city. St Francis is particularly associated with birds and animals, whose patron he is and which feature among his attributes; he is said to have asked that they be cared for by law.

St George and the Dragon, Tintoretto (1518–94)

Doubt has been cast in recent years on the very existence of St George, despite his popularity as a charismatic emblem of good vanquishing evil. Tintoretto's painting shows the saint, as in many other pictures, clad in armour and seated on his bounding charger at the moment of spearing the dragon. Though the picture's main subject, however, he is off in the middle distance while the foreground is taken up by the fleeing Princess of Silene, from Libya. He is the patron saint of army officers as well as of England itself, and his attribute is a shield bearing a red cross.

Mass of St Gregory, Master of Flémalle (1378/9–1444)

Born c540 into a patrician Roman family, St Gregory is associated with the conversion of the English, to whom he sent St Augustine of Canterbury as a missionary. As Pope, from 590, he did much to make the Church a great power in matters earthly as well as spiritual. The Master of Flémalle has shown him celebrating Mass as a naked Christ appears before the kneeling saint, standing on the altar.

St Helena's Vision of the Cross, Paolo Veronese (*c*1528–88)

The Emperor Constantine, the first Roman ruler to embrace Christianity, was converted by Helena, his mother. She had previously been an innkeeper, from Asia Minor. Subsequently she was credited, while travelling in Palestine, with finding the remains of the cross on which Jesus had died, and which became her attribute. She is the patron saint of dyers.

Miracle of St Ignatius Loyola, Peter Paul Rubens (1577–1640)

A hard recovery from a war wound was the background against which the saint (*b*1491) had a life-changing vision of the Virgin and Child. In 1534 he became a founder of the Society of Jesus, which subsequently, during the Counter-Reformation, developed into a neo-military organisation. Among his attributes is a dragon trampled underfoot.

St James the Greater, Giovanni Battista Tiepolo (1696–1770)

So called to distinguish him from St James the Less, an Apostle who is thought to have been a blood relation of Jesus. In depictions of the Agony in the Garden, among the Apostles it is James the Greater, together with Peter and John, who are shown as a group closer to Christ than the other disciples. A legend of some centuries later has him being murdered by Herod Agrippa. His body is alleged to be buried in north-west Spain, at Compostela, which was to be the climax of a pilgrimage route that crossed nearly two countries. St James' attributes reflect his importance to pilgrims, comprising a staff, wallet and shell. He is the patron of furriers as well as of the Spanish nation.

St Jerome in a Landscape, Giovanni Battista Cima (1459/60–1517/18)

It was Jerome, born *c*342 into a prosperous Dalmatian family, who translated the Bible into Latin, thus making its contents more accessible throughout the Roman world. This portrait, showing him as an ancient – if muscular – semi-naked hermit, gives due emphasis to his reputation for fist-shaking rage. Jerome is often shown, as here, with his pet lion. The story goes that he befriended the lion after removing a thorn from its paw. The monastery where he was living ruled that the lion should be put to work; accordingly its job was to lead out Jerome's ass each day in search of firewood. The ass disappeared, with the result that the lion was accused of having eaten it; however the lion was able to vindicate itself by returning not only the ass but the robbers who had taken it. The saint's attributes, understandably, include his lion.

Decapitation of John the Baptist, Juan de Flandes (*fl* 1496–*c*1519)
John is seen both as the Old Testament's last prophet and as the first saint of the New Testament. He baptised Jesus, whose coming as the Messiah he had foretold. The Gospel according to St Matthew describes him thus: 'John had his raiment of camel's hair, and a leathern girdle about his loins: and his meat was locusts and wild honey.' In the painting by Juan de Flandes all that is shown of him is his severed head, cut off on the orders of Herod in response to being denounced by John and here being put onto a silver salver. Traditionally the head was delivered in this mode at a banquet. John the Baptist is the patron saint of tailors, missionaries, and several individual cities.

St John at Patmos, Hieronymus Bosch (*c*1450–1516)
The youngest Apostle, author of one of the four Gospels, was the brother of St James the Greater. It was during an exile to the island of Patmos that he was said to have written The Book of the Revelation. He is said to have escaped more than one violent death including poisoning and scalding in boiling oil. His attributes are his Book of the Gospel, a chalice from which a serpent is issuing, and an eagle, often represented in churches as part of the lectern.

St Lawrence, Francisco de Zurbarán (1598–1664)
Richly robed, he is here shown holding his attribute, the gridiron on which he was roasted to death. He was a C3 Spaniard, martyred in his role as a treasurer of the Church. When the authorities demanded that he give them the treasures in his charge, having already given these away as alms St Lawrence preferred instead the local poor and disabled. Tradition says that during his execution he uttered the words, 'Thou hast roasted that one side, turn that over and eat.' He is the patron saint of cooks.

St Lucy, Francesco del Cossa (*c*1435–77)
Little in this bland piece of portraiture betrays the pious horror of one story about its subject – that is, until it becomes apparent that the saint is holding not some flower, but a pair of eyes on what looks like a stalk. Lucy was a Sicilian virgin, martyred by decapitation in the C4. One of her suitors allegedly found her eyes so alluring that, to save him from moral compromise, she had his own eyes pulled out. She is nonetheless invoked for protection against ocular disease.

St Luke painting the Virgin, Rogier van der Weyden
(1399/1400–1464)
As the Virgin breastfeeds the infant Jesus, her likeness is being taken here by St Luke, said in legend to have been a painter. Both main figures sit

in a well-appointed room against an alluring late-medieval vista of townscape plus a broad river and open country. Luke, a physician thought to have been a Greek native of Antioch, was author of the Gospel bearing his name, and of the Acts of the Apostles. He is patron saint of painters, doctors and butchers, and his attribute is a winged ox.

Martyrdom of St Mark, Tintoretto

The Last Supper is said to have taken place in the home of Mark's mother; he himself wrote one of the Gospels. He became bishop of Alexandria, where he was martyred by being dragged through the city's streets. In 829 his remains were taken from Alexandria to Venice and buried in St Mark's church. He is patron saint of Venice, where he is referred to in the form of several emblematic statues of a winged lion.

Mary Magdalene, Titian (c1487/90–1576)

Said to be a repentant prostitute who washed Jesus' feet with her tears and anointed them having dried them with her own hair. Her name may come from her birthplace, Magdala, near the Sea of Galilee. Many portraits show her wearing scarlet and with quantities of flowing red hair; they also depict her with a skull, evoking an awareness of mortality and, as here, looking heavenwards in a state of contrition. Her attribute is a jar of ointment.

The Calling of St Matthew, Marinius van Roymersvaele (1497–1567)

Matthew was the Apostle who wrote the first of the four Gospels. Before his conversion he was a tax-gatherer. After being present at the Ascension, he travelled extensively, to countries including Persia and Ethiopia. His attribute is an angel, and he is patron saint of bankers and taxmen.

St Michael, Domenico Ghirlandaio (1449–94)

An archangel traditionally shown, as here, wearing armour, in his role as the leader of the forces that defeated Satan when there was war in heaven. This portrait shows him holding his attributes: a pair of scales, for the weighing of souls, and a sword. He is the protector of Israel and of soldiers, and is invoked against danger at sea and in battle.

Consecration of St Nicholas, Veronese (c1528–88)

A C4 saint, bishop of Myra. He has little reliable history, but is the subject of several legends. In several countries he is identified with Santa Claus, and in Germany and the Netherlands St Nicholas is the bringer of presents for children each 6 December. Among his attributes is the pawnbrokers' sign of three golden balls, representing the bags of gold he was

said to have given to three girls as a dowry to save them from prostitu-
tion. In 1087 his remains were stolen and brought to Bari; it has been
claimed that from time to time they give off a form of oil with healing
properties. He is patron saint of children, pawnbrokers, bankers and
travellers.

Conversion of St Paul, Niccolò dell'Abbate (c1509–71)

A tentmaker by trade, born in Tarsus in the present-day Turkey, Paul is
thought to have been a Pharisee; his conversion came as he was on his
way to Damascus to persecute the local Christians. In this painting, as
elsewhere, he is shown as part of a composition dominated by the horse
from which he has just fallen. This is the instant when Paul became
temporarily blind, while a voice demanded of him; 'Why persecutest
thou me?' He came to be one of the most prominent figures of early
Christianity; having been arrested for incitement to riot, he was shipwrecked on his way to trial in Rome, on the island of Malta, where he had
a hair's-breadth escape from a poisonous snake. He was beheaded in
Rome, and his attributes are the sword of his execution, a book, and a
viper being cast into a fire.

Martyrdom of St Peter, Caravaggio (c1573–1610)

A fisherman from Galilee, whose name was also Simon. He was called
Peter by Jesus, this being the equivalent word for 'rock' in several
languages of the region: '... thou art Peter, and upon this rock I will build
my church; and the gates of hell shall not prevail upon it. And I will give
unto thee the keys of the kingdom of heaven ...' Peter was martyred in
Rome during the reign of Nero; traditionally he asked to be crucified
upside down, and died on the subsequent site of St Peter's Church. His
attributes include two keys.

Martyrdom of St Sebastian, Antonio (c1432–98) and
Piero Pollaiuolo (c1441–96)

By tradition he was an officer in the Praetorian guard of the Emperor
Diocletian, who ordered him to be shot (with an arrow) on discovering
that Sebastian was a Christian. Left for dead, he was nursed by the widow
of a fellow-Christian and subsequently showed himself to the Emperor as
proof of the power of Christ. Diocletian responded by having him beaten
to death. His assault by the imperial bowmen has been a popular subject;
in this painting the atrocity is being carried out against a vast and blissful
landscape. Understandably his attribute is an arrow, and he is patron saint
of pinmakers.

Martyrdom of St Stephen, School of Pietro da Cortona (1596–1669)

Stephen is known as the first Christian martyr, stoned to death in Jerusalem on a charge of blasphemy. Among those present was Paul, who at that stage was still bent on the persecution of the Christians. In this picture the execution itself only takes up the lower half of the canvas; above, a heavenly host awaits the deliverance of the martyr's soul. As well as a stone, Stephen's attributes include a palm, symbolically associated with martyrdom, here being held out by a hovering angel.

Martyrdom of St Thomas, Stefan Lochner (c1400–1451)

'Doubting Thomas' is the description commonly given to this Apostle, in reference to his disbelief on being told of Christ's resurrection. 'Except I shall see in his hands the prints of the nails, and put my finger into the print of the nails, and thrust my hand into his side, I will not believe ... then came Jesus ... and said ... reach hither thy finger and behold my hands: and reach hither thy hand, and thrust it into my side: and be not faithless, but believing.' Tradition has it that Thomas died in southern India, having been sent by Christ to do building work for the King of India. There he converted the Kerulans, who for several centuries were known as 'St Thomas Christians'. He was put to death, as shown in this violent painting featuring both clubbing and a sword through his throat, after persuading the king's wife to avoid her husband's bed. Thomas is the patron saint of Christian Indians, and of carpenters, masons and architects, and his attributes are a carpenter's rule and a spear.

Embarkation of St Ursula, Claude (Le) Lorraine né Gelée (1600–1682)

This Cornish princess of medieval legend had consented to marry the son of the English king, on condition that he converted to Christianity and waited for her to return from a pilgrimage to Rome. On her homecoming voyage she, and the eleven thousand virgins accompanying her, were attacked by Huns and massacred; her attribute is an arrow. In this painting, Ursula and her small group of companions are almost incidentally visible as a group in the middle distance; the main subject of the picture appears to be the peaceful quayside with its apparatus of shipping, its pearly sunlight and a general atmosphere of hushed anticipation.

St Veronica, Hans Memlinc (c1430/35–1494)

St Veronica does not appear in the Bible itself; instead, a subsequent legend credits her with being present at the Crucifixion. There, she was said to have given her handkerchief to Christ on his way to Calvary to wipe his sweating face. A cloth bearing the imprint of a man's face does exist, in Rome, in the possession of St Peter's Church, where it has been since C8. Such a cloth is the attribute of St Veronica, who is patron saint of washerwomen and linen-drapers.

St Zenobius restoring a dead man to life, Sandro Botticelli (c1445–1510)

A bishop of Florence and one of the city's patron saints, who died early C5. Several miracles are credited to him, most of which involved bringing the dead back to life. In Botticelli's painting the saint is performing one such resurrection, in a severe, sparsely populated streetscape. His own corpse is said to have brought a dead tree back to life, having accidentally come into contact with it. His attribute is usually the image of a dead child.

Literature – Classical

Greek and Roman classical mythology

The Romans took over the Greek pantheon of gods and gave them Roman equivalents – though with a distinctly local flavour. The Romans tended to draft them in as needed. Aesculapius, for example, the Greek god of healing, was brought to Rome after the plague of 293BCE.

Role	Greek name	Roman name
Agriculture	Demeter	Ceres
Dawn	Eos	Aurora
The Earth	Gaea [or Gaia]	Tellus
The Three Fates	Moirae	Parcae
The Forge	Hephaestus	Vulcan
The Three Furies	Erinyes	Furiae
Good Luck	Tyche	Fortuna
The Three Graces	Graces	Gratiae
Health and Medicine	Asclepius	Aesculapius
Hearth and Home	Hestia	Vesta
King of the Gods	Zeus	Jupiter
Queen of the Gods	Hera	Juno
Love and Beauty	Aphrodite	Venus
Love and Desire	Eros	Cupid
The Messenger	Hermes	Mercury
The Moon	Selene	Luna
Moon and Hunting	Artemis	Diana
The Sea	Poseidon	Neptune
Strength	Herakles	Hercules
Sun	Helios	Sol
Sun, Youth and Reason	Apollo	Apollo
King of the Underworld	Hades	Pluto
Queen of the Underworld	Persephone	Proserpina
Time	Cronus	Saturn
War	Ares	Mars
Wine	Dionysus	Bacchus
Wisdom	Athene	Minerva
Woods and Shepherds	Pan	Faunus

Who's who in classical mythology

Monsters, giants and other unusual beings

Argus Monster with one hundred eyes; slain by Hermes; his eyes placed by Hera into the peacock's tail.

Briareus Monster of hundred hands; son of Uranus and Gaea.

Cerberus Three-headed dog guarding the entrance to Hades.

Centaurs Beings half man and half horse; lived in the mountains of Thessaly.

Charybdis Female monster; personification of whirlpool.

Chimera Female monster with head of lion, body of goat, tail of serpent; killed by Bellerophon.

Chiron Most famous of centaurs.

Cyclopes Race of single-eyed giants (singular: Cyclops).

Gorgons Female monsters; Euryale, Medusa, and Stheno; had snakes for hair; their glances turned mortals to stone.

Harpies Monsters with heads of women and bodies of birds.

Hydra Nine-headed monster in marsh of Lerna; slain by Hercules.

Minotaur Monster, half man and half beast, kept in Labyrinth in Crete; slain by Theseus.

Pegasus Winged horse that sprang from Medusa's body at her death; ridden by Bellerophon when he slew Chimera.

Polyphemus a Cyclops; devoured six of Odysseus's men; then blinded by Odysseus.

Procrustes Giant; stretched or cut off legs of victims to make them fit iron bed; slain by Theseus.

Python Serpent born from slime left by Deluge; slain by Apollo.

Scylla Female monster inhabiting rock opposite Charybdis; menaced passing sailors.

Sinis Giant; he bent pines, with which he hurled victims against side of mountain; slain by Theseus.

Sphinx Monster of Thebes; killed those who could not answer her riddle; slain by Oedipus. Name also refers to other monsters having body of lion, wings, and head and bust of woman.

Gods and demigods

Aesculapius God of health; Greek Asclepius.

Amor The Roman equivalent of Eros.

Amphitrite Sea goddess; wife of Poseidon.

Anteros God who avenged unrequited love.

Aphrodite (Venus) Goddess of love and beauty; daughter of Zeus and Dione; mother of Eros. Loved Adonis.

Apollo God of beauty, poetry, music; later identified with Helios as Phoebus Apollo; son of Zeus and Leto.

Ares (Mars) God of war; son of Zeus and Hera.

Artemis (Diana) Goddess of moon; huntress; twin sister of Apollo.

Asclepius Greek equivalent of Aesculapius.

Astarte Phoenician goddess of love; variously identified with Aphrodite, Selene, and Artemis.

Astraea Goddess of Justice; daughter of Zeus and Themis.

Athena (Minerva) Goddess of wisdom; known poetically as Pallas Athene; sprang fully armed from head of Zeus.

Aurora Roman equivalent of Eos.

Bacchus Roman equivalent of Dionysus.

Bellona Roman goddess of war.

Ceres Roman equivalent of Demeter, goddess of Harvest.

Cronus (Saturn) Titan; god of harvests; son of Uranus and Gaea; dethroned by his son Zeus.

Cupid Roman equivalent of Eros.

Cybele Anatolian nature goddess; adopted by Greeks and identified with Rhea.

Demeter (Ceres) Goddess of agriculture; mother of Persephone.

Diana Roman equivalent of Artemis.

Dionysus (Bacchus) God of wine; son of Zeus and Semele.

Dis Roman equivalent of Pluto.

Eos (Aurora) Goddess of dawn.

Eris Goddess of discord.

Eros (Amor or Cupid) God of love; son of Aphrodite.

Fauns Roman deities of woods and groves.

Faunus Roman equivalent of Pan.

Flora Roman goddess of flowers.

Fortuna Roman goddess of fortune.

Gaea (Tellus) Goddess of earth; daughter of Chaos; mother of Titans; known also as Ge, Gea, Gaia, etc.

Hebe (Juventas) Goddess of youth; cupbearer of gods before Ganymede; daughter of Zeus and Hera.

Hecate Goddess of sorcery and witchcraft.

Helios (Sol) God of sun; later identified with Apollo.

Hephaestus (Vulcan) God of fire; celestial blacksmith; son of Zeus and Hera; husband of Aphrodite.

Hera (Juno) Queen of heaven; wife of Zeus.

Hermes (Mercury) God of physicians and thieves; messenger of gods; son of Zeus and Maia.

Hestia (Vesta) Goddess of hearth; sister of Zeus.

Hymen God of marriage.

Hyperion Titan; early sun god; father of Helios.

Hypnos (Somnus) God of sleep.

Iris Goddess of rainbow; messenger of Zeus and Hera.

Istra The Greek goddess of Psyche

Janus Roman god of gates and doors; represented with two opposite faces.

Juno Roman equivalent of Hera.

Jupiter Roman equivalent of Zeus.

Juventas Roman equivalent of Hebe

Latona Roman equivalent of Leto.

Leto (Latona) Mother by Zeus of Artemis and Apollo.

Lucina Roman goddess of childbirth; identified with Juno.

Luna Roman equivalent of Selene.

Mars Roman equivalent of Ares.

Mercury Roman equivalent of Hermes.

Minerva Roman equivalent of Athena.

Mnemosyne Goddess of memory; mother by Zeus of Muses.

Momus God of ridicule.

Morpheus God of dreams.

Mors Roman equivalent of Thanatos.

Nemesis Goddess of retribution.

Neptune Roman equivalent of Poseidon.

Nike Goddess of victory.

Nomiki Law

Nox Roman equivalent of Nyx.

Nyx (Nox) Goddess of night.

Ops Roman equivalent of Rhea.

Pales Roman goddess of shepherds and herdsmen.

Pan (Faunus) God of woods and fields; part goat; son of Hermes.

Penates Roman household gods.

Phaethon Son of Helios; drove his father's sun chariot and was struck down by Zeus before he set world on fire.

Pluto (Dis) God of Hades; brother of Zeus.

Plutus God of wealth.

Pomona Roman goddess of fruits.

Pontus Sea god; son of Gaea.

Poseidon (Neptune) God of sea; brother of Zeus.

Priapus God of regeneration.

Proserpine Roman equivalent of Persephone.

Proteus Sea god; assumed various shapes when called on to prophesy.

Quirinus Roman war god.

Saturn Roman equivalent of Cronus.

Selene (Luna) Goddess of the moon.

Silvanus Roman god of woods and fields.

Sirens Minor deities who lured sailors to destruction with their singing.

Sol Roman equivalent of Helios.

Somnus Roman equivalent of Hypnos.

Tellus Roman goddess of earth.

Terminus Roman god of boundaries and landmarks.

Terra Roman earth goddess.

Thanatos (Mors) God of death.

Themis Titan goddess of laws of physical phenomena; daughter of Uranus; mother of Prometheus.

Triton Demigod of sea; son of Poseidon.

Venus Roman equivalent of Aphrodite.

Vertumnus Roman god of fruits and vegetables; husband of Pomona.

Vesta Roman equivalent of Hestia.

Vulcan Roman equivalent of Hephaestus.

Zeus (Jupiter) Chief of Olympian gods; son of Cronus and Rhea; husband of Hera; father of the three Graces.

Fates, Moirae (Parcae); daughters of Nox and Erebus (or of Jupiter and Themis)

Clotho Spinner of the thread of life.

Lachesis Determiner of the length of the thread of life.

Atropos Cutter of the thread of life.

Decuma, Morta and Nona Roman equivalents of Atopos, Clotho and Lachesis

Graces, Charites or Gratiae: beautiful goddesses

Aglaia Brilliance; One of the graces; daughters of Zeus and Eurynome

Euphrosyne Joy; One of the graces; daughters of Zeus and Eurynome

Thalia Bloom; One of the graces; daughters of Zeus and Eurynome

The Old Women, Graeae

Deino One of the Graeae; daughters of Phorcys and Ceto; shared a tooth and an eye with Enyo and Pephredo, which they passed from one to another.

Enyo One of the Graeae; daughters of Phorcys and Ceto; shared a tooth and an eye with Deino and Pephredo, which they passed from one to another.

Pephredo One of the Graeae; daughters of Phorcys and Ceto; shared a tooth and an eye with Enyo and Deino, which they passed from one to another.

Pleiades

The seven daughters of Atlas, transformed into a heavenly constellation, of which only six stars are visible.

Alcyone
Asterope (Sterope)
Celaeno
Electra
Maia
Taygeta

The seventh Pleiad, **Merope**, is said to have hidden in shame from loving a mortal.

Muses; goddesses presiding over arts and sciences; daughter of Zeus and Mnemosyne

Calliope Muse of epic poetry.
Clio Muse of history.
Erato Muse of lyric and love poetry.
Euterpe Muse of music.
Melpomene Muse of tragedy.
Polymnia (Polyhymnia) Muse of sacred poetry.
Terpsichore Muse of choral dance and song.
Thalia Muse of comedy and bucolic poetry.
Urania Muse of astronomy.

Nymphs and satyrs

Calypso Sea nymph; kept Odysseus on her island Ogygia for seven years.
Daphne Nymph; pursued by Apollo; changed to laurel tree.
Dryads Wood nymphs.
Dryope Maiden changed to Hamadryad.

Echo Nymph who fell hopelessly in love with Narcissus; faded away except for her voice.

Eurydice Nymph; wife of Orpheus.

Galatea Sea nymph; loved by Polyphemus.

Hamadryads Tree nymphs.

Naiads Nymphs of waters, streams, and fountains.

Napaeae Wood nymphs.

Nereids Sea nymphs; attendants on Poseidon.

Nymphs Beautiful maidens; minor deities of nature.

Oceanids Ocean nymphs; daughters of Oceanus.

Oenone Nymph of Mount Ida; wife of Paris, who abandoned her; refused to cure him when he was poisoned by arrow of Philoctetes at Troy.

Oreads Mountain nymphs.

Satyrs Hoofed demigods of woods and fields; companions of Dionysus.

Sileni Minor woodland deities similar to satyrs (singular: silenus). Sometimes Silenus refers to eldest of satyrs, son of Hermes or of Pan.

Syrinx Nymph pursued by Pan; changed to reeds, from which he made his pipes.

Thalia a sea-nymph, attendant upon Poseidon.

Gorgons: three women with serpents for hair and a glance that turned its recipients to stone; children of Phorcys and Ceto

Euryale One of the Gorgons.

Medusa One of the Gorgons; slain by Perseus, who cut off her head.

Stheno One of the Gorgons.

Personifications

Aether Personification of sky.

Chaos Formless void; personified as first of gods.

Chronos Personification of time.

Hesperus Evening star.

Hygeia Personification of health.

Phosphor Morning star.

Uranus Personification of Heaven; husband of Gaea; father of Titans; dethroned by his son Cronus.

Kings, queens and princesses

Admetus King of Thessaly; his wife, Alcestis, offered to die in his place.

Aeëtes King of Colchis; father of Medea; keeper of the Golden Fleece.

Aeson King of Ioclus; father of Jason; overthrown by his brother Pelias; restored to youth by Medea.

Agamemnon King of Mycenae; son of Atreus; brother of Menelaus; leader of Greeks against Troy; slain on his return home by Clytemnestra and Aegisthus.

Antigone Daughter of Oedipus; accompanied him to Colonus; performed burial rite for Polynices and hanged herself.

Atalanta Princess who challenged her suitors to a foot race; Hippomenes won race and married her.

Atreus King of Mycenae; father of Menelaus and Agamemnon; bro of Thyestes, three of whose sons he slew and served to him at banquet; slain by Aegisthus.

Cepheus King of Ethiopia; father of Andromeda.

Danaë Princess of Argos; mother of Perseus by Zeus, who appeared to her in form of a golden shower.

Dido Founder and queen of Carthage; stabbed herself when deserted by Aeneas.

Eurystheus King of Argos; imposed twelve labours on Hercules.

Hecuba Wife of Priam.

Hippolyte Queen of Amazons; wife of Theseus.

Iobates King of Lycia; sent Bellerophon to slay the Chimera.

Iphigenia Daughter of Agamemnon; offered as sacrifice to Artemis at Aulis; carried by Artemis to Tauris where she became priestess; escaped from there with Orestes.

Ismene Daughter of Oedipus; sister of Antigone.

Ixion King of Lapithae; for making love to Hera he was bound to endlessly revolving wheel in Tartarus.

Memnon Ethiopian king; made immortal by Zeus; son of Tithonus and Eos.

Menelaus King of Sparta; son of Atreus; brother of Agamemnon; husband of Helen.

Mezentius Cruel Etruscan king; ally of Turnus against Aeneas; slain by Aeneas.

Midas King of Phrygia; given gift of turning all he touched to gold.

Minos King of Crete; after death, one of three judges of dead in Hades; son of Zeus and Europa.

Nestor King of Pylos; noted for wise counsel in expedition against Troy.

Odysseus (Ulysses) King of Ithaca; husband of Penelope; wandered ten years after fall of Troy before arriving home.

Oedipus King of Thebes; son of Laius and Jocasta; unwittingly murdered Laius and married Jocasta; tore his eyes out when relationship was discovered.

Pandion King of Athens, son of Erichthonius, father of Procne and Philomela.

Pelias King of Ioclus; seized throne from his brother Aeson; sent Jason for Golden Fleece; slain unwittingly by his daughters at instigation of Medea.

Persephone (Proserpine) Queen of infernal regions; daughter of Zeus and Demeter; wife of Pluto.

Philomela Daughter of King Pandion of Athens; loved by her brother-in-law Tereus (*qv*); turned into a swallow (or a nightingale)

Polyxena Daughter of Priam; betrothed to Achilles, whom Paris slew at their betrothal; sacrificed to shade of Achilles.

Priam King of Troy; husband of Hecuba; ransomed Hector's body from Achilles; slain by Neoptolemus.

Procne Daughter of King Pandion of Athens; wife of Tereus (*qv*); turned into a nightingale (or a swallow).

Pygmalion King of Cyprus; carved ivory statue of maiden which Aphrodite gave life as Galatea.

Sarpedon King of Lycia; son of Zeus and Europa; slain by Patroclus at Troy.

Sisyphus King of Corinth; condemned in Tartarus to roll huge stone to top of hill; it always rolled back down again.

Tantalus Cruel king; father of Pelops and Niobe; condemned in Tartarus to stand chin-deep in lake surrounded by fruit branches; as he tried to eat or drink, water or fruit always receded.

Tereus Son of Ares (Mars); King of the Thracians; husband of Procne and father of Itys, slain by Procne and served to Tereus when she found that he was wooing her sister Philomela; turned into a hoopoe (or a hawk).

Turnus King of Rutuli in Italy; betrothed to Lavinia; slain by Aeneas.

Ulysses See **Odysseus**.

Titans: Early gods from which Olympian gods were derived; children of Uranus and Gaea

Atlas Titan; held world on his shoulders as punishment for warring against Zeus; son of Iapetus; father of the Pleiades.

Cronus (Saturn) Titan; god of harvests; son of Uranus and Gaea; dethroned by his son Zeus.

Dione Titan goddess; mother by Zeus of Aphrodite.

Epimetheus Titan; Brother of Prometheus; husband of Pandora.

Hyperion Titan; early sun god; father of Helios.

Iapetus Titan; father of Atlas, Epimetheus, and Prometheus.

Oceanus Eldest of Titans; god of waters.

Prometheus Titan; stole fire from heaven for man. Zeus punished him by chaining him to rock in Caucasus where vultures devoured his liver daily.

Saturn See **Cronus**.

Themis Titan goddess of laws of physical phenomena; daughter of Uranus; mother of Prometheus.

Underworld

Acheron One of the Rivers of the Underworld.

Aeacus One of three judges of dead in Hades; son of Zeus.

Avernus Infernal regions; name derived from small vaporous lake near Vesuvius which was fabled to kill birds and vegetation.

Cerberus Three-headed dog guarding entrance to Hades.

Ceres Roman equivalent of Demeter. Goddess of Harvest.

Charon Boatman on Styx who carried souls of dead to Hades; son of Erebus.

Cocytus One of the Rivers of Underworld.

Dis Roman equivalent of Pluto.

Elysium Abode of blessed dead.

Hades (Dis) Name sometimes given to Pluto; also, the abode of the dead, ruled by Pluto.

Lares Roman ancestral spirits protecting descendants and homes.

Lethe One of the Rivers of Underworld.

Manes Souls of dead Romans, particularly of ancestors.

Persephone (Proserpine) Queen of the infernal regions; daughter of Zeus and Demeter; wife of Pluto.

Phlegethon One of the Rivers of Underworld.

Rhadamanthus One of three judges of dead in Hades; son of Zeus and Europa.

Rivers of the Underworld Acheron (woe), Avernus (poison), Cocytus (wailing), Lethe (forgetfulness), Phlegethon (fire), Styx (across which souls of dead were ferried by Charon).

Styx One of the Rivers of Underworld. The souls of the dead were ferried across the Styx by Charon with a coin (obelus) on the tongue.

Tartarus Underworld below Hades; often refers to Hades.

Winds

Aeolus Keeper of the Winds.

Aquilo One of the Winds. See **Boreas**.

Auster One of the Winds. See **Notus**.

Boreas One of the Winds – the north wind.

Eurus One of the Winds – the east wind

Favonius One of the Winds. See **Zephyrus**.

Notus (Auster) One of the Winds – the south wind.

Winds Aeolus (keeper of winds).

Zephyrus (Favonius) One of several Winds – the west wind.

Miscellaneous

Alethia Greek name meaning Wisdom

Amazons Female warriors in Asia Minor; supported Troy against Greeks.

Ancile Sacred shield that fell from heavens; palladium of Rome.

Andra A Greek name meaning Strong and Courageous.

Argo Ship in which Jason and followers sailed to Colchis for Golden Fleece.

Castalia In Greek Mythology the most powerful Oracle was the oracle of Delphi. People would come from all around with question, seeking answers. The oracle's source of inspiration sprang forth from a fountain called Castalia.

Erebus Spirit of darkness; son of Chaos.

Galatea Statue of maiden carved from ivory by Pygmalion; given life by Aphrodite.

Golden Fleece Fleece from ram that flew Phrixos to Colchis; Aeëtes placed it under guard of dragon; carried off by Jason.

Philippa A Greek name meaning Lover of Horses.

Symplegades Clashing rocks at entrance to Black Sea; Argo passed through, causing them to become forever fixed.

The Furies or avenging spirits – Erinyes or Furiae

Alecto One of the Furies, also known as Erinyes or Eumenides.

Megaera One of the Furies, also known as Erinyes or Eumenides.

Tisiphone One of the Furies, also known as Erinyes or Eumenides.

Heroes, heroines and others

Achilles Greek warrior; slew Hector at Troy; slain by Paris, who wounded him in his vulnerable heel.

Actaeon Hunter; surprised Artemis bathing; changed by her to a stag; and then killed by his dogs.

Adonis Beautiful youth loved by Aphrodite.

Aegeus Father of Theseus; believing Theseus killed in Crete, he drowned himself; Aegean Sea named for him.

Aegisthus Son of Thyestes; slew Atreus; with Clytemnestra, his paramour, slew Agamemnon; slain by Orestes.

Aegyptus Brother of Danaus; his sons, except Lynceus, slain by Danaides.

Aeneas Trojan; son of Anchises and Aphrodite; after fall of Troy, led his followers eventually to Italy; loved and deserted Dido.

Aesculapius See **Asclepius**.

Aethra Mother of Theseus.

Ajax Greek warrior; killed himself at Troy because Achilles's armor was awarded to Odysseus.

Alcestis Wife of Admetus; offered to die in his place but saved from death by Hercules.

Alcmene Wife of Amphitryon; mother by Zeus of Hercules.

Alectryon Youth changed by Ares into cock.

Althaea Wife of Oeneus; mother of Meleager.

Amphion Musician; husband of Niobe; charmed stones to build fortifications for Thebes.

Amphitryon Husband of Alcmene.

Anchises Father of Aeneas.

Andraemon Husband of Dryope.

Andromache Wife of Hector.

Andromeda Daughter of Cepheus; chained to cliff for monster to devour; rescued by Perseus.

Anteia Wife of Proetus; tried to induce Bellerophon to elope with her.

Antinoüs Leader of suitors of Penelope; slain by Odysseus.

Arachne Maiden who challenged Athena to weaving contest; changed to spider.

Ariadne Daughter of Minos; aided Theseus in slaying Minotaur; deserted by him on island of Naxos and married Dionysus.

Arion Musician; thrown overboard by pirates but saved by dolphin.

Asclepius (Aesculapius) Mortal son of Apollo; slain by Zeus for raising dead; later deified as god of medicine. Also known as Asklepios.

Bellerophon Corinthian hero; killed Chimera with aid of Pegasus; tried to reach Olympus on Pegasus and was thrown to his death.

Briseis Captive maiden given to Achilles; taken by Agamemnon in exch for loss of Chryseis, which caused Achilles to cease fighting, until death of Patroclus.

Cadmus Brother of Europa; planter of dragon seeds from which first Thebans sprang.

Cassandra Daughter of Priam; prophetess who was never believed; slain with Agamemnon.

Castor One of Dioscuri.

Cephalus Hunter; accidentally killed his wife Procris with his spear.

Chryseis Captive maiden given to Agamemnon; his refusal to accept ransom from her father Chryses caused Apollo to send plague on Greeks besieging Troy.

Circe Sorceress; daughter of Helios; changed Odysseus's men into swine.

Clytemnestra Wife of Agamemnon, whom she slew with aid of her paramour, Aegisthus; slain by her son Orestes.

Creon Father of Jocasta; forbade burial of Polynices; ordered burial alive of Antigone.

Creüsa Princess of Corinth, for whom Jason deserted Medea; slain by Medea, who sent her poisoned robe; also known as Glaüke.

Creusa Wife of Aeneas; died fleeing Troy.

Daedalus Athenian artificer; father of Icarus; builder of Labyrinth in Crete; devised wings attached with wax for him and Icarus to escape Crete.

Danaïdes Daughters of Danaüs; at his command, all except Hypermnestra slew their husbands, the sons of Aegyptus.

Danaüs Brother of Aegyptus; father of Danaïdes; slain by Lynceus.

Diomedes Greek hero; with Odysseus, entered Troy and carried off Palladium, sacred statue of Athena.

Diomedes Owner of man-eating horses, which Hercules, as ninth labour, carried off.

Dioscuri Twins Castor and Pollux; sons of Leda by Zeus.

Electra Daughter of Agamemnon and Clytemnestra; sister of Orestes; urged Orestes to slay Clytemnestra and Aegisthus.

Endymion Mortal loved by Selene.

Eteocles Son of Oedipus, whom he succeeded to rule alternately with Polynices; refused to give up throne at end of year; he and Polynices slew each other.

Europa Mortal loved by Zeus, who, in form of white bull, carried her off to Crete.

Ganymede Beautiful boy; successor to Hebe as cupbearer of gods.

Glaucus Mortal who became sea divinity by eating magic grass.

Haemon Son of Creon; promised husband of Antigone; killed himself in her tomb.

Hector Son of Priam; slayer of Patroclus; slain by Achilles.

Helen Fairest woman in world; daughter of Zeus and Leda; wife of Menelaus; carried to Troy by Paris, causing Trojan War.

Heliades Daughters of Helios; mourned for Phaëthon and were changed to poplar trees.

Helle Sister of Phrixos; fell from ram of Golden Fleece; water where she fell named Hellespont.

Hercules Hero and strong man; son of Zeus and Alcmene; performed twelve labours or deeds to be free from bondage under Eurystheus; after death, his mortal share was destroyed, and he became immortal. Also known as Herakles or Heracles. Labours: (1) killing Nemean lion; (2) killing Lernaean Hydra; (3) capturing Erymanthian boar; (4) capturing Cerynean hind; (5) killing man-eating Stymphalian birds; (6) procuring girdle of Hippolyte; (7) cleaning Augean stables; (8) capturing Cretan bull; (9) capturing man-eating horses of Diomedes; (10) capturing cattle of Geryon; (11) procuring golden apples of Hesperides; (12) bringing Cerberus up from Hades.

Hero Priestess of Aphrodite; Leander swam Hellespont nightly to see her; drowned herself at his death.

Hippolytus Son of Theseus and Hippolyte; falsely accused by Phaedra of trying to kidnap her; slain by Poseidon at request of Theseus.

Hippomenes Husband of Atalanta, whom he beat in race by dropping golden apples, which she stopped to pick up.

Hyacinthus Beautiful youth accidentally killed by Apollo, who caused flower to spring up from his blood.

Hypermnestra Daughter of Danaüs; refused to kill her husband Lynceus.

Icarus Son of Daedalus; flew too near sun with wax-attached wings, fell into sea and was drowned.

Io Mortal maiden loved by Zeus; changed by Hera into heifer.

Iulus Son of Aeneas.

Jason Son of Aeson; to gain throne of Ioclus from Pelias, went to Colchis and brought back Golden Fleece; married Medea; deserted her for Creüsa.

Jocasta Wife of Laius; mother of Oedipus; unwittingly became wife of Oedipus; hanged herself when relationship was discovered.

Laius Father of Oedipus, by whom he was slain.

Laocoön Priest of Apollo at Troy; warned against bringing wooden horse into Troy; destroyed with his two sons by serpents sent by Poseidon.

Lavinia Wife of Aeneas after defeat of Turnus.

Leander Swam Hellespont nightly to see Hero; drowned in storm.

Leda Mortal loved by Zeus in form of swan; mother of Helen, Clytemnestra, Dioscuri.

Lynceus Son of Aegyptus; husband of Hypermnestra; slew Danaüs.

Maia Daughter of Atlas; mother of Hermes.

Marsyas Shepherd; challenged Apollo to music contest and lost; flayed alive by Apollo.

Medea Sorceress; daughter of Aeëtes; helped Jason obtain Golden Fleece; when deserted by him for Creüsa, killed her children and Creüsa.

Meleager Son of Althaea; his life would last as long as brand burning at his birth; Althaea quenched and saved it but destroyed it when Meleager slew his uncles.

Narcissus Beautiful youth loved by Echo; in punishment for not returning her love, he was made to fall in love with his image reflected in a pool; he pined away and became a flower.

Neoptolemus Son of Achilles; slew Priam; also known as Pyrrhus.

Niobe Daughter of Tantalus; wife of Amphion; her children slain by Apollo and Artemis; changed to stone but continued to weep her loss.

Ops See **Rhea**.

Orestes Son of Agamemnon and Clytemnestra; brother of Electra; slew Clytemnestra and Aegisthus; pursued by Furies until his purification by Apollo.

Orion Hunter; slain by Artemis and made heavenly constellation.

Orpheus Famed musician; son of Apollo and Muse Calliope; husband of Eurydice.

Palinurus Aeneas' pilot; fell overboard in his sleep and was drowned.

Pandora Owner of box containing human ills; mortal wife of Epimetheus.

Paris Son of Priam; gave apple of discord to Aphrodite, for which she enabled him to carry off Helen; slew Achilles at Troy; slain by Philoctetes.

Patroclus Great friend of Achilles; wore Achilles' armor and was slain by Hector.

Pelops Son of Tantalus; his father cooked and served him to gods; restored to life; Peloponnesus named for him.

Penelope Wife of Odysseus; waited faithfully for him for many years while putting off numerous suitors.

Periphetes Giant; son of Hephaestus; slain by Theseus.

Perseus Son of Zeus and Danaë; slew Medusa; rescued Andromeda from monster and married her.

Phaedra Daughter of Minos; wife of Theseus; caused the death of her stepson, Hippolytus.

Philoctetes Greek warrior who possessed Hercules's bow and arrows; slew Paris at Troy with poisoned arrow.

Phineus Betrothed of Andromeda; tried to slay Perseus but turned to stone by Medusa's head.

Phrixos Brother of Helle; carried by ram of Golden Fleece to Colchis.

Pirithous Son of Ixion; friend of Theseus; tried to carry off Persephone from Hades; bound to enchanted rock by Pluto.

Pollux One of the Dioscuri.

Polynices Son of Oedipus; he and his brother Eteocles killed each other; burial rite, forbidden by Creon, performed by his sister Antigone.

Procris Wife of Cephalus, who accidentally slew her.

Proetus Husband of Anteia; sent Bellerophon to Iobates to be put to death.

Psyche Beloved of Eros; punished by jealous Aphrodite; made immortal and united with Eros.

Pyramus Babylonian youth; made love to Thisbe through hole in wall; thinking Thisbe slain by lion, killed himself.

Pyrrhus See **Neoptolemus**.

Remus Brother of Romulus; slain by him.

Rhea (Ops) Daughter of Uranus and Gaea; wife of Cronus; mother of Zeus; identified with Cybele.

Romulus Founder of Rome; he and Remus suckled in infancy by she-wolf; slew Remus; deified by Romans.

Sciron Robber; forced strangers to wash his feet, then hurled them into sea where tortoise devoured them; slain by Theseus.

Semele Daughter of Cadmus; mother by Zeus of Dionysus; demanded Zeus appear before her in all his splendour and was destroyed by his lightning bolts.

Sibyls Various prophetesses; most famous, Cumaean sibyl, accompanied Aeneas into Hades.

Telemachus Son of Odysseus; made unsuccessful journey to find his father.

Theseus Son of Aegeus; slew Minotaur; married and deserted Ariadne; later married Phaedra.

Thisbe Beloved of Pyramus; killed herself at his death.

Thyestes Brother of Atreus; Atreus killed three of his sons and served them to him at a banquet.

Tiresias Blind soothsayer of Thebes.

Tithonus Mortal loved by Eos; changed into a grasshopper.

Ulysses Roman equivalent of Odysseus.

Literature – Modern

Booker Prizewinners

Winners of the Booker Prize for Fiction, launched by Booker McConnell Ltd in 1968; the announcement of the winner had been shown on television since 1981; it is now the Man Booker Prize, sponsored by the finance house Man Group PLC.

1969 P H Newby, *Something to Answer For*, Faber
1970 Bernice Rubens, *The Elected Member*, Eyre & Spottiswoode
1971 V S Naipaul, *In a Free State*, Andre Deutsch
1972 John Berger, *G*, Weidenfeld
1973 J G Farrell, *The Siege of Krishnapur*, Weidenfeld
1974 Nadine Gordimer, *The Conservationist*, Cape
          Stanley Middleton, *Holiday*, Hutchinson
1975 Ruth Prawer Jhabvala, *Heat and Dust*, Murray
1976 David Storey, *Saville*, Cape
1977 Paul Scott, *Staying On*, Heinemann
1978 Iris Murdoch, *The Sea, The Sea*, Chatto & Windus
1979 Penelope Fitzgerald, *Offshore*, Collins
1980 William Golding, *Rites of Passage*, Faber
1981 Salman Rushdie, *Midnight's Children*, Cape
1982 Thomas Keneally, *Schindler's Ark*, Hodder & Stoughton
1983 J M Coetzee, *Life and Times of Michael K*, Secker & Warburg
1984 Anita Brookner, *Hotel du Lac*, Cape
1985 Keri Hulme, *The Bone People*, Hodder & Stoughton
1986 Kingsley Amis, *The Old Devils*, Hutchinson
1987 Penelope Lively, *Moon Tiger*, Deutsch
1988 Peter Carey, *Oscar and Lucinda*, Faber
1989 Kazuo Ishiguro, *The Remains of the Day*, Faber
1990 A S Byatt, *Possession*, Chatto & Windus
1991 Ben Okri, *The Famished Road*, Cape
1992 Michael Ondaatje, *The English Patient*, Bloomsbury
          Barry Unsworth, *Sacred Hunger*, Hamish Hamilton
1993 Roddy Doyle, *Paddy Clark, Ha, Ha, Ha*, Secker & Warburg
1994 James Kelman, *How Late It Was, How Late*, Secker & Warburg
1995 Pat Barker, *The Ghost Road*, Viking
1996 Graham Swift, *Last Orders*, Picador
1997 Arundhati Roy, *The God of Small Things*, Flamingo

1998 Ian McEwan, *Amsterdam*, Cape
1999 J M Coetzee, *Disgrace*, Secker & Warburg
2000 Margaret Atwood, *The Blind Assassin*, Bloomsbury
2001 Peter Carey, *The True History of the Kelly Gang*, Faber
2002 Yann Martel, *Life of Pi*, Canongate
2003 D B C Pierre, *Vernon God Little*, Faber

Twentieth-century English-language writers

'If you can't be just, be arbitrary.' This widely appreciated aphorism may have originated from the workings of the law, but it describes perfectly the problems of compiling a list such as this. The twentieth-century saw the development of more literary genres than any other time in history would have believed possible; in fact the rise of science fiction has made it necessary to put this category into a separate list (*qv*). It follows that the best one can say of a selection like this, however carefully made, is that readers might disagree with it. Any other response would mean failure indeed!

Douglas Adams (1952–2001) British writer who successfully blended fantasy and science fiction with comedy.

Kingsley Amis (1922–95) English poet and novelist best known for his particular vein of comic satire.

Martin Amis (1949–) Son of Kingsley; rated for the arresting edginess of language in his novels and journalism alike.

Maya Angelou (1928–) American dramatist and poet drawing much of her work from the experience of growing up as poor and black.

Margaret Atwood (1939–) Canadian novelist and poet who takes inspiration from the themes of national and gender identity.

W(ystan) H(ugh) Auden (1907–73) American poet, English-born; informal, innovative style with left-wing emphasis in his earlier years.

Alan Ayckbourn (1939–) English playwright, immensely popular for his comedies of middle-class manners, which are often given an usual structure.

James Baldwin (1924–87) American novelist and essayist whose work challenged the culture of white supremacy and dwelt on issues of homosexuality.

Julian Barnes (1946–) English novelist and essayist, writing in several modes that combine large ideas with an admixture of historical fact.

Samuel Beckett (1906–89) Irish playwright and novelist; a leading figure in the mid-century movement known as the theatre of the absurd. His dramas combine darkness and complexity with surrealism.

Saul Bellow (1915–) American, born in Canada, whose novels are both introspective and concerned with the decay of city life.

Alan Bennett (1934–) English playwright and screenwriter, author of subtle, reflective dramas dwelling on such things as class awareness and national identity, with a fine ear for everyday speech.

Arnold Bennet (1867–1931) English observer of social and domestic life, known for his series of novels set in the pottery towns of the Midlands.

Lawrence Block (1938–) American crime novelist whose works, set mostly in New York, cover a range from comic and entertaining through to unblinkered realism.

Rupert Brooke (1887–1915) English poet best known for his verse written during WW1 in anticipation of active service.

John Buchan (1875–1940) British novelist, author of patriotically flavoured adventure stories.

(John) Anthony Burgess (Wilson) (1917–93) Prolific English novelist whose works, witty and often satirical, range through historical settings to fantasy.

William Burroughs (1914–97) American writer of surreal 'cut-up' novels freighted with drugs and violence.

Erskine Caldwell (1903–87) American novelist writing with an emphasis on the lives of poor whites in the Deep South of the US.

Truman Capote (1924–84) American novelist who drew material from his own southern childhood, and from real-life cases of murder.

Angela Carter (1940–92) English novelist and short-story writer with an odd, elliptical narrative method and a tendency towards modern gothic.

Willa Cather (1876–1947) American novelist, recorder of life as experienced by Plains immigrants.

Raymond Chandler (1888–1959) American, educated in England; his crime novels, downbeat and sharply observed, did much to raise the genre's standing.

Paddy Chayefsky (1923–81) American screenwriter and television playwright, whose works used ordinary circumstances to explore large subjects. In movies such as *The Hospital* and *Network* he dealt in a strain of uncompromising satire.

Dame Agatha (Mary Clarissa) Christie née Miller, *aka* **Mary Westmacott** (1890–1976) English writer of detective novels from the 'classic' era of crime writing; creator of some enduring central characters.

Joseph Conrad (1857–1924) Polish-born British writer who distinguished himself in a language learned relatively late in life; author of novels both violent and contemplative, dealing with international politics and adventure at sea.

John Dos Passos (1896–1970) American novelist, author of the panoramic trilogy *The 42nd Parallel*, *1919* and *The Big Money*.

Theodore Dreiser (1871–1945) American author of doom-laden novels whose characters are trapped both by nature and the workings of society.

Lawrence (George) Durrell (1912–90) English novelist and poet noted for his accounts of wartime and expatriate life.

T(homas) S(tearns) Eliot (1888–1965) English poet, American-born; a foremost figure of his time as a writer who combined learning with invention.

James Ellroy (1948–) American crime writer whose novels present a vivid account of Los Angeles over the second half of the century, as a place of chaos in which people from every part of society are open to corruption.

William Faulkner (1897–1962) American novelist best known for his depictions of the Deep South and its conflicts, social and sexual, arising from its foundation in slavery.

F(rancis) Scott (Key) Fitzgerald (1896–1940) American novelist and short story writer, seen as an outstanding observer of the Jazz Age. Beneath their outward glamour, his works hint at a world of dismay.

Ian Fleming (1908–64) English writer of journalism and novels. His spy stories have been posthumously much extended by others, due to the popularity of his hero James Bond.

E(dward) M(organ) Forster (1879–1970) Liberal-minded English novelist dwelling on attempted conciliation between the cultures of different classes and nationalities, as expressed in closely observed personal relationships.

Robert Lee Frost (1874–1963) American poet, closely associated with the people and landscapes of New England.

John Galsworthy (1867–1933) English dramatist and novelist with a wide overview of daily life in his own social class; nowadays more likely to be televised than read.

Allen Ginsberg (1926–97) American Beat poet, sometime object of notoriety for his exploration of sexuality and the anti-establishment theme of his work.

William Golding (1911–93) English novelist, poet and playwright; an award-laden author of works that document the human potential for chaos.

Nadine Gordimer (1923–) South African novelist and short–story writer, a witness over several decades to the ill effects on white and black people alike of her country's former policy of apartheid.

Robert Graves (1895–1985) English novelist and poet, celebrated for his historical novels set in ancient Rome, and his autobiographical account of World War I, *Goodbye to All That*, which gets much of its effect from being set largely in the period just before the war.

Graham Greene (1904–91) English novelist whose fiction combines what he saw as a popular aspect with a widely regarded intellectual content, mostly on religious or political themes. The term 'Greeneland' has been used, in a semi-geographical sense, to describe his world of international intrigue and personal compromise.

Ernest (Miller) Hemingway (1899–1961) American writer with a style famously influenced by the verbal economies of journalism; his novels celebrated a largely strenuous world of masculine values.

Patricia Highsmith (1921–95) American novelist, author of crime fictions that emphasize the secret workings of the human mind as much as its outward effect.

James Langston Hughes (1902–67) American poet who wrote of life in Harlem and the hardships suffered by his fellow city-dwelling black compatriots.

Ted Hughes (1930–98) British poet, associated in his work with the world of nature and a somewhat maudlin cast of perception.

Aldous Huxley (1894–1963) English novelist, author of sharp social satires and philosophically searching fantasies. His later work was, he claimed, much influenced by hallucinogens. Huxley was denied much obituary space, by the coincidence of his dying on the same day as J F Kennedy.

James Joyce (1882–1941) Irish novelist and short story writer, much of whose work features his native Dublin. His masterful *Ulysses* is famously experimental in form, and was at first censored for its detailed carnality. The day, 16 June 1904, on which its action takes place, is now known as Bloomsday, after its central character, Leopold Bloom, and was the source of much centenary celebration.

Thomas Keneally (1935–) Australian novelist, playwright and short-story writer, creator of works threaded through with historical fact and peopled by characters who must make difficult moral choices. 'Factoid' may be the best description of book such as *Schindler's Ark*, based on the recollections of several Holocaust survivors.

Jack Kerouac (1922–69) Most celebrated of America's beat writers, who caught the preoccupations of his time with his autobiographical *On the Road*.

Stephen King (1947–) American horror writer, a leader in the genre, whose books have been extensively filmed. One compelling quality is his ability to draw out monsters from settings of immaculate ordinariness.

Philip Larkin (1922–85) English poet of melancholy and satiric lyricism; bard of colloquially described urban and provincial ordinariness.

D(avid) H(erbert) Lawrence (1885–1930) English painter, poet and novelist, partly banned until thirty years after his death for his explicit, if not quite convincing, accounts of sexuality. In response to the social and aesthetic ravages of industrialisation, he advocated a better balance between humankind and the rest of nature.

John Le Carré (1931–) English thriller writer, whose novels explore in close detail the subjects of deception, loyalty, and the need or otherwise for moral compromise.

Ursula Le Guin (1929–) American writer of science-fantasy novels, of which the Earthsea trilogy, written for a young-adult readership, has been particularly well regarded for the breadth and sureness of its imaginings.

C(live) S(taples) Lewis (1898–1963) English novelist and scholar, author of critical works such as *The Allegory of Love* and religious writings including *The Screwtape Letters*. He is best known for the science fiction trilogy which started with *Out of the Silent Planet*, and his Narnia series of novels written for children. As in his non-fiction, all these stories carried a preoccupation with Christianity.

Sinclair Lewis (1885–1951) American novelist acclaimed largely for the realism and satire of his novels describing the values and constraints of mid-Western small-town life.

Jack London né John Griffith Chaney (1876–1916) American novelist, who drew for his writings upon a life of struggle and incident, including serving as a sailor, tramp and gold miner. His experience of extreme poverty made him outspoken in his descriptions of such hardship and his comments on the social order, both American and British.

Robert Lowell (1917–77) American poet for whom huge claims were made in his lifetime: a dissident but aristocratic voice, whose intellectually satisfying style combined with a substance largely drawn from his disorganised private life.

Carson McCullers (1917–67) American novelist and writer of short stories, whose fictions are mostly set in her native Georgia. Some carry a Gothic flavour and centre on misfits; she herself declared that her works dealt in 'spiritual isolation'.

Norman Mailer (1923–) American novelist whose career began resoundingly with the publication of *The Naked and the Dead*, based on his own time in the Pacific with the American military. Taken as a whole, his other work comprises an unorthodox mixture of genres.

Arthur Miller (1915–) American playwright, in whose works the theme of self-knowledge is often conspicuous, together with evocation of Greek tragedy and the drama of Ibsen. Despite this provenance, his plays tend to be set against a realistic description of modern America. They include *All My Sons*, *Death of a Salesman*, *The Crucible*, and *The Misfits*, a screenplay written for Marilyn Monroe (1926–62), his then wife.

Henry Miller (1891–1980) American essayist and novelist, author of several works initially seen as notorious for describing his own sexual exploits and rackety expatriate life. The erotic content of his work is nowadays found more 'innocent'. He was to become became a counter-cultural influence on the Beat generation of writers.

A(lan) A(lexander) Milne (1882–1956) English playwright and children's novelist; best known by the stories he wrote for his young son Christopher Robin, which feature a child of the same name and his toy animals, notably Winnie-the-Pooh, a bear of little brain, Piglet, Eeyore *et al*.

Iris Murdoch (1919–99) English scholar and novelist, whose fictions describe an intellectual, middle-class, obliquely comic world of offbeat eroticism.

Vladimir Nabokov (1899–1977) American novelist, exiled from his native Russian at the time of the Bolshevik revolution. He wrote initially in Russian, later becoming one of the most inventive and resourceful of English-language fictioneers.

V(idiadhar) S(urajprasad) Naipaul (1932–) British novelist, born in Trinidad; Naipaul's work has expanded in geographical and thematic scope, from his early humorous descriptions of life in Trinidad, to darker times in countries of the Third World.

Ogden Nash (1902–71) American writer of catchy, humorous and inventive verse, which owes much to the abilities that supported his career in advertising.

George Orwell (1903–50) English novelist and essayist, several of whose turns of phrase have passed into everyday speech. He wrote of poverty in realistic terms, having lived as a tramp; in *Homage to Catalonia* he recorded his experiences in the Spanish Civil War; and in the fantasy *Animal Farm* and the futuristic *Nineteen Eighty-four* he commented on the nature of political tyranny.

Wilfred Owen (1893–1918) Foremost British poet of World War I, forthright in his account of warfare as horror and waste; died in action a week before the end of hostilities.

Sylvia Plath (1932–63) American poet, author of often bizarrely worded verse whose substance was apt to be intensely personal. Her unsatisfactory marriage to Ted Hughes (see above), and the conflict between family life and the creative imperative both contributed to her suicide.

Ezra Pound (1885–1972) American poet, experimental and technically ambitious, and influential in helping the careers of James Joyce and

T S Eliot. Much of his life, including WW2, was spent in Italy, where he made radio broadcasts supporting the fascist government and blaming the war on the Jews. For this he was confined by the US authorities for many years in a mental asylum.

Damon Runyon (1884–1946) American short story writer, whose career was forged early in journalism; he wrote pithy, imaginative tales of low life based on his own researches in the New York underworld. Some of his stories were adapted to make the musical *Guys and Dolls*.

Salman Rushdie (1947–) British novelist, a source of much controversy, born in India into a wealthy Muslim family. His fiction uses a large canvas, drawing on elements of magical realism. However, *The Satanic Verses* was seen by some Muslims as blaspheming, and the Iranian leader of the time, the Ayatollah Khomeini, gave out a ruling that urged the assassination of Rushdie; there followed ten years in which Rushdie was forced to live in hiding.

J(erome) D(avid) Salinger (1919–) Reclusive American novelist and short story writer; his novel *The Catcher in the Rye* stands as a benchmark account of adolescence.

Carl Sandburg (1878–1967) American poet, seen as a successor to Walt Whitman because of his celebration of nationhood, in particular the people of his native mid-West. Sandburg also had a distinguished career as a biographer of Abraham Lincoln.

(George) Bernard Shaw (1856–1950) Irish critic, novelist, essayist and playwright. A dismaying childhood and an emphatically religious education helped shape him as an adversary of the British class system. He was – a founder – member of the Fabian Society, which worked to advance a fairer life for all, and an advocate of a system of simpler spelling and punctuation which has had as little success since his death as before it.

Isaac Bashevis Singer (1904–91) Polish-born American writer of novels and short stories. His work draws on the folk-tales and legends of traditional Jewish culture, and describes Polish and American Jewish life before the Holocaust, emphasising the effects of advancing modernity.

John Steinbeck (1902–68) American novelist, best known for his powerful depiction of the Great Depression, in *Of Mice and Men* and *The Grapes of Wrath*.

Tom Stoppard (1937–) British playwright and screenwriter, born Tomas Straussler in what is now the Czech Republic. Stoppard came quite early to fame with *Rosencrantz and Guildenstern Are Dead*, a play exemplifying his verbal panache and originality of approach.

Dylan (Marlais) Thomas (1914–53) Welsh poet, whose excellence was undiminished by the fact that he died of drink. He is best known through his description of the small town where he lived for part of his life, in the form of the radio play *Under Milk Wood*.

James Thurber (1894–1961) American essayist, cartoonist and short story writer, who characteristically describe the absurdities of an ordinary world. His most famous creation is the eponymous anti-hero of his story, 'The Secret Life of Walter Mitty'.

J(ohn) R(onald) R(euel) Tolkien (1892–1973) British scholar and fantasy writer, South-African born, whose fiction drew heavily on his career as a philologist and teacher of Nordic mythology. His trilogy *The Lord of the Rings*, fifteen years in the writing, continues to grow in popularity, largely because current technology has finally allowed the making of an impressive film version.

Gore Vidal (1925–) Novelist and critic, descended on both sides from families as long established as any in what is now the United States of America. His upbringing included a precocious first-hand knowledge of politics, a fact that has declared itself in novels set in several times and nations.

Evelyn Waugh (1903–66) English novelist whose earlier works were satirical, comic and sharply observed. His later work, such as *Brideshead Revisited*, expressed an unwitting, sometimes aggressive, anxiety about his own place in society.

Edith Wharton (1862–1937) American novelist and writer of short stories. Instead of merely inhabiting America's gilded age, as she had been raised and funded to do, Wharton recorded it, in a series of novels that held up her world to be examined from many aspects.

Patrick White (1912–90) Australian novelist, not always honoured in his own country due to a view of his countrymen as largely suburban and soulless. His books emphasise man as a creature living in isolation and extremity.

William Carlos Williams (1883–1963) American poet and novelist whose verse uses ordinary speech and, as a subject, everyday life.

Sir P(elham) G(renville) Wodehouse (1881–1975) Anglo–American writer, a master of comic fiction. His work included novels, short stories, song lyrics and screenplays. 'The performing flea' of English letters is one description given him; this does little justice however to the painstaking – and invisible – craft he bestowed on such works as the novels featuring the intellectually finite Bertie Wooster and his omnicompetent valet, Jeeves.

Thomas (Clayton) Wolfe (1900–1938) American writer of strongly autobiographical novels, much of whose published work was organised into several books by his publisher after Wolfe had died suddenly from tuberculosis of the brain.

(Adeline) Virginia Woolf *née* **Stephen** (1882–1941) English novelist at the heart of the Bloomsbury group of writers, artists and scholars; author of several intensely stream-of-consciousness fictions. Though her life was privileged, it was overshadowed by several bereavements that ploughed into her mental well-being, and she ended it by drowning herself.

W(illiam) B(utler) Yeats (1865–1939) Irish poet, whose work progressed through an initial modish feel for fairy-tale, to a strongly voiced account of his personal experience and an enduring expression of Irish nationalism.

Dickens characters

Pickwick Papers

ALLEN, Arabella and Benjamin – AYRESLEIGH, Mr – BAGMAN, The One-eyed – BAMBER, Jack – BANTAM, Angelo Cyrus, Esq, MC – BARDELL, Mrs Martha and Master Tommy – BETSEY – BLADUD, Prince – BLOTTON, Mr – BOLDWIG, Captain – BOLO, Miss – BUDGER, Mrs – BULDER, Colonel, Mrs Colonel and Miss – BUZFUZ, Serjeant – CHANCERY PRISONER, The – CLERGYMAN, The – CLUBBER, Sir Thomas, Lady and The Misses – CLUPPINS, Mrs Betsey – CRADDOCK, Mrs – CROOKEY – CRUSHTON, The Honourable Mr – DISMAL JEMMY – DODSON and FOGG – DOWLER, Captain and Mrs – DUBBLEY – DUMKINS, Mr – EDMUNDS, John, Mr and Mrs – EMMA – FITZ-MARSHALL, Charles – FIZKIN, Horatio, Esq – FLASHER, Wilkins – FOGG, Mr – GOODWIN – GROFFIN, Thomas – GRUB, Gabriel – GRUMMER, Daniel – GRUNDY, Mr – GUNTER, Mr – GWYNN, Miss – HARRIS – HENRY – HEYLING, George and Mary – HOPKINS, Jack – HUMM, Anthony – HUNT – HUNTER, Mrs Leo and Mr Leo – HUTLEY, Jem – ISAAC – JACKSON, Mr –

JEMMY, Dismal – JINGLE, Alfred – JINKINS, Mr – JINKS, Mr – JOE, The Fat Boy – JOHN – KATE – LOBBS, Maria – LOBBS, Old – LOWTEN, Mr – LUCAS, Solomon – LUFFEY, Mr – MAGNUS, Peter – MALLARD, Mr – MARTIN, Mr – MARTIN – MARTIN – MARTIN, Jack – MARY – MATINTER, The two Misses – MILLER, Mr – MIVINS, Mr – MUDGE, Mr Jonas – MUTHANED, Lord – MUZZLE, Mr – NAMBY, Mr – NEDDY – NODDY, Mr – NUPKINS, George, Esq, Mrs and Miss Henrietta – PAYNE, Doctor – PEEL, Mr Solomon – PERKER, Mr – PHUNKY, Mr – PICKWICK, Samuel – PIPKIN, Nathaniel – PODDER, Mr – POTT, Mr and Mrs – PRICE, Mr – PRUFFLE – RADDLE, Mr and Mrs Mary Ann – ROGERS, Mrs – ROKER, Mr Tom – SAM – SANDERS, Mrs Susannah – SAWYER, Bob – SHEPHERD, The – SIMMERY, Frank, Esq – SIMPSON, Mr – SKIMPIN, Mr – SLAMMER, Doctor – SLUMKEY, The Honourable Samuel – SLURK, Mr – SMANGLE – SMART, Tom – SMAUKER, John – SMIGGERS, Joseph – SMITHERS, Miss – SMITHIE, Mr, Mrs and the Misses – SMORLTORK, Count – SMOUCH, Mr – SNIPE, The Honourable Wilmot – SNODGRASS, Augustus – SNUBBIN, Serjeant – SNUPHANUPH, Lady – STAPLE, Mr – STARELEIGH, Mr Justice – STIGGINS, The Reverend Mr – STRUGGLES, Mr – TADGER, Brother – TAPPLETON, Lieutenant – TOMKINS, Miss – TOMLINSON, Mrs – TOMMY – TROTTER, Job – TRUNDLE, Mr – TUCKLE – TUPMAN, Tracy – UPWITCH, Richard – WARDLE, Mr, Miss Emily, Miss Isabella, Miss Rachael and Mrs – WATTY, Mr – WELLER, Samuel – WELLER, Tony and Mrs Susan – WHIFFERS – WICKS, Mr – WILKINS – WINKLE, Mr, Senior and Nathaniel – WITHERFIELD, Miss – WUGSBY, Mrs Colonel – ZEPHYR, The

Oliver Twist

ANNY – ARTFUL DODGER, The – BARNEY – BATES, Charley – BAYTON – BECKY – BEDWIN, Mrs – BET or BETSY – BILL – BLATHERS and DUFF – BOLTER, Morris – BRITTLES – BROWNLOW, Mr – BULL'S-EYE – BUMBLE, Mr – CHARLOTTE – CHITLING, Tom – CLAYPOLE, Noah – CORNEY, Mrs – CRACKIT, Toby – DAWKINS, John – DICK, Little – DODGER, The Artful – DUFF – FAGIN – FANG, Mr – FLEMING, Agnes and Rose – GAMFIELD – GILES, Mr – GRIMWIG, Mr – KAGS – LEEFORD, Edward – LIMBKINS – LIVELY, Mr – LOSBERNE, Mr – MANN, Mrs – MARTHA – MAYLIE, Harry, Mrs and Rose – MONKS – NANCY – SALLY, Old – SIKES, Bill – SOWERBERRY, Mr and Mrs – TWIST, Oliver

Mudfog Assoc

BELL, Mr Knight – BLANK, Mr – BLUBB, Mr – BLUNDERUM, Mr – BROWN, Mr – BUFFER, Doctor – CARTER, Mr – COPPERNOSE, Mr – CRINKLES, Mr – DOZE, Professor – DRAWLEY, Mr – DULL, Mr – DUMMY, Mr – FEE, Doctor W

R – FLUMMERY, Mr – GRIME, Professor – GRUB, Mr – GRUMMIDGE, Doctor – JOBBA, Mr – JOLTERED, Sir William – KETCH, Professor John – KUTANKUMAGEN, Doctor – KWAKLEY, Mr – LEAVER, Mr – LEDBRAIN, Mr X – LONG EARS, The Honourable and Reverend Mr – MALLET, Mr – MISTY, Mr X –MISTY, Mr X X – MORTAIR, Mr – MUDDLEBRAINS, Mr – MUFF, Professor – MULL, Professor – NEESHAWTS, Doctor – NOAKES, Mr – NOGO, Professor – PESSELL, Mr – PIPKIN, Mr – PROSEE, Mr – PUMPKINSKULL, Professor – PURBLIND, Mr – QUEERSPECK, Professor – RUMMUN, Professor – SCROO, Mr – SLUG, Mr – SMITH, Mr – SNIVEY, Sir Hookham – SNORE, Professor – SNUFFLETOFFLE, Mr O J A – SOEMUP, Doctor – SOWSTER – STYLES, Mr – TICKLE, Mr – TIMBERED, Mr – TOORELL, Doctor – TRUCK, Mr – WAGHORN, Mr – WHEEZY, Professor – WIGSBY, Mr – WOODENSCONCE, Mr

Nicholas Nickleby

ADAMS, Captain – AFRICAN KNIFE-SWALLOWER, The – ALICE – ALPHONSE – BELLING, Master – BELVAWNEY, Miss – BLOCKSON, Mrs – BOBSTER, Mr and Miss – BOLDER – BONNEY, Mr – BORUM, Mr, Mrs, Augustus, Charlotte and Emma – BRAVASSA, Miss – BRAY, Madeline and Mr Walter – BROOKER – BROWDIE, John – BULPH, Mr – CHEERYBLE BROTHERS, (Charles and Edwin) – CHEERYBLE, Frank – CHOWSER, Colonel – COBBEY – CROWL, Mr – CRUMMLES, Mr Vincent, Mrs, Master, Master Percy and Miss Ninetta – CURDLE, Mr and Mrs – CUTLER, Mr and Mrs – DAVID – DIGBY – FOLAIR, Mr – GAZINGI, Miss – GENTLEMAN, The, In Small-Clothes – GEORGE – GRAYMARSH – GREEN, Miss – GREGSBURY, Mr – GRIDE, Arthur – GROGZWIG, Baron of – GRUDDEN, Mrs – HANNAH – HAWK, Sir Mulberry – INFANT PHENOMENON – JOHNSON, Mr – KENWIGS, Mr, Mrs and Morleena – KNAG, Miss and Mr Mortimer – KOLËDWETHOUT, Baron Von and his wife – LA CREEVY, Miss – LANE, Miss – LEDROOK, Miss – LENVILLE, Thomas and Mrs – LILLYVICK, Mr – LINKINWATER, Miss and Tim – LUMBEY, Mr – MANTALINI, Madame and Mr Alfred – MOBBS – NICKLEBY, Mr Godfrey, Nicholas the elder, Nicholas the younger, Ralph, Kate and Mrs – NOGGS, Newman – PETOWKER, Miss Henrietta – PHOEBE, or PHIB – PLUCK, Mr – PRICE, Matilda – PUGSTYLES, Mr – PUPKER, Sir Matthew – PYKE, Mr – SCALEY, Mr – SIMMONDS, Miss – SLIDERSKEW, Peg – SMIKE – SNAWLEY, Mr and Mrs – SNEVELLICCI, Miss, Mr and Mrs – SNEWKES, Mr – SNOBB, The Honourable Mr – SQUEERS, Wackford, Mrs, Miss Fanny, Master Wackford Junior – SWILLENHAUSEN, Baron Von and his wife – TIMBERRY, Mr Snittle – TIX, Mr Tom – TOM – TOMKINS – TRIMMERS, Mr – VERISOPHT, Lord Frederick – WESTWOOD, Mr –WILLIAM – WITITTERLY, Mrs Julia and Mr Henry – YORK, The Five Sisters of

Master Humphrey's Clock

ALICE, Mistress – BELINDA – BENTON, Miss – DEAF GENTLEMAN, The – GOG – GRAHAM, Hugh – JINKINSON – MAGOG – MARKS, Will – MASTER HUMPHREY – MILES, Mr Owen – PICWICK, Mr Samuel – PODGERS, John – REDBURN, Jack – SLITHERS, Mr – TODDYHIGH, Joe – WELLER, Samuel and Tony the elder

The Old Curiosity Shop

BACHELOR, The – BARBARA – BARBARA'S MOTHER – BRASS, Sally and Sampson – CHEGGS, Mr and Miss – CHUCKSTER, Mr – CLERGYMAN, The – CODLIN, Tom – DAVID, Old – EDWARDS, Miss – EVANS, Richard – GARLAND, Mr, Mrs and Mr Abel – GEORGE – GEORGE, Mrs – GRANDFATHER, Little Nell's – GRINDER, Mr – GROVES, James – HARRIS, Mr – HARRY – JARLEY, Mrs – JERRY – JINIWIN, Mrs – JOWL, Joe – LIST, Isaac – MARCHIONESS, The – MARTON, Mr – MONFLATHERS, Miss – NELL, Little – NUBBLES, Christopher or Kit, Jacob and Mrs – OWEN, John – QUILP, Daniel and Mrs Betsey – SCOTT, Tom – SEXTON, The Old – SHORT – SIMMONS, Mrs Henrietta – SINGLE GENTLEMAN, The – SLUM, Mr – SPHYNX, Sophronia – SWEET WILLIAM – SWIVELLER, Dick – TRENT, Frederick and Little Nell – TROTTERS – VUFFIN – WACKLES, Miss Jane, Miss Melissa, Miss Sophy and Mrs – WEST, Dame – WHISKER – WILLIAM, Sweet – WITHERDEN, Mr

Barnaby Rudge

AKERMAN, Mr – BLACK LION, The – CHESTER, Mr and Edward – COBB, Tom – CONWAY, General – DAISY, Solomon – DENNIS, Ned – GASHFORD, Mr – GILBERT, Mark – GORDON, Colonel – GORDON, Lord George – GREEN, Tom – GRIP – GRUEBY, John – HAREDALE, Mr Geoffrey and Miss Emma – HUGH – LANGDALE, Mr – MIGGS, Miss – PARKES, Phil – PEAK – RUDGE, Barnaby, Mrs and Mr – STAGG – TAPPERTIT, Simon – VARDEN, Dolly, Gabriel and Mrs Martha – WILLET, John and Joe

A Christmas Carol

BELLE – CAROLINE – CRATCHIT, Bob, Mrs, Belinda, Martha, Master Peter and Tiny Tim – DILBER, Mrs – FAN – FEZZIWIG, Mr, Mrs and The Three Misses – FRED – GHOST OF CHRISTMAS PAST, PRESENT AND YET TO COME – JOE – MARLEY, The Ghost of Jacob – SCROOGE, Ebenezer – TOPPER, Mr – WILKINS, Dick

Martin Chuzzlewit

BAILEY, Junior – BEVAN, Mr – BIB, Julius Washington Merryweather – BRICK, Jefferson and Mrs Jefferson – BUFFUM, Mr Oscar – BULLAMY – CHOKE, General Cyrus – CHOLLOP, Major Hannibal – CHUFFEY, Mr – CHUZZLEWIT, Anthony, George, Jonas, Martin Senior and Martin the Younger – CICERO – CODGER, Miss – CRIMPLE, David – DIVER, Colonel – DUNKLE, Doctor Ginery – FIPS, Mr – FLADDOCK, General – GAMP, Sairey – GANDER, Mr – GRAHAM, Mary – GROPER, Colonel – HOMINY, Mrs – IZZARD, Mr – JACK – JANE – JINKINS, Mr – JOBLING, Doctor John – JODD, Mr – KEDGICK, Captain – KETTLE, Lafayette – LEWSOME, Mr – LUPIN, Mrs – MODDLE, Mr Augustus – MONTAGUE, Tigg – MOULD, Mr, Mrs and the Two Misses – MULLIT, Professor – NADGETT, Mr – NORRIS, Mr, Mrs and the Two Misses – PAWKINS, Major and Mrs – PECKSNIFF, Seth and Mercy – PINCH, Ruth and Tom – PIP, Mr – PIPER, Professor – POGRAM, The Honourable Elijah – PRIG, Betsey – SCADDER, Zephaniah – SIMMONS, William – SLYME, Chevy – SMIF, Putnam – SOPHIA – SPOTTLETOE, Mr and Mrs – SWEEDLEPIPE, Paul – TACKER – TAMAROO – TAPLEY, Mark – TIGG, Montague – TODGERS, Mrs M – TOPPIT, Miss – WESTLOCK, John – WOLF, Mr

The Chimes

BOWLEY, Lady, Master and Sir Joseph – CHICKENSTALKER, Mrs Anne – CUTE, Alderman – FERN, Lilian and Will – FILER, Mr – FISH, Mr – LILIAN – RICHARD – TUGBY – VECK, Margaret and Toby

The Cricket on the Hearth

BOXER – FIELDING, May and Mrs – PEERYBINGLE, John and Mrs Mary – PLUMMER, Caleb, Bertha and Edward – SLOWBOY, Tilly – TACKLETON

The Battle of Life

BRITAIN, Benjamin – CRAGGS, Mr Thomas and Mrs – HEATHFIELD, Alfred – JEDDLER, Doctor Anthony, Grace and Marion – MARTHA, Aunt – NEWCOME, Clemency – SNITCHEY, Jonathan and Mrs – WARDEN, Michael

Dombey and Son

ANNE – BAGSTOCK, Major Joseph – BAPS, Mr and Mrs – BERINTHIA – BILER – BITHERSTON, Master – BLIMBER, Doctor, Mrs and Miss Cornelia – BLOCKITT, Mrs – BOKUM, Mrs – BRIGGS – BROGLEY, Mr – BROWN, Alice and Mrs – BUNSBY, Captain Jack – CARKER, Harriet, James and Mr John – CHICK, Mr John and Mrs Louisa – CHICKEN, The Game – CHOWLEY –

CLARK, Mr – CLEOPATRA – CUTTLE, Captain Edward – DAWS, Mary – DIOGENES – DOMBEY, Mrs Edith, Mrs Fanny, Florence, Little Paul and Mr Paul – FEEDER, Reverend Alfred, M A and Mr B A – FEENIX, Cousin – FLOWERS – GAME CHICKEN, The – GAY, Walter – GILLS, Solomon – GLUBB, Old – GRANGER, Mrs Edith – HOWLER, The Reverend Melchisedech – JEMIMA – JOE – JOHN – JOHNSON – KATE – MacSTINGER, Alexander, Charles, Juliana and Mrs – MARTHA – MARWOOD, Alice – 'MELIA – MIFF, Mrs – MORFIN, Mr – NATIVE, The – NIPPER, Susan – PANKEY, Miss – PEPS, Doctor Parker – PERCH, Mr and Mrs – PILKINS, Mr – PIPCHIN, Mrs – RICHARDS – ROB THE GRINDER – SKETTLES, Lady, Sir Barnet and Barnet Junior – SKEWTON, The Hon. Mrs – SOWNDS – TOODLE, Mr, Mrs Polly and Robin – TOOTS, Mr P and Mrs – TOWLINSON, Thomas – TOX, Miss Lucretia – TOZER – WICKAM, Mrs – WITHERS

The Haunted Man

DENHAM, Edmund – LONGFORD, Edmund – REDLAW, Mr – SWIDGER, George, Milly, Philip and William – TETTERBY, Mr Adolphus, Mrs Sophia, 'Dolphus, Johnny and Sally

David Copperfield

ADAMS – BABLEY, Richard – BAILEY, Captain – BARKIS, Mr and Miss – CHARLEY – CHESTLE, Mr – CHILLIP, Mr – CLICKETT – COPPERFIELD, Mrs Clara, David and Mrs Dora – CREAKLE, Mr, Mrs, Miss – CREWLER, Mrs, Miss Caroline, Miss Louisa, Miss Lucy, Miss Margaret, Miss Sarah, Miss Sophy and The Reverend Horace – CRUPP, Mrs – DARTLE, Rosa – DEMPLE, George – DOLLOBY, Mr – DORA – EM'LY, Little – ENDELL, Martha – FIBBETSON, Mrs – GEORGE – GRAINGER – GRAYPER, Mr and Mrs – GULPIDGE, Mr and Mrs – GUMMIDGE, Mrs – HAMLET'S AUNT – HEEP, Mrs and Uriah – HOPKINS, Captain – JANET – JIP – JORAM, Mr and Mrs – JORKINS, Mr – LARKINS, Miss and Mr – LITTIMER – MALDON, Jack – MARKHAM – MARKLEHAM, Mrs – MEALY POTATOES – MELL, Mr Charles and Mrs – MICAWBER, Master Wilkins, Miss Emma and Mr Wilkins – MILLS, Miss Julia and Mr – MOWCHER, Miss – MURDSTONE, Mr Edward and Miss Jane – NETTINGALL, The Misses – OLD SOLDIER, The – OMER, Minnie and Mr – PARAGON, Mary Anne – PASSNIDGE, Mr – PEGGOTTY, Clara, Mr Daniel and Ham – QUINION, Mr – SHARP, Mr – SHEPHERD, Miss – SPENLOW, Miss Clarissa, Miss La Vinia, Miss Dora and Mr Francis – SPIKER, Mr Henry and Mrs Henry – STEERFORTH, James and Mrs – STRONG, Doctor and Mrs Annie – TIFFEY, Mr – TIPP – TRADDLES, Thomas – TROTWOOD, Miss Betsey and her husband – TUNGAY – WALKER, Mick – WATERBROOK, Mr and Mrs – WICKFIELD, Agnes and Mr – WILLIAM – WILLIAM

Bleak House

BADGER, Mr and Mrs Bayham – BAGNET, Matthew, Mrs, Malta, Quebec and Woolwich – BARBARY, Miss – BLINDER, Mrs – BOGSBY, James George – BOODLE, Lord – BOYTHORN, Lawrence – BUCKET, Mr Inspector and Mrs – BUFFEY, The Right Honourable William, MP – CARSTONE, Richard – CHADBAND, The Reverend Mr and Mrs – CHARLEY – CLARE, Ada – COAVINSES – DARBY – DEDLOCK, Sir Leicester, Lady Honoria and Volumnia – DONNY, Miss – FLITE, Miss – GEORGE – GRIDLEY, Mr – GRUBBLE, W – GUPPY, Mrs and William – GUSHER, Mr – GUSTER – HAWDON, Captain – HORTENSE, Mademoiselle – JARNDYCE, John – JELLYBY, Caroline, Mrs, Mr and 'Peepy' – JENNY – JO – JOBLING, Tony – KENGE, Mr – KROOK, Mr – LIZ – THE MAN FROM SHROPSHIRE – MELVILLESON, Miss M – MERCURY – MOONEY – NECKETT, Charlotte, Emma, Mr and Tom – NEMO – PARDIGGLE, Mr O A, FRS, Mrs, Alfred, Egbert, Felix, Francis and Oswald – PERKINS, Mrs – PIPER, Mrs – PRISCILLA – QUALE, Mr – RACHAEL, Mrs – ROSA – ROUNCEWELL, Mrs, Mrs, George and Watt – SHROPSHIRE, The Man from – SKIMPOLE, Arethusa, Harold, Mrs, Kitty and Laura – SMALLWEED, Bartholomew, Grandfather, Grandmother and Judy – SNAGSBY, Mr and Mrs – SQUOD, Phil – STABLES, The Honourable Bob – SUMMERSON, Esther – SWILLS, Little – TANGLE, Mr – THOMAS – TOUGHEY – TULKINGHORN, Mr – TURVEYDROP, Mr and Prince – VHOLES, Mr – WEEVLE, Mr – WISK, Miss – WOODCOURT, Allan and Mrs

Hard Times

BITZER – BLACKPOOL, Mrs and Stephen – BOUNDERBY, Josiah and Mrs Louisa – CHILDERS, Mr E W B – GORDON, Emma – GRADGRIND, Mr Thomas, Mrs, Adam Smith, Jane, Louisa, Malthus and Thomas – HARTHOUSE, Mr James – JUPE, Cecilia and Signor – KIDDERMINSTER, Master – M'CHOAKUMCHILD, Mr – MERRYLEGS – PEGLER, Mrs – RACHAEL – SCADGERS, Lady – SLACKBRIDGE – SLEARY, Josephine and Mr – SPARSIT, Mrs

The Seven Poor Travellers

BEN – DOUBLEDICK, Richard – MARSHALL, Mary – TAUNTON, Captain – TAUNTON, Mrs

The Holly Tree

BOOTS – CHARLEY – COBBS – EDWIN – EMMELINE – GEORGE – LEATH, Angela – NORAH – WALMERS, Master Harry, Junior and Mr

Little Dorrit

AUNT, Mr F's – BANGHAM, Mrs – BARNACLE, Clarence, Lord Decimus Tite, Ferdinand and Mr Tite – BEADLE, Harriet – BLANDOIS – BOB – CASBY, Christopher – CALVETTO, John Baptist – CHIVERY, John, Young John and Mrs – CLENNAM, Arthur and Mrs – CRIPPLES, Master and Mr – DAWES – DORRIT, Amy, Edward, Fanny, Mr Frederick and Mr William – DOYCE, Daniel – F'S AUNT, Mr – FINCHING, Mrs Flora – FLINTWINCH, Affery, Ephraim and Jeremiah – GENERAL, Mrs – GOWAN, Henry, Mrs and Mrs Henry – HAGGAGE, Doctor – JENKINSON – LAGNIER – MAGGY – MAROON, Captain – MARSHALSEA, Father of The – MEAGLES, Mr, Mrs and Minnie – MERDLE, Mr and Mrs – MR F'S AUNT – NANDY, John Edward – PANCKS, Mr – PET – PLORNISH, Mr and Mrs – RIGAUD – RUGG, Miss Anastasia – RUGG, Mr – SPARKLER, Mr Edmund and Mrs Edmund – STILTSTALKING, Lord Lancaster – TATTYCORAM – TICKIT, Mrs – TINKLER, Mr – TIP – WADE, Miss – WOBBLER, Mr

A Tale of Two Cities

BARSAD, John – CARTON, Sydney – CLY, Roger – CRUNCHER, Jerry, Young Jerry and Mrs – DARNAY, Charles and Mrs Lucie – DEFARGE, Madame Thérèse and Monsieur Ernest – EVRÉMONDE, Charles – GABELLE, Monsieur Théophile – GASPARD – JACQUES ONE, TWO, THREE, FOUR and FIVE – JOE – LORRY, Mr Jarvis – MANETTE, Doctor Alexander – MANETTE, Lucie – PROSS, Miss and Solomon – ST EVRÉMONDE, Marquis, Marquis, Marquise, Charles and Lucie – STRYVER, Mr –TELLSON AND COMPANY – TOM – VENGEANCE, The

Hunted Down

ADAMS, Mr – BANKS, Major – BECKWITH, Mr Alfred – MELTHAM, Mr – NINER, Miss Margaret – SAMPSON, Mr – SLINKTON, Mr Julius

The Uncommercial Traveller

ANDERSON, John and Mrs – ANTONIO – BATTENS, Mr – BONES, Mr and Mrs Banjo – CARLAVERO, Giovanni – CHIPS – CLEVERLY, Susannah and Williams – DIBBLE, Mr Sampson and Mrs Dorothy – FACE-MAKER, Monsieur The – FLANDERS, Sally – FLIPFIELD, Mr, Mrs, Miss and Mr Tom – GLOBSON, Bully – GRAZINGLANDS, Mr Alexander and Mrs Arabella – JACK, Dark – JACK, Mercantile – JOBSON, Jesse, Number Two – KING, Horace – KINDHEART, Mr – KLEM, Mr, Mrs and Miss –MELLOWS, Mr J – MERCY – MITTS, Mrs – MURDERER, Captain – OAKUM-HEAD – ONOWENEVER, Mrs – PANGLOSS – PARKLE, Mr – QUICKEAR – QUINCH, Mrs – REFRACTORY, Chief and Number Two – SAGGERS, Mrs – SALCY, P, Family – SHARPEYE –

SPECKS, Joe and Mrs – SQUIRES, Olympia – STRAUDENHEIM – SWEENEY, Mrs – TESTATOR, Mr – TRAMPFOOT – VENTRILOQUIST, Monsieur The – VICTUALLER, Mr Licensed – WEEDLE, Anastasia – WILTSHIRE

Great Expectations

AGED, The – AMELIA – AVENGER, The – BARLEY, Clara and Old Bill – BIDDY – BRANDLEY, Mrs – CAMILLA, Mr John or Raymond and Mrs – CLARRIKER – COILER, Mrs – COMPEYSON – DRUMMLE, Bentley – ESTELLA – FLOPSON – GARGERY, Joe and Mrs Georgiana Maria – GEORGIANA – HAVISHAM, Miss – HUBBLE, Mr and Mrs – JACK – JAGGERS, Mr – MAGWITCH, Abel – MARY ANNE – MIKE – MILLERS – MOLLY – ORLICK, Dolge – PEPPER – PIRRIP, Philip – POCKET, Herbert, Alice, Jane, Joe, Fanny, Mr Matthew, Mrs Belina and Sarah – POTKINS, William – PROVIS – PUMBLECHOOK, Uncle – SKIFFINS, Miss – SOPHIA – SPIDER, The – STARTOP, Mr – TRABB, Mr – WALDENGARVER, Mr – WEMMICK, Mr John, Mr Senior and Mrs – WHIMPLE, Mrs – WILLIAM – WOPSLE, Mr

Somebody's Luggage

BOUCLET, Madame – CHRISTOPHER – GABRIELLE – LANGLEY, Mr – MARTIN, Miss – MUTUEL, Monsieur – PRATCHETT, Mrs – THÉOPHILE, Corporal

Mrs Lirriper's Lodgings

BOBBO – EDSON, Mr and Mrs Peggy – JACKMAN, Major Jemmy – JANE – LIRRIPER, Jemmy Jackman and Mrs Emma – MAXEY, Caroline – PERKINSOP, Mary Anne – SERAPHINA – SOPHY – WOZENHAM, Miss

Mrs Lirriper's Legacy

BUFFLE, Mr, Mrs and Miss Robina – EDSON, Mr – GEORGE – GRAN, Mrs – JACKMAN, Major Jemmy – LIRRIPER, Doctor Joshua, Mrs and Jemmy Jackman – MADGERS, Winifred – RAIRYGANOO, Sally – WOZENHAM, Miss

Our Mutual Friend

AKERSHEM, Miss Sophronia – BLIGHT, Young – BOFFIN, Mrs Henrietta and Nicodemus – BOOTS, Mr and BREWER, Mr – CHERUB, The – CLEAVER, Fanny and Mr – DOLLS, Mr – FLEDGEBY, Mr – GLAMOUR, Bob – GLIDDERY, Rob – GOLDEN DUSTMAN, The – HANDFORD, Julius – HARMON, John and Mrs John – HEADSTONE, Bradley – HEXAM, Jesse, Charley and Lizzie – HIGDEN, Mrs Betty – INSPECTOR, Mr – JOEY, Captain – JONATHAN – JOHNNY – JONES, George – KIBBLE, Jacob – LAMMLE, Mr and Mrs Alfred – MORTIMER – MARY ANNE – MILVEY, Mrs Margaretta and The Reverend

Frank – MULLINS, Jack – PEECHER, Miss Emma – PODDLES – PODSNAP, Miss Georgiana, Mr John and Mrs – POTTERSON, Miss Abbey and Job – PUBSEY AND CO – RIAH, Mr – RIDERHOOD, Pleasant and Roger – ROKESMITH, Mr and Mrs John – SAMPSON, George – SLOPPY – SNIGSWORTH, Lord – SPRODGKIN, Mrs – TAPKINS, Mrs – TIPPINS, Lady – TODDLES – TOOTLE, Tom – TWEMLOW, Mr Melvin – VENEERING, Mr Hamilton and Mrs Anastasia – VENUS, Mr – WEGG, Silas – WILFER, Miss Bella, Miss Lavinia, Reginald and Mrs Reginald – WILLIAMS, William – WRAYBURN, Mr and Mrs Eugene – WREN, Jenny

Doctor Marigold

MARIGOLD, Doctor, Mrs, Little Sophy and Willum – MIM – PICKLESON – SOPHY

Barbox Brothers

BARBOX BROTHERS – BEATRICE – JACKSON, Mr – 'LAMPS' – PHŒBE – POLLY –TRESHAM

Boy at Mugby

EZEKIEL – PIFF, Miss – SNIFF, Mr and Mrs – WHIFF, Miss

The Trial for Murder (2 Ghost Stories)

DERRICK, John – HARKER, Mr

Holiday Romance

ALICIA, Princess – ALICUMPAINE, Mrs – ASHFORD, Miss Nettie – BLACK, Mrs – BOLDHEART, Captain – BOOZEY, William von – BROWN – CERTAINPERSONIO, Prince – DROWVEY, Miss – GRANDMARINA, Fairy – GRIMMER, Miss – LATIN-GRAMMAR MASTER, The – LEMONY Mrs – ORANGE, Mr James and Mrs – PEGGY – PICKLES – RAINBIRD, Alice – REDFORTH, Lieutenant-Colonel Robin –TINKLING, William, Esquire –TOM – WATKINS THE FIRST, King

George Silverman

FAREWAY, Adelina, Lady and Mr – GIMBLET, Brother – HAWKYARD, Mr Verity – SILVERMAN, George – SYLVIA – WHARTON, Mr Granville

Edwin Drood

BAZZARD, Mr – BILLICKIN, Mrs – BUD, Miss Rosa – CRISPARKLE, The Reverend Septimus and Mrs – DATCHERY, Dick – DEPUTY – DROOD, Edwin – DURDLES – FERDINAND, Miss – GIGGLES, Miss – GREWGIOUS, Hiram,

Esquire – HONEYTHUNDER, Mr Luke – JASPER, John – JENNINGS, Miss – JOE – LANDLESS, Helena and Neville – LOBLEY, Mr – REYNOLDS, Miss – RICKITTS, Miss – THOMAS – SAPSEA, Mr Thomas – TARTAR, Lieutenant – TISHER, Mrs – TOPE, Mr and Mrs – TWINKLETON, Miss

Some Uncollected Pieces – The Strange Gentleman

BROWN, Miss Emily – DOBBS, Miss Julia – JOHN – JOHNSON, John – NOAKES, Mrs – OVERTON, Mr Owen – PETER, Lord – SPARKS, Tom – STRANGE GENTLEMAN, The – TOMKINS, Charles – TROTT, Mr Walker – WILSON, Fanny and Mary

The Village Coquettes

BENSON, Lucy, Old and Young – EDMUNDS, George – FLAM, The Honourable Sparkins – MADDOX, John – NORTON, Squire – ROSE – STOKES, Mr Martin

Is She His Wife? Or, Something Singular

JOHN – LIMBURY, Mr Peter and Mrs – LOVETOWN, Mr Alfred and Mrs – TAPKINS, Mr Felix

Public Life of Mr Tulrumble (Once Mayor of Mudfog)

JENNINGS, Mr – SNIGGS, Mr – TULRUMBLE, Mrs, Mr Nicholas and Nicholas Junior – TWIGGER, Edward and Mrs

The Pantomime of Life

DO'EM – FIERCY, The Honourable Captain Fitz-Whisker

The Lamplighter's Story

BARKER, Miss Fanny – EMMA – GALILEO ISAAC NEWTON FLAMSTEAD – GRIG, Tom – MOONEY, Mr

Some important Science Fiction writers of modern times

Science Fiction is a genre with an unusually close relationship between authors and fans. Every year in most major markets there is at least one convention where the readers can meet the writers, and there are regular 'World Cons' for serious buffs. Much fun is had on these occasions, and industrial quantities of beer are consumed. The genre is, however, prone to navel-gazing about what it is exactly. One important distinction is that

SF is not fantasy; some kind of consistent rationale must prevail without the plot resorting to magic. For this reason writers such Philip Pulman, Terry Pratchett and J K Rowling – though wonderful – are not regarded as practitioners of SF. The history of the genre has been traced back as far as *The Epic of Gilgamesh*, but in its modern form it is generally seen as starting with Jules Verne, H G Wells and magazines such as Hugo Gernsback's *Amazing Stories*. The biggest prize in SF – The Hugo – is named in Gernsback's honour. Once dominated by the grand old names (Asimov, Heinlein, Clarke and Herbert), the field was invigorated by a new generation of wildly inventive writers, both British and American, of the so-called cyber-punk variety.

This selection gives only a flavour of the delights of Science Fiction.

Brian Aldiss (1925–) is one of Britain's foremost SF writers and part of the experimental 'New Wave' that was associated with *New Worlds* magazine. Also a mainstream writer and poet. *Hothouse*, *Report on Probability A*, and the *Helliconia* series are essential reading.

Poul Anderson (1926–2001) Versatile, clever American writer, creator of the future history series of novels, The Technic Civilization, featuring the wily but ultimately human and humane trader, Nicolas van Rijn. *Brain Wave*, *Tau Zero* and *The Avatar* should not be missed.

Neal Asher (1961–), a rising British star born in Essex. He writes in the edgy, turbo-charged cyber-punk manner. The future does not show any improvement in human nature, but the technology allows us to be horrible in hitherto unimaginable ways. *The Skinner* and *Gridlinked* are uncomfortably compelling.

Isaac Asimov (1920–92), American though born in Russia, his prodigious output and fertile imagination dominated the field from the 1940s to the 1960s. He invented the three Laws of Robotics in a series of novels about a robot detective, and is best known for the epic Foundation Trilogy which spanned the entire galaxy. Later, for commercial reasons, this was unwisely expanded. He also wrote over one hundred volumes of popular non-fiction, mainly on science. See *The Caves of Steel*, *The Naked Sun*, *Foundation and Empire*.

J G Ballard (1930–), British, born in Shanghai, China, is one of the most original voices in the field with an intense, melodic style. His childhood experiences in a prison camp informed his mainstream biographical novel, *The Empire of the Sun* (filmed by Spielberg in 1987). His SF is atmospheric and strange, often full of images of rust, decay and urban alienation. *Crash* (1972) explored the off-beat eroticism of traffic accidents. The *Drowned World* and *High Rise* are must-read titles.

Iain M Banks (1954–), Scottish, has two incarnations and the one with the initial 'M' writes bravura SF often featuring the 'Culture', a galaxy-wide alliance of species with roughly similar values. Many of the most engaging personalities are the giant sentient starships. His more literary output gets smart reviews, but for sheer exhilaration the SF is hard to match. *Excession* and *The Player of Games* are the two to start with.

Stephen Baxter (1957–), British, has a PhD in mathematics and specialises in big concept SF of a mind-expanding nature. The Xeelee stories concern the nature of matter itself. *Creation*, *Time* and *Evolution* are typical titles.

Greg Bear (1951–), American, has a deservedly great reputation as a modern master who combines scientific rigour with a sense of wonder. *Blood Music* won both the Hugo and the Nebula awards. Also read *Eon*, *Slant* and *Darwin's Radio*.

Alfred Bester (1913–87), American. Though his output was small, his inventiveness was high. *The Demolished Man* (1953) opened up many possibilities and *Tiger! Tiger!* (published in the USA as *The Stars my Destination*) is deservedly a minor classic of revenge and teleportation in extreme peril.

James Blish (1921–75), American expatriate in Britain, explored moral and religious issues in very entertaining SF. His 'Cities in Flight' stories took whole cities into space. *A Case of Conscience* won a Hugo for its account of a Jesuit priest led into a moral trap of terrible implications.

Ray Bradbury (1920–), American, is one of the genre's great stylists who evokes a sense of the homely and familiar made sinister by being in the wrong place or suborned in some creepy way. *The Martian Chronicles* is a classic, but he is perhaps best known for *Fahrenheit 451* (the temperature at which books burn), a title alluded to by Michael Moore (the bestseller author of *Stupid White Men*) in his latest documentary, *Fahrenheit 9–11*.

Kenneth Bulmer (1921–), prolific British writer of SF adventure and space opera who took over editing the influential New Writings in SF anthologies after Ted Carnell. Energetic and fast-paced; try *Worlds for the Taking* (1966). He also wrote in other genres and for TV under a variety of pseudonyms.

Algis Budrys (1931 –), born in Prussia but emigrated to the USA, a master short story writer and occasional novelist (*Rogue Moon* is excellent). Rather more literary than many SF writers, Budrys's output was often uncomfortably paranoia-inducing. *Who?*, a story about identity, still makes for uneasy reading.

Lois McMaster Bujold (1949–), American, has won more Hugo Awards for Best Novel than anyone else apart from Robert Heinlein, and has also received several other awards. Most are for her character-driven Vorkosigan series, beginning with *Shards of Honor*, in which she imagines what could be the worst possible thing that could happen to her hapless characters, then writes about it. Her books are intelligent space opera with humour and humanity, and although Miles Vorkosigan is a military genius and, in many of the books, a space mercenary, there are hardly any 'big guns'.

Arthur C Clarke (1917–), British living in Sri Lanka, is one of the great names of SF. Often credited with foreseeing the communications satellite, his work has a mix of hard science and a sense of man's cosmic destiny. *Childhood's End* and *Rendez-vous with Rama* are religious SF at its best – entertaining and laden with ideas. His short story, *The Sentinel*, later expanded into a series of novels, was the basis for Kubrick's brilliant film *2001– A Space Odyssey* (1968).

Hal Clement (1922–2003), American, a science teacher, he is famous for his meticulously worked-out hard science stories in which the laws of physics are applied to interestingly alien environments. *A Mission of Gravity* is the best known, and it influenced a generation of writers who married imagination with scientific plausibility.

Philip K Dick (1928–82), American, was one of the leaders of the field and one of the great imaginations of the century. Decades after his death, his stories are still being used as an ideas mine by Hollywood. The films *Bladerunner* (based on *Do Androids Dream of Electric Sheep*), *Total Recall*, *Minority Report*, *Imposter*, *Screamers* and *Paycheck* were all inspired by PKD (as he is known to aficionados). His novels and short stories were preoccupied with problems of identity, though this bleak theme was always suppressed into a brilliantly imagined narrative. *Ubik*, *The Man in the High Castle*, *A Scanner Darkly* and (though it is one of the saddest things you'll ever read) *Valis* are all essential reading.

Gordon R Dickson (1923–2001), American, was a master of rollicking space opera on an epic scale often in a military context. Gordon Dickson had been a soldier in WW2, but was by no means an endorser of martial values. His *Dorsai* trilogy is great fun for lovers of this form of SF.

Harlan Ellison (1934–), American, a radical innovator and controversialist, always pushing the limits of his own style and those of the genre. Mainly a master of dark, intense short stories, his famous 'A Boy and his Dog' gave the familiar post-nuclear apocalypse story an even more disturbing twist than usual. His story 'I have no mouth, but I must scream' was highly influential though often parodied.

Philip José Farmer (1918–), American, is usually credited with putting sex into SF. His *The Lovers* (with sex and love across the alien species barrier) inspired many a story on a similar theme. Best known for his huge *Riverworld* series in which Mark Twain wakes up after death to find that every human being who ever lived has been resurrected on an alien planet on the banks of a river 10 million miles long. He caused controversy in the SF world by once using the name Kilgore Trout, a fictional invention of Kurt Vonnegut. Vonnegut was not amused though Farmer maintained that it was a tribute.

William Gibson (1948–), American, gave the whole field an enormous boost when he wrote edgy, dystopian stories in which technology was sometimes hostile and often misused by humans. His fast, urban dangerous novels inhabit the virtual world of electronic information. This was the cyber-punk revolution. *Neuromancer*, *Burning Chrome* and *Virtual Light* are great novels that leave the reader wondering if we are evolving into a species that may be enhanced by technology while at the same time becoming appreciably less human.

Peter F Hamilton (1960–), British, born in the now resurrected county of Rutland that occasionally figures in his books, is one of the brilliant new voices on the SF scene. His Night's Dawn trilogy of giant volumes, of which *The Reality Dysfunction* is the first, blends the gothic with the scientific.

Harry Harrison (1925–), American living in Ireland then UK, hugely energetic entertainer and inventor of anarchic characters such as 'the stainless-steel rat' and Bill, the Galactic Hero. Both feature strongly in non-stop adventures often aimed at undermining various tyrannies. His glorious *Deathworld* trilogy is set on a heavy-gravity planet in which the ecology is not only mind-numbingly competitive and hostile, but also to some degree telepathic. Read also *A Transatlantic Tunnel, Hurrah!* for sheer hubris and fun.

Robert A(nson) Heinlein (1907–88), prolific American, came close to dominating the field in the 1960s though he was a very unlikely person to inspire the flower-power generation. This stemmed from *Stranger in a Strange Land*, a novel used as a platform for endless philosophising about religion, the individual versus the State, and shared emotional and sexual experience. Heinlein, an ex-navy man until ill health invalided him out of service, often used his stories as a means of expounding his right-wing views on how society should be organised. *Starship Troopers* (1959) made much of patriotic military values. It won a Hugo in 1960 but aroused much controversy. *The Moon is A Harsh Mistress*, about a mutiny in a lunar penal colony, reinforced the message. Always given to diatribes that got ever longer as he got older, Heinlein's early work nevertheless delivered his views with terrific narrative skill.

Frank Herbert (1920–86), American, is best known for his huge novel *Dune* (1965) and its four sequels. He was the first to devise an entire fictional ecology worked out in subtle detail, and to extrapolate its economic and political side-effects With its environmental concerns, hints of mysticism and an epic plot based loosely on the doomed House of Atreides from Greek tragedy, *Dune* is a heady mixture that sold in huge numbers and is still in print today. *Hellstom's Hive*, a non-*Dune* title, is also very fine.

Robert E Howard (1906–36), American, important more for spawning a genre – Sword and Sorcery – than for his literary skill, though his writing has energy. Conan the Barbarian is his best known creation. It was filmed years later with Arnold Schwarzenegger in the title role, and is worth seeing as it is hilariously bad. Bizarrely, Howard shot himself when he learned of his mother's imminent death.

Aldous Huxley (1894–1963), British, a celebrated novelist and writer (see especially *Point, Counter Point* and *Eyeless in Gaza*) from a famous family (Thomas Huxley, his grandfather, was the celebrated Darwinian biologist). He is included as a corrective to the idea that once a book wins literary esteem it somehow ceases to be SF. *Brave New World* (1932) is classic SF, quite prescient, and written in part as a corrective to the Wellsian idea that technology would improve the human condition. He became interested in the effects of mind-altering drugs such as mescaline which he wrote about with piercing intelligence. He died on the day (22/11/1963) when John F Kennedy was assassinated.

Daniel Keyes (1927–), American, a fine writer of short stories. 'Flowers for Algernon' is famous for the way it charts the rise and fall of the narrator's IQ under the influence of drugs. Stylistically it is a tour-de-force that is much anthologised.

C M Kornbluth (1923–58), American, a brilliant short-story writer and novelist perhaps best known for his collaborations with Fred Pohl of which *The Space Merchants* achieved the biggest success. Kornbluth's novel *The Syndic* anticipated the power of corporations. His collection *The Marching Morons* makes compelling reading.

Murray Leinster (1896–1975), American, influenced the genre in part through his prodigious output. His first story appeared in *Argosy* magazine in 1919 and he was still writing when he died. *War with the Gizmos* (1951) portrays an alien invasion. Leinster was adept at putting adventure stories into an SF context.

Stanislaw Lem (1921–), Polish, writes literary SF. The authorities regarded it as harmless fantasy, but he used it subversively. Reality is always an elastic concept in the works of Lem, and it certainly is not defined by the State. His best known book *Solaris* (1961) was filmed by Tarkovsky and, more recently, Soderbergh. *The Cyberiad* is also well worth reading.

Anne McCaffrey (1926–), American but resident in Ireland, broadened the appeal of the genre with her successful Dragonflight series which was more feminine than the Boys' Own blasters and spaceship stuff. The short story 'The Ship that Sang' is a little gem.

Vonda McIntyre (1948–), American, is less techie than many of the men and more concerned with characterisation. *The Exile Waiting* is an unusual take on post-catastrophe Earth. She is also an expert compiler and editor. Her novel *Dreamsnake* won the Hugo.

John Meaney (1957–), British, is one of the talented newcomers who has been described as post-cyber-punk tech noir. Edgy and well imagined, *To Hold Infinity* and *Paradox* should not be missed.

China Miéville (1972–), British, is an extraordinary new voice. His SF is steamy, organic and sexy and the worlds he creates throb with vitality The technology is well imagined, but it tends to be genetic and biological rather than electronic. *Scar* and *Perdido Station* are essential for anyone interested in the genre.

Walter M Miller (1923–96), American, fought at Monte Cassino in WWII. He is a noted writer of short stories, but his fame rests on the classic Hugo-winning *A Canticle for Leibowitz* (1960) which charts the destruction, rise and fall again of civilisation itself. A book that should be read by all, SF fans or not.

Michael Moorcock (1939–), British, was important as the editor of New Worlds magazine and as a prolific writer of SF, fantasy and well regarded mainstream novels such as *Byzantium Endures*. He produced vast quantities of sword and sorcery stuff and the deeply cool Jerry Cornelius stories, one of which, *The Final Programme*, was filmed. His short story 'Behold the Man' (1967) featured a time traveller who returns to biblical times and is crucified as Christ.

Richard Morgan (1965–), British, is another young writer who made a spectacular debut with *Altered Carbon*, a turbo-charged tech noir thriller. *Broken Angels* is just as exciting. Publishers hype him as the next Big Thing – and they may be right.

Larry Niven (1938–), American, is the author of the stupendous *Ringworld* series with one of the most attractive aliens, the Kzin, giant bipedal felines of an utterly untrustworthy nature. He often collaborates with Jerry Pournelle as in *The Mote in God's Eye* and other novels.

William F Nolan (1928–), American, was an editor and reviewer for the *Los Angeles Times* as well as an SF writer. He caught a mood about the hegemony of youth with his story *Logan's Run* in which nobody is allowed to live beyond twenty-one. In the film (1976) based upon it the fatal age was extended to thirty.

Frederick Pohl (1919–97), American, a veteran writer of consistent quality and imagination. *Drunkard's Walk*, *A Plague of Pythons*, *Man Plus* are all excellent. *Gateway* was the first of a series of stories that featured a hyperspace jump-off point. He also collaborated with C M Kornbluth and Jack Williamson.

Christopher Priest (1943–), British, wrote inventive Wellsian SF like *Inverted World* and *The Space Machine* but later moved away from the genre into well-reviewed mainstream novels such as *The Separation* and *The Glamour*. His fascination with the problem of deciding what is real survived the transition.

Keith Roberts (1935–1997), British, a clever short story writer and novelist. *The Inner Wheel* is excellent. However, his fame rests largely on *Pavane* (1968), an evocative alternative history story in which the Reformation never happened.

Robert Sheckley (1928–), American but expatriate resident in Ibiza then UK, is inventive and funny. His writing is often humorous, satirical and with a strong sense of the absurd. *Mindswap* is a good place to start on the off-beat pleasures of this author.

Clifford D Simak (1904–88), American, an ex-journalist and one of the fathers of modern SF, whose stories often had a radical bent. *Way Station* (1952) is important. In *City* he has a series of linked tales in which intelligent dogs make a much better job of building a civilised society than human beings.

Dan Simmons (1948–), American, one of the new voices, is a former teacher whose beautifully wrought and allusive space opera reconsiders myth and literature through an SF lens. His novel based on Homer's *Iliad* is mind-bending (see *Ilium*) and his series in which the protagonist in an incarnation of the poet Keats quite compelling. Once you read *Hyperion* you'll find it hard to resist the rest.

E E 'Doc' Smith (1890–1965), American, the chief chemist for a doughnut manufacturer and also the father of space opera, the extravagant subgenre featuring huge artefacts, colossal powers, over-the-top aliens, breathless action, and galaxy-wide scale. His *Skylark* and *Lensmen* series were commercially huge though now somewhat out of fashion.

Olaf Stapledon (1886–1950), British, was influential despite relatively modest sales. His *Last and First Men* (1930) has such an incredible scope, charting as its does the entire life-span of our species, that it fired the imaginations of many who followed. It is still very readable.

William Tenn (1920–), American, pseudonym of Philip Klass, was a gifted writer of ideas who specialised in short stories of which there are many distinguished collections. *The Seven Sexes* features an alien species that is so sexually polymorphic that seven varieties need to get together for reproduction. Tenn cleverly holds back the purpose of the meeting until the end of the story.

Neal Stephenson (1959–), American, is a dazzling high-tech writer with an eclectic mind and a gift for conspiracies. His *Cryptonomicon* has been favourably compared to Thomas Pynchon. *Snowcrash* and *The Diamond Age* are brilliant. He is one of the most important of the new generation of American SF writers.

A E van Vogt (1912–2000), Canadian, hugely inventive and productive writer with mystical leanings. *Slan*, a novel about telepaths, is regarded as a classic and *The World of Null-A* (non-Aristotelian logic) and its sequel turned many readers onto the work of Alfred Korzybski and his Institute for General Semantics. In the 1950s van Vogt became interested in Dianetics, the quasi-scientific religion of L Ron Hubbard.

Kurt Vonnegut (1922–), American, fresh, funny, thought-provoking, wise and a bit melancholy, his fame has claimed him for the mainstream though his early work was packaged and sold as SF. *Player Piano* and *Cat's Cradle* are SF at its best. Vonnegut was captured in WW2 and sent to work in a factory in Dresden. There he witnessed the catastrophic fire-bombing of the city, an experience that he found impossible to write about until *Slaughterhouse-Five* published twenty-five years later.

Roger Zelazny (1937–95), American, one of the greats, author of fifty novels and over one hundred and fifty short stories, opened up the genre by moving it away from space technology. Many of his characters are inspired by mythology or religion. *Lord of Light* is based on Hinduism. His Amber series was set on a higher and more intense plane than everyday experience and its characters have god-like powers. It is enormously popular. One of his novels, *Damnation Alley*, was turned into an indifferent movie.

Who was really who in literature?

The Ancient Mariner in Coleridge's poem *The Rime of the Ancient Mariner* is said to be based upon Fletcher Christian, the Acting Mate who led the infamous mutiny on HMS *Bounty* in 1789. There was a rumour that Christian had escaped from Pitcairn with gold from the *Bounty* and made his way back to England, and thence to the Lake District, where the story reached Samuel Taylor Coleridge.

Biggles, or James Bigglesworth, the ace pilot in the stories of Capt WE Johns, was based upon Air Commodore Cecil George Wigglesworth. The literary detective, William Amos, traces this to an interview Johns gave on the radio in 1949 in which he said that his hero was based on a pilot with a similar name. Historical context provided the rest, though the real Biggles started in the Royal Naval Air Service before being transferred to the RAF. He spent most of WW2 in Iceland.

James Bond in Ian Fleming's spy novels has many who have claimed to be the original. The name came from the ornithologist author of *Birds of the West Indies*. Candidates for the original Bond stem from Fleming's service in British Naval Intelligence in the Second World War. Commander William ('Bill') Dunderdale was a Russian-speaking veteran of many operations in the Black Sea. Lt-Commander Michael Mason was a RN boxing champion and involved in the plot to cut off German oil supplies by blocking the Danube. The Yugoslav double agent, Dusko Popov, has also been suggested. Sidney Reilly (who disappeared in 1925), a British spy against the Russians, has been posited mainly on account of his prodigious sexual appetites, but Fleming disparaged that idea.

Robinson Crusoe, by Daniel Defoe né Foe; (1660–1731) was published in 1719. The character was probably based on Alexander Selkirk (or Selacraig; 1676–1721) who ran away to sea in 1695. In 1704 he quarrelled with Willaim Dampier, his Captain, and asked to be put ashore on Juan Fernández, an uninhabited island, where he lived for four years before being rescued and continuing his naval career.

Sebastian Flyte in Evelyn Waugh's *Brideshead Revisted* (1945) was based loosely on the Hon Hugh Lygon, the second son of the Earl of Beauchamp, who was a friend of Waugh's at Oxford. Waugh visited the family home at Madresfield Court, Great Malvern, many times and it made a big impression on him. Hugh Lygon died in 1936.

Sherlock Holmes in Sir Arthur Conan Doyle's detective stories was acknowledged by his creator to have been inspired by Dr Joseph Bell, a surgeon and professor at Edinburgh University. Many other candidates have been put forward, but Bell, who was famously observant, employed Doyle as an outpatient clerk when he was a medical student, so the actor would have had ample opportunity to study Bell's methods.

Augustus Melmotte is the chief character in the novel *The Way We Live Now* (1875) by Anthony Trollope (1815–82). Those who doubt that life imitates art should ponder on the careers of Horatio William Bottomley (1860–1933) and (Ian) Robert Maxwell (né Jan Ludvik Hoch; 1923–91) – and, indeed, of George Hudson, The Railway King (1800–71), who may well have been an inspiration to Trollope.

Mr Merdle in Charles Dickens's *Little Dorrit* (published in serial form 1855–7) was based upon John Sadleir, MP, an Irish banker who cut his own throat on Hampstead Heath after swindling the Tipperary Joint Stock Bank and the Royal Swedish Railway out of many hundreds of thousands of pounds.

Orlando in Virginia Woolf's novel (1928) of that name was modelled on the Hon Victoria ('Vita') Sackville-West, the wife of Sir Harold Nicolson.

Vita was a novelist, poet, garden designer (Sissinghurst) and buoyant seducer of other women, including Virginia Woolf.

George Smiley, the protagonist in many of John Le Carré's espionage novels, has had three possible models. Michael Ward Bingham, Earl of Clanmorris, was one, though this was disputed by Le Carré's publishers and the Ministry of Defence when Lady Clanmorris wrote her memoirs *Smiley's Wife*. There are elements also of the Reverend Vivian Hubert Howard Green who taught the author at Sherbourne School. Sir Maurice Oldfield, formerly the Director of MI6, was also a possibility, though he was known to doubt the idea. However, Le Carré did arrange for him to have lunch with Alec Guinness, the actor, when he was preparing for the excellent TV version of *Tinker, Tailor, Soldier, Spy*.

Sir Luke Strett in Henry James's *The Wings of the Dove* is said to be based in part on the American doctor, WW Baldwin, who had a practice in Florence. He attended the wife of Mark Twain (Sam Clemens) during her final illness.

Subtle in Ben Jonson's *The Alchemist* (1610) is modelled on Dr John Dee (1527–1608), the powerful physician and astrologer in the court of Elizabeth I. Elements of Dr Dee are also to be found in Prospero in *The Tempest* (1607) by Shakespeare.

Svengali in George du Maurier's novel *Trilby* (1894) was based upon the mesmerist Felix Moscheles (1833–1917) whom the author met in Belgium. Despite the dark nature of the portrait, Moscheles was pleased to have the power of mesmerism recognised. He and Du Maurier later collaborated on other books.

Poets who died young

There's at least one reason why prematurely dead writers include a large proportion of poets. Many poets find their voice earlier than, say, novelists or playwrights; a potential author of several prose masterworks simply won't have got into the swing of things if he or she is destined to perish too soon. Among the causes of poets' lives cut short, war is the guiltiest party, possibly followed by hostilities of a domestic kind.

Sir Walter Raleigh (1552–1618) Beheaded on an uncertain suspicion of treason.

Sir Philip Sidney (1554–86) Fatally wounded while fighting in the Netherlands against the Spaniards.

Christopher Marlowe (1564–93) Stabbed in a fight at a tavern in Deptford, London.

Thomas Chatterton (1752–70) Committed suicide by poisoning after early success deserted him.

George Gordon, Lord Byron (1788–1824) Died of marsh fever after joining the Greek uprising against rule by Turkey.

Percy Bysshe Shelley (1792–1822) Drowned when the boat he was sailing foundered off the coast of Italy.

John Keats (1795–1821) Died of consumption.

Alexandr Sergevich Pushkin (1799–1837) Killed in a duel over his wife.

Charlotte, Emily and Anne Brontë (1816–55, 1818–48, 1820–49) Charlotte died of a pregnancy-related illness, Emily and Anne from a pulmonary disease.

Edward Thomas (1878–1917) Killed at Arras.

Rupert Brooke (1887–1915) Died of blood poisoning on the Greek island of Skyros, having been posted to the Dardanelles.

Wilfred Owen (1893–1918) Killed on the Western Front.

Dylan Thomas (1914–53) Died of alcohol poisoning.

Sylvia Plath (1932–63) Committed suicide by gassing.

Poets laureate

After this royal appointment was made official, with the apt choice of Dryden, a number of poets were to be appointed for their politics than their ability to write tolerable verse. Before its good name was restored, in the nineteenth century, at least one Laureate, Henry Pye, was considered so bad that Walter Scott declared him 'respectable in everything but his poetry'. Luckily, sycophancy has long ceased to be part of the job description, but the other no-longer-compulsory duty of writing poetry for royal occasions sometimes seems, when practised, to lead to work of self-conscious banality.

1688–88	John Dryden
1689–92	Thomas Shadwell
1692–1715	Nahum Tate
1715–18	Nicholas Rowe

1718–30   Laurence Eusden
1730–57   Colley Cibber
1757–85   William Whitehead
1785–90   Thomas Warton
1790–1813 Henry James Pye
1813–43   Robert Southey
1843–50   William Wordsworth
1850–92   Alfred, Lord Tennyson
1896–1913 Alfred Austin
1913–30   Robert Bridges
1930–67   John Masefield
1968–72   Cecil Day-Lewis
1972–84   Sir John Betjeman
1984–98   Ted Hughes
1998–   Andrew Motion

Nobel laureate winners of the prize for literature

Year	Name	Country and dates
1901	Rene Sully-Prudhomme	(France) 1837–1907
1902	Theodor Mommsen	(France) 1817–1903
1903	Bjornstjerne Bjornson	(Norway) 1832–1910
1904	Frederic Mistral	(France) 1830–1914
	Jose Echegaray	(Spain) 1832–1916
1905	Henryk Sienkiewicz	(Poland) 1846–1916
1906	Giosue Carducci	(Italy) 1835–1907
1907	Rudyard Kipling	(UK) 1865–1936
1908	Rudolf Eucken	(Germany) 1846–1926
1909	Selma Lagerlof	(Sweden) 1858–1940
1910	Paul von Heyse	(Germany) 1830–1914
1911	Maurice Maeterlinck	(Belgium) 1862–1949
1912	Gerhart Hauptmann	(Germany) 1862–1946
1913	Rabindranath Tagore	(India) 1861–1941
1914	—	
1915	Romain Rolland	(France) 1866–1944
1916	Verner von Heidenstam	(Sweden) 1859–1940
1917	Karl Gjellerup	(Denmark) 1857–1919
	Henrik Pontoppidan	(Denmark) 1857–1943
1918	—	
1919	Carl Spitteler	(Switzerland) 1845–1924
1920	Knut Hamsun	(Norway) 1859–1952
1921	Anatole France	(France) 1844–1924

1922	Jacinto Benavente y Martinez	(Spain) 1866–1954
1923	William Butler Yeats	(Ireland) 1865–1939
1924	Wladyslaw Reymont	(Poland) 1868–1925
1925	George Bernard Shaw	(Ireland) 1856–1950
1926	Grazia Deledda	(Italy) 1875–1936
1927	Henri Bergson	(France) 1859–1941
1928	Sigrid Undset	(Norway) 1882–1949
1929	Thomas Mann	(Germany) 1875–1955
1930	Sinclair Lewis	(USA) 1885–1951
1931	Erik Axel Karlfeldt	(Sweden) 1864–1931
1932	John Galsworthy	(UK) 1867–1933
1933	Ivan Bunin	(USSR) 1870–1953
1934	Luigi Pirandello	(Italy) 1867–1936
1935	—	
1936	Eugene O'Neill	(USA) 1888–1953
1937	Roger Martin du Gard	(France) 1881–1958
1938	Pearl Buck	(USA) 1892–1973
1939	Frans Emil Sillianpaa	(Finland) 1888–1964
1940–43	—	
1944	Johannes V Jensen	(Denmark) 1873–1950
1945	Gabriela Mistral	(Chile) 1889–1957
1946	Hermann Hesse	(Switzerland) 1877–1962
1947	Andre Gide	(France) 1869–1951
1948	T S Eliot	(UK) 1888–1965
1949	William Faulkner	(USA) 1897–1962
1950	Bertrand Russell	(UK) 1872–1970
1951	Par Lagerkvist	(Sweden) 1891–1974
1952	Francois Mauriac	(France) 1885–1970
1953	Winston Churchill	(UK) 1874–1965
1954	Ernest Hemingway	(USA) 1898–1961
1955	Haldor K Laxness	(Iceland) 1902–
1956	Juan Ramon Jimenez	(Spain) 1881–1952
1957	Albert Camus	(France) 1913–60
1958	Boris Pasternak (declined)	(USSR) 1890–1960
1959	Salvatore Quasimodo	(Italy) 1901–68
1960	Alexis Leger	(France) 1887–1975
1961	Ivo Andric	(Yugoslavia) 1892–1975
1962	John Steinbeck	(USA) 1902–68
1963	Giorgos Seferis	(Greece) 1900–1971
1964	Jean-Paul Sartre (declined)	(France) 1905–80
1965	Mikhail Sholokhov	(USSR) 1905–84

1966	S Y Agnon	(Poland) 1888–1970
	Nelly Sachs	(Sweden) 1891–1970
1967	Miguel Asturias	(Guatemala) 1891–1970
1968	Yasunari Kawabata	(Japan) 1899–1972
1969	Samuel Beckett	(Ireland) 1906–89
1970	Alexander Solzhenitsyn	(USSR) 1918–
1971	Pablo Neruda	(Chile) 1904–73
1972	Heinrich Böll	(Germany) 1917–85
1973	Patrick White	(Australia) 1912–90
1974	Harry Martinson	(Sweden) 1904–78
	Eyvind Johnson	(Sweden) 1900–1976
1975	Eugenio Montale	(Italy) 1896–1981
1976	Saul Bellow	(USA) 1915–
1977	Vincente Aleixandre	(Spain) 1898–1984
1978	Isaac Bashevis Singer	(USA) 1904–91
1979	Odysseus Elytis	(Greece) 1911–
1980	Czeslaw Milosz	(Poland) 1911–
1981	Elias Canetti	(Bulgaria) 1905–
1982	Gabriel Marquez	(Colombia) 1928–
1983	William Golding	(UK) 1911–
1984	Jaroslav Seifert	(Czechoslavakia) 1901–86
1985	Claude Simon	(France) 1913–
1986	Wole Soyinka	(Nigeria) 1934–
1987	Joseph Brodsky	(USSR) 1940–
1988	Naquib Mahfouz	(Egypt) 1911–
1989	Camilo Jose Cela	(Spain) 1916–
1990	Octavio Paz	(Mexico) 1914–
1991	Nadine Gordimer	(South Africa) 1923–
1992	Derek Walcott	(Trinidad) 1930–
1993	Toni Morrison	(USA) 1931–
1994	Kenzaburo Oe	(Japan) 1935–
1995	Seamus Heaney	(Ireland) 1939–
1996	Wislawa Szymborska	(Poland) 1923–
1997	Dario Fo	(Italy) 1920–
	José Saramago	(Portugal) 1922–
1999	Gunter Grass	(Germany) 1927–
2000	Gao Xingjian	(China) 1940–
	V S Naipaul	(Trinidad) 1932–
	Imre Kertész	(Hungary) 1929–
2003	J M Coetzee	(South Africa) 1940–

Music

Composers

Tomaso Albinoni (*b* Venice, 1671; *d* 1751) A wealthy amateur whose output, notably of operas and concerti grossi, was vast.

Johann Sebastian Bach (*b* Eisenach, 1685; *d* 1750) Organist and composer of cantata, oratorio and keyboard music. In his own lifetime he lacked the acclaim, as the greatest of composers, that he has received over the last century or more. He was buried in an unmarked grave, whose location was not established until 1894.

Béla Bartók (*b* Nagyszentmiklos, Hungary, 1881; *d* 1945) Composer whose works acquired a national style. Later however, his output was conspicuously atonal and dissonant. He died disillusioned by the disintegration, in recent decades, of his native land.

Ludwig van Beethoven (*b* Bonn, 1770; *d* 1827) Born in poverty, the offspring of alcoholics. He had little education and found it hard to express himself verbally. Nonetheless his mentors came to include Mozart and Haydn, and he greatly expanded the possibilities of the concerto and the symphony. His deafness, starting from the age of thirty and eventually total, failed to diminish him as a composer.

Alban Berg (*b* Vienna, 1885; *d* 1935) A pupil of Schoenberg, whose influence appears in the atonal quality of many works. After years of failing health, he died of blood poisoning following an insect bite.

Hector Berlioz (*b* near Grenoble, 1803; *d* 1869) Innovative in his orchestration; often inspired by non-musical influences especially Shakespeare. For twenty-five years, from his early thirties, he had to work as a critic to earn his living.

Pierre Boulez (*b* Montbrizon, France, 1925) As an orchestral conductor he has had an extensive career; as a composer he has experimented widely with serial techniques and electronic sounds.

Johannes Brahms (*b* Hamburg, 1833; *d* 1897) In an era of romantic tastes, his orchestral music remained predominantly classical. Later in life he favoured songs and chamber music. He was greatly influenced by his friendship with the Schumann family.

Benjamin Britten (*b* Lowestoft, 1913; *d* 1976) He studied under Frank Bridge and John Ireland. As a member of the GPO Film Unit for four years from 1935, he wrote incidental music; he was greatly influenced by working with W H Auden. He composed chamber music, operas and choral works, sometimes writing for the voice of his friend Peter Pears, with whom he founded the Aldeburgh Festival.

Anton Bruckner (*b* Ansfelden, Upper Austria, 1824; *d* 1896) Composer of choral works and symphonies, largely informed by a profound religious sense. As a committed Wagnerian, he tended to alienate adherents of Brahms' music.

William Byrd (*b* Lincolnshire 1543; *d* 1623) His religious pieces, written for Catholic and Protestant churches alike, were supreme; however, he followed all the fashions of the time, including madrigals and compositions for virginals. From 1572 he shared the post of organist at the Chapel Royal with Thomas Tallis.

Frédéric François Chopin (*b* Zelazowa Wola, Poland, 1810; *d* 1849) Pianist and composer, who wrote many pieces intended to show off technique in performance; influenced in early life by the traditions of Polish music.

Aaron Copland (*b* Brooklyn, 1900; *d* 1992) Pianist, lecturer, and conductor; and a composer whose work often reflects American themes. His compositions vary in accessibility.

Arcangelo Corelli (*b* Fusignano, Italy, 1653; *d* 1713) As a violinist he had a huge influence on subsequent musicians; as a composer it was he who defined the form of the concerto grosso.

François Couperin (*b* Paris, 1668; *d* 1733) A court musician in the service of Louis XIV, and member of a celebrated family. He is remembered in particular by his compositions written for the harpsichord.

Peter Maxwell Davies (*b* Manchester, 1934) His range as an experimental composer is large, and since 1970 has been influenced by the land- and seascapes around his home in the Orkney islands.

Claude Debussy (*b* St Germain-en-Laye, 1862; *d* 1918) Composer of fragmentary melody and unconstrained rhythms in pieces evoking a variety of places and emotions.

Frederick Delius (*b* Bradford, Yorkshire, 1862; *d* 1934) The son of a Prussian industrialist, he is mostly known for his orchestral tone poems, though his work also includes pieces for full orchestra, concertos and operas. Having contracted syphilis in 1890, over the last decade or more of his life he became blind and paralytic; he owed much in these years to his amanuensis Eric Fenby.

John Dowland (*b* London(?), 1563; *d* 1626) Author of several books of compositions for the lute; he was himself a famous lutenist. After spending much of his life travelling throughout Europe, in 1612 he was appointed as one of the King's Musicians for the Lute.

Edward Elgar (*b* Broadheath, near Worcester, 1857; *d* 1934) Only in 1899, with the *Enigma Variations*, did he achieve wide recognition. His choral work and symphonies often show a feeling for English people and landscape. He did not identify, though, with much of the nationalist enthusiasm for his *Land of Hope and Glory*, a strain in his *Pomp and Circumstance March* No 1 in D, written as a coronation ode for Edward VII.

Gabriel Fauré (*b* Pamiers, Ariege, 1845; *d* 1924) A pupil of Saint-Saens; composer of music for the theatre; also chamber music, a Requiem, and a large number of songs.

George Gershwin (*b* New York, 1898; *d* 1937) Born into a family of Russian immigrants that included his brother Ira, the song lyricist, with whom he had a life-long collaboration. An early enthusiasm for ragtime and jazz became a permanent influence on his work, which includes orchestral pieces, musicals and popular songs.

Orlando Gibbons (*b* Oxford, 1583; *d* 1625) For the second half of his life he was organist of the Chapel Royal and also, from 1623, at Westminster Abbey. He wrote church music, including about forty anthems; also keyboard pieces, music for viols and a number of memorable madrigals.

Christoph Willibald von Gluck (*b* Erasbach, Bavaria, 1714; *d* 1787) Performer on cello, violin and keyboard instruments; composer of opera and ballet music who sought to make music combine with a dramatic narrative instead of just ornamenting it.

Edvard Grieg (*b* Bergen, 1843; *d* 1907) Born into an accomplished musical family with Scottish antecedents; composer of tuneful orchestral works, sonatas and songs. Much of his work breathes the spirit of Norwegian traditions of music and dance. He is buried in a cliffside overlooking a fjord close to his home, near Bergen.

George Frederic Handel (*b* Halle, Saxony, 1685; *d* 1759) He trained in composition and harpsichord, oboe, organ and violin despite opposition to a musical career from his father, a barber-surgeon. During several years in London, he was to enjoy huge success with his Italian-style operas; a trend that was reversed with the instant popularity of John Gay's *The Beggar's Opera*. Handel restored this loss of fortune by writing oratorios, and died wealthy.

Franz Joseph Haydn (*b* Rohrau, Austria, 1732; *d* 1809) Composer who established the form of the string quarter and had much influence on the development of the symphony. In 1781/2 he met Mozart, whom he held in great – and reciprocated – esteem; from 1792 to 1794 Beethoven was his pupil.

Gustav Holst (*b* Cheltenham, 1874; *d* 1934) He came from a musical family of Swedish descent, and studied at the Royal College of Music, where his classmate Vaughan Williams became a life-long friend. He wrote operas, military music, and choral and orchestral works and was much influenced by folk music.

Charles Ives (*b* Danbury CT 1874; *d* 1954) His involvement with a successful insurance company, Ives and Myrick, which he founded in 1907, enabled him to pursue a career in experimental music which included polyrhythms and polytonality and the concatenation of different style – always exciting. His *Symphony No3* won a Pulitzer Prize in 1904.

Leos Janácek (*b* Hukvaldy, Moravia, 1854; *d* 1928) Born into a family of fourteen children, he faced a steep climb out of poverty in his early years. His foremost works were all composed during the final quarter-century of his life; they expressed much national feeling and reflected Czech folk song and everyday speech.

Franz Liszt (*b* Raiding, Hungary, 1811; *d* 1886) Piano virtuoso and composer of much music for the piano, along with concertos and the first symphonic poems. Of the three children born of his affair with the Comtesse Marie d'Agoult, Cosima was to marry Richard Wagner.

Jean-Baptiste Lully (*b* Florence, 1632; *d* 1687) A dancer as well as a musician, Lully enjoyed the patronage of Louis XIV, for whom, in collaboration with Molière, he wrote a number of ballets; he is also credited with creating the French form of opera. He died after accidentally stabbing himself in the foot while conducting a *Te Deum* for the king.

Gustav Mahler (*b* Kaliste, Bohemia, 1860; *d* 1911) Composer of long symphonic works using idiosyncratic orchestral resources. Since his death the draft of his tenth symphony has been completed in various inspired forms. His reputation, once lessened, has risen again in the late twentieth-century.

Felix Mendelssohn-Bartholdy (*b* Hamburg, 1809; *d* 1847) The form of his music is classical; its spirit is expressively lyrical. He was recognised early as a major composer, in 1826 with works including the *Midsummer Night's Dream* overture. In 1843 he founded the Leipzig Conservatory.

Olivier Messiaen (*b* Avignon, 1908; *d* 1992) A strongly felt Catholicism is the basis for much of his work, whose inspirations include Gregorian chant and bird song; it also features electronic music and inventive use of percussion.

Claudio Monteverdi (*b* Cremona, 1567; *d* 1643) He had a prosperous career, largely as a writer of madrigals, but with unexpected setbacks. Monteverdi was one of Europe's most famous composers, when the death of his wife, in 1607, plunged him into several years of depression. In 1630 the outbreak of plague was a huge disruption; he joined the priesthood and almost gave up composition. A time of great creativity followed, especially with his operatic works.

Wolfgang Amadeus Mozart (*b* Salzburg, 1756; *d* 1791) As a harpsi-chordist and composer, a child prodigy who wrote his first – and already Mozartian-sounding – symphony at eight years old. He had a preference for writing opera, but also turned his extraordinary fluency to keyboard, orchestral and chamber works. He has a claim to be foremost among musical geniuses and had much success in his lifetime; nonetheless he died in poverty and was buried in a pauper's grave.

Niccolo Paganini (*b* Genoa, 1782; *d* 1840) An early virtuoso on violin, for which instrument he wrote several works. By his mid-teens he had rescued himself from a life of poverty; but drink and gambling thereafter threatened more than once to overturn his life. He made a legendary pact with the Devil, forbidding his burial in consecrated ground; the upshot of this was that until 1926 his body was moved continuously.

Giovanni Palestrina (*b* Palestrina, c1525; *d* 1594) Composer of some madrigals and much church music, distinguished for its flowing choral melodies. It was he who brought to completion the polyphonic style developed in the Low Countries. He had planned to spend a prosperous retirement in his birthplace, but died as he was about to set out.

Sergey Prokofiev (*b* Sontsovka, Ukraine, 1891; *d* 1953) Pianist, conductor and composer of works including ballets, film scores, and operas; his early music in particular was dissonant but nonetheless melodic. He fell from favour with the Soviet authorities in 1948, to be restored to official approval in 1959.

Giacomo Puccini (*b* Lucca, 1858; *d* 1924) A major contributor to operatic repertoire world-wide, as the composer of melodic works with a strong dramatic narrative.

Henry Purcell (*b* London, 1659; *d* 1695) Known mainly for his theatre music and opera, in which he anticipated Handel. From 1679 he was organist at Westminster Abbey. He wrote prolifically and was recognised during his tragically shortened life as the first among English composers of his time.

Sergei Rachmaninov (*b* Oneg, near Novgorod, 1873; *d* 1943) Pianist and composer, whose music is romantic and emotive in style. Having freed himself from depression and poverty, he gained international success. However, after the revolution of 1917 he left Russia, where his music was now seen as decadent. The rest of his life was spent in exile; he was grati-fied nonetheless when the Soviet authorities accepted that his work should no longer be denounced as 'bourgeois'.

Maurice Ravel (*b* Ciboure, 1875; *d* 1937) A composer of orchestral music both lyrical and strongly rhythmic. During WW1, though found unfit for active service, he went to the front as a driver; afterwards he suffered from insomnia which was to make him increasingly ill to the end of his life.

Nikolai Rimsky-Korsakov (*b* Tikhvin, 1844; *d* 1908) While he was at the Naval College in St Petersburg he was introduced by his piano teacher to Balakirev and, together with fellow composers Borodin and Mussorgsky, Rimsky-Korsakov became part of the group known as 'the Five'. It was his re-orchestration of works by Borodin and Mussorgsky that helped make them famous.

Gioachino Rossini (*b* Pesaro, Italy, 1792; *d* 1868) Known mainly as a composer of opera, he also wrote church music, pieces for piano, and songs. His operas are a young man's oeuvre, seen at the time as rather noisy; after 1829 he never wrote another.

Eric Satie (*b* Honfleur, 1866; *d* 1925) Witty and modernist; largely specialising in pieces for the piano. Though Debussy was older, he was much influenced by Satie, who was also had an effect on 'the Six', *ie* Auric, Durey, Honegger, Milhaud, Poulenc and Tailleferre.

Arnold Schoenberg (*b* Vienna, 1874; *d* 1951) His twelve-tone technique of atonal composition had a permanent effect on western forms of composition. He had little formal training in music, though as a child he was taught several instruments. After WW1, opposition to his work began to be replaced by success.

Franz Schubert (*b* Vienna, 1797; *d* 1828) He is best known for his piano works and his many song settings. Early success favoured him, but he became ill with syphilis in 1822 and was killed a few years later by typhoid.

Robert Schumann (*b* Zwickau, 1810; *d* 1856) Pianist, composer and conductor, whose career as a performer ended in 1832 when his right hand became crippled. It was partly this that redirected him towards composing. From the early 1840s his mental health declined, perhaps in response to syphilis. In 1853 he failed to kill himself by jumping into the Rhine, but died not long after in a lunatic asylum.

Dmitri Shostakovich (*b* St Petersburg, 1906; *d* 1975) Opera, ballet and film music were all part of his oeuvre; but most of all he is known for his symphonies celebrating the best and the most terrible of current Soviet history. Following criticism by the authorities, alternating with their approval, eventually he wrote as two people: privately as himself, and for public purposes.

Jean Sibelius (*b* Hameenlinna, Finland, 1865; *d* 1957) Following early success as a composer he enjoyed an international career. His music shows the powerful effect of Finnish mythology. No composition by him survives from after the mid–1920s.

Bedrich Smetana (*b* Litomysl, 1824; *d* 1884) Founder of a patriotic move-ment within Czech music through works that drew much from national folk rhythms; the upheavals of 1848 helped lighten his patriotic fervour. A disorganised life, including deafness, from 1874, did not prevent him from composing. He died of syphilis.

Johann Strauss (*b* Vienna, 1825; *d* 1899) The 'Waltz King' of Vienna came from an extensive family of performers and composers. His works mostly comprised polkas, waltzes and operettas.

Richard Strauss (*b* Munich, 1864; *d* 1949) His earlier work, in a career featuring songs, ballets, operas and symphonic poems, tended towards grandiloquence; later they became more intimate.

Igor Stravinsky (*b* Oranienbaum, near St Petersburg, 1882; *d* 1971) Famously composer of the music for Diaghilev's *Rite of Spring* (1913), whose first night provoked a riot. After the October Revolution of 1917 he lived in exile, returning to Russia only once: on a visit forty-eight years later.

Thomas Tallis (*b* London(?), c1505; *d* 1585) Organist, and composer of Latin masses, pieces for keyboard, and motets such as the ingenious *Spem in alium*, for forty-part choir. From 1543 he remained a Gentleman of the Chapel Royal, through some formidable changes of regime.

Pyotr Ilyich Tchaikovsky (*b* Kamsko-Votkinsk, 1840; *d* 1893) Whether reflective or exultant, his Russian-accented music was direct and powerful. He wrote ballet scores, symphonies, concertos, and operas, though for a long time he met with little success. The threat of failure, with a terrible marriage and guilt at his own homosexuality, combined to depress him to the point where he tried to drown himself. It was in the last five years of his life that he wrote some of his best pieces. He died of cholera.

Georg Philipp Telemann (*b* Magdeburg, 1681; *d* 1767) Deploying all the styles of his time, he was enormously prolific: his works include forty operas and six hundred overtures. For much of his later life he was musical director for five of Hamburg's main churches.

Ralph Vaughan Williams (*b* Down Ampney, Gloucestershire, 1872; *d* 1958) His music, which included symphonies, operas, choral works and orchestral pieces, carried a great feeling for the English countryside. A private income allowed him a lot of time for researching folk music, and much of his last three decades were spent on composing.

Giuseppi Verdi (*b* Le Roncole, 1813; d. 1901) Mainly a composer of operas, although he did devote five years, from 1860, to the parliament of the newly united Italy. In his later operas, the musical themes are increasingly based on character and action.

Antonio Vivaldi (*b* Venice, 1676; *d* 1741) His hair gained him the nickname 'the red priest'; it seems, though, that he took his priesthood lightly. He wrote church music, oratorios and operas, but is best known for his concerto *The Four Seasons*, written for the Foundling Hospital for girls in Venice.

Richard Wagner (*b* Leipzig, 1813; *d* 1883) Opera, to him, combined all the arts; for his four-opera masterwork *The Ring* he wrote his own libretti and oversaw every aspect of production. His life, surprising in its anti-semitism given his Jewish ancestry, was disorganised, and featured escape attempts from debtors, from political persecution, and from sexual scandal.

Kurt Weill (*b* Dessau, 1900; *d* 1950) Jazz was an influence on his orchestral work; he also wrote musicals and theatre pieces. He collaborated to formidable effect with Bertolt Brecht; but after Hitler came to power his music was banned in Germany. He lived a life of hardship and exile from 1933, until achieving success in America.

Some Jazz musicians

Jazz emerged as a home-grown American music at the end of C19. It grew out of the many musical influences in that country at that time: ballads, music traditional and popular, religious and brass band music, and what might be termed 'serious' music; with the addition of ragtime (itself influenced by the list above); and the blues, which emerged as one of the gifts of those who had arrived as slaves. Early jazz is generally thought of as springing up in the New Orleans area but, even without the benefit of radio and recordings, there was a more widespread musical groundswell that was conducive to what came to be called jazz.

In this section we will list some of the more important names associated with the development of jazz, categorised as the benefit of hindsight enables us to see a pattern where, perhaps, little was visible at the time.

Charles 'Buddy' Bolden (1877–1931), cornet and leader.
Joe 'King' Oliver (1885–1938), cornet and leader.
Edward 'Kid' Ory (1886–1973), trombone.
Freddie Keppard (1890–1933), trumpet.
Ferdinand 'Jelly Roll' Morton (1890–1941), piano, composer and leader.
Johnny St Cyr (1890–1966), banjo.
Johnny Dodds (1892–1940), clarinet.
Jimmie Noone (1895–1944), clarinet.
Warren 'Baby' Dodds (1898–1959), drums.
Louis Armstrong (1901–71), trumpet, composer, leader.
The Hot Five (and Hot Seven): Armstrong, Dodds, Ory, St Cyr and Lil Hardin (Mrs Armstrong); + Baby Dodds and Pete Briggs (tuba).
The Original Dixieland Jazz Band (ODJB): Nick La Rocca (cornet), Larry Shields (clarinet), Eddie Edwards (trombone), Henry Ragas (piano), Tony Sbarbaro (Spargo) (drums).

The New Orleans Rhythm KIngs (NORK): Paul Mares (trumpet), Leon Roppolo or Rappolo (clarinet), George Brunis (trombone), *et al*.

The Austin High School Gang: Jimmy McPartland (trumpet), Bud Freeman (tenor), Frank Teschemacher (C-melody sax), *et al*.

Leon 'Bix' Beiderbecke (1903–31), cornet, piano, composer.

The Blues

W(illiam) C(hristopher) Handy (1873–1958), composer, arranger and leader.

Huddie Ledbetter, 'Leadbelly' (1885–1949), guitar and vocals.

Gertrude 'Ma' Rainey (1886–1939), vocals.

Lonnie Johnson (1889–1970), guitar and vocals.

William Lee Conley 'Big Bill' Broonzy (1893–1958), guitar and vocals.

Bessie Smith (1894–1937), vocals.

Lizzie Miles (1895–1963), vocals.

'Blind Lemon' Jefferson (1897–1929), guitar and vocals.

Ida Cox (1905–50), vocals.

Josh White (1908–69), guitar and vocals.

Sonny Terry (1911–86) and **Brownie McGhee** (1915–96)

Muddy Waters (1915–83), guitar and vocals.

Ragtime and Stride piano

Scott Joplin (1868–1917), piano and composer.

James P Johnson (1894–1955), piano and composer.

Willie 'The Lion' Smith (1897–1973), piano and composer.

Edward Kennedy 'Duke' Ellington (1899–1974), piano, composer and leader.

Thomas 'Fats' Waller (1904–43), piano and composer.

William 'Count' Basie (1904–84), piano, composer and leader

Earl 'Fatha' Hines (1905–83), piano, composer and leader.

Big Bands – leaders and arrangers

Paul Whiteman (1890–1967).

Fletcher Henderson (1898–52), piano.

Don Redman (1900–64).

Chick Webb (1902–39), drummer.

Jimmie Lunceford (1902–47).

Cab Calloway (1907–94).

Boogie Woogie pianists

Jimmy Yancey (1894–1951).

Charles 'Cow Cow' Davenport (1894–1955).
Clarence 'Pine Top' Smith (1904–29).
Pete Johnson (1904–67).
Meade 'Lux' Lewis (1905–64).
Albert Ammons (1907–49).

The Swing era

Glen Gray's Casa Loma Orchestra.
Glenn Miller (1904–44), trombone and leader.
The Dorsey Brothers – Jimmy (1904–57), reeds and leader; Tommy (1905–56), trumpet and leader.
Lionel Hampton (1908–2002), piano and vibraphone.
Benny Goodman (1909–86), clarinet and leader.
Artie Shaw (1910–), clarinet and leader.
Woody Herman (1913–87), clarinet and leader.
Charlie Barnet (1913–91), reeds and leader.
Harry James (1916–83), trumpet and leader.

Bop pioneers

Kenny Clarke (1914–85), drums.
John Birks 'Dizzy' Gillespie (1917–93), trumpet and leader.
Charlie Christian (1919–42), guitar.
Charlie 'Yardbird' or 'Bird' Parker (1920–55), tenor.
Thelonius Sphere Monk (1920–82), piano.
Oscar Pettiford (1922–60), bass.
Buddy de Franco (1923–), clarinet.
Earl 'Bud' Powell (1924–66), piano.
Jay Jay Johnson (1924–2001) trombone.

Further developments

Gil Evans (1912–88), composer and arranger.
Pete Rugolo (1915–), composer and arranger.
Tadd Dameron (1917–65), composer and arranger.
Lennie Tristano (1919–78), piano.
Art Blakey (1919–90), Drums and leader.
Dave Brubeck (1920–), piano.
Charles Mingus (1922–79), bass, composer and leader.
Fats Navarro (1923–50), trumpet.
Sonny Stitt (1924–82), piano and reeds.
Oscar Peterson (1925–), piano.
Max Roach (1925–), drums.

John Coltrane (1926–67), reeds.
Miles Davis (1926–91), trumpet.
Stan Getz (1927–91), tenor.
Gerry Mulligan (1927–96) baritone sax.
Horace Silver (1928–), piano and composer.
Sonny Rollins (1929–). tenor and leader.
Ornette Coleman (1930–), reeds.

Singing voices

Alto This term, the Italian for 'high', is used to describe a male voice higher than that of any tenor. Mostly it now refers to the lower range of female voice or, in church choirs, the voices of boys and women.

Baritone In male singers this is the nearest to normal speech, being an intermediate range of voice.

Bass Among male voices, the lowest – though not necessarily the most limited.

Basso profundo An even deeper bass.

Castrato In a woman the equivalent would be either soprano or contralto. In males it was produced by castration, practised for this purpose in C17 and C18 Europe, mostly in the interests of church music.

Coloratura soprano An extravagantly styled form of soprano voice.

Contralto Among types of female voice, this is the lowest.

Counter-tenor An adult male soloist singing unusually high, *ie* as an alto.

Falsetto Usually this term describes an adult male alto, but with less fullness than the voice of a counter-tenor.

Heldentenore German expression describing a 'hero tenor', one who can sing above the volume of a full orchestra.

Mezzo-soprano This voice falls between the ranges of soprano and alto. Its potential richness is useful for operatic roles.

Soprano Among female singers, the highest type of voice, with a wide dramatic range.

Tenor Apart from castrato, this is the highest male voice; like sopranos, tenors can produce a variety of sounds, from light to dramatically profound.

Theatre

Shakespeare's players

From the preliminary pages of the First Folio (1623) of Shakespeare's plays

THE WORKES OF WILLIAM SHAKESPEARE, CONTAINING ALL HIS COMEDIES, HISTORIES, AND TRAGEDIES: TRUELY SET FORTH, ACCORDING TO THEIR FIRST ORIGINALL.

THE NAMES OF THE PRINCIPALL ACTORS IN ALL THESE PLAYES.

William Shakespeare.   Samuel Gilburne.
Richard Burbadge.   Robert Armin.
John Hemmings.   William Ostler.
Augustine Phillips.   Nathan Field.
William Kempt.   John Underwood.
Thomas Poope.   Nicholas Tooley.
George Bryan.   William Ecclestone.
Henry Condell.   Joseph Taylor.
William Slye.   Robert Benfield.
Richard Cowly.   Robert Goughe.
John Lowine.   Richard Robinson.
Samuell Crosse.   Iohn Shancke.
Alexander Cooke.   Iohn Rice.

The plays of Shakespeare

Title	TLA	Class	Date	X
The early plays				
1 The Two Gentlemen of Verona	TGV	C	1588–96	12
2 The Taming of the Shrew	ToS	C	1588–96	16
3 The Comedy of Errors	CoE	C	1588–96	13
4 Henry VI, Part I	H61	H	1588–96	34
5 Henry VI, Part II	H62	H	1588–96	40
6 Henry VI, Part III	H63	H	1588–96	35
7 King John	LDJ	H	1588–96	22
8 Titus Andronicus	TAn	T	1588–96	20
9 Richard III	RIII	H	1588–96	40
The Elizabethan middle plays				
10 The Merchant of Venice	MoV	C	1596–1603	18
11 A Midsummer Night's Dream	MND	C	1596–1603	21

12	Love's Labour's Lost	LLL	C	1596–1603	17
13	Richard II	RII	H	1596–1603	24
14	Henry IV, Part I	H41	H	1596–1603	23
15	Henry IV, Part II	H42	H	1596–1603	52
16	The Merry Wives of Windsor	MWW	C	1596–1603	20
17	Romeo and Juliet	R&J	T	1596–1603	23
18	Much Ado About Nothing	MAN	C	1596–1603	14
19	Henry V	KHV	H	1596–1603	43
20	As You Like It	AYL	C	1596–1603	21
21	Julius Caesar	JlC	T	1596–1603	32
22	Twelfth Night	12N	C	1596–1603	13
23	Hamlet, Prince of Denmark	Ham	T	1596–1603	22

The Jacobean middle plays

24	Troilus and Cressida	T&C	T	1603–07	24
25	Othello	OMV	T	1603–07	25
26	Measure for Measure	M4M	C	1603–07	18
27	King Lear	KLr	T	1603–07	16
28	All's Well That Ends Well	AWW	C	1603–07	15
29	Macbeth	Mac	T	1603–07	21
30	Antony and Cleopatra	A&C	T	1603–07	34
31	Coriolanus	COR	T	1603–07	15

The late plays

32	Pericles, Prince of Tyre	PPT	T	1607–13	22
33	Timon of Athens	ToA	T	1607–13	17
34	The Winter's Tale	WnT	C	1607–13	20
35	The Tempest	TEM	C	1607–13	14
36	Cymbeline	Cym	T	1607–13	17
37	The Two Noble Kinsmen	2NK	TC	1607–13	21
38	Henry VIII	KH8	H	1607–13	24

C = Comedy
H = History
T = Tragedy
X = Number of characters in the following list

Shakespearean characters

No	Play	Character
0814	Tan	Aaron the Moor, lover of Tamora
0312	CoE	Abbess, Courtesan
1322	RII	Abbot of Westminster
2611	M4M	Abhorson, the executioner
2404	T&C	Achilles, Commander
2017	AYL	Adam, Oliver's Servant
3114	COR	Adrian
3512	TEM	Adrian, a Lord
0306	CoE	Adriana, Wife of Antipholus of Syracuse
3115	COR	Aediles
0815	Tan	Aemilius, Noble Roman
2419	T&C	Aeneas, commander
2401	T&C	Agamemnon, commander in chief
3014	A&C	Agrippa, Follower of Caesar
3106	COR	Agrippa, Menenius, Coriolanus's friend
2405.	T&C	Ajax, Commander
0811	Tan	Alarbus, son of Tamora
2706	KLr	Albany, Goneril's Husband
3302	ToA	Alcibiades, Timon's true friend
2424	T&C	Alexander, Servant to Cressida
3029	A&C	Alexas
1943	KHV	Alice, Katharine's Maid (French side)
3501	TEM	Alonso, King of Naples
3311	ToA	Amazons
1941	KHV	Ambassador (French side)
2019	AYL	Amiens
2602	M4M	Angelo
0310	CoE	Angelo, a goldsmith
2911	Mac	Angus, Nobleman of Scotland
1813	MAN	Anotio
2420	T&C	Antenor, commander
3412	WnT	Antigonus, Lord
3207	PPT	Antiochus, Daughter of
3206	PPT	Antiochus, King of Corinth
0303	CoE	Antipholus, of Syracuse
2211	12N	Antonio, a sea captain, friend of Sebastian
1006	MoV	Antonio, a Venetian merchant
3506	TEM	Antonio, Brother and usurper of Prospero

0104	TGV	Antonio, Father of Proteus
2103	JlC	Antonius, Marcus, Lieutenant to Julius Caesar
3001	A&C	Antony, Mark, Joint Ruler of Rome
3307	ToA	Apemantus, a churlish philosopher
1720	R&J	Apothecary
3617	Cym	Apparitions: of Posthumus's father, mother and brothers
0913	RIII	Archbishop of Canterbury
1911	KHV	Archbishop of Canterbury (English side)
0914	RIII	Archbishop of York
1408	H41	Archbishop of York, Rebel
1508	H42	Archbishop of York, Rebel
1524	H42	Archbishop of York, Rebel
0716	LDJ	Archduke of Austria
3413	WnT	Archidamus, Lord
3702	2NK	Arcite, Nephew of the King Creon of Thebes
3509	TEM	Ariel, an airy spirit
0704	LDJ	Arthur, Nephew of King John
3607	Cym	Arviragus, known as Polydore son of Belarius banished to Wales by King Cymbeline, but actually the latter's long-lost son
2012	AYL	Audrey, goatherd
3112	COR	Aufidius, Tullus
3113	COR	Aufidius, Tullus, his Lieutenant
3407	WnT	Autolycus, rouge
1320	RII	Bagot
1016	MoV	Balthasar, a servant
1715	R&J	Balthasar, a servant
0309	CoE	Balthazar, a merchant
2906	Mac	Banquo, Nobleman of Scotland
0202	ToS	Baptista
1418	H41	Bardolph – from the Boar's Head Tavern
1537	H42	Bardolph – from the Boar's Head Tavern
1923	KHV	Bardolph (English side)
1602	MWW	Bardolph, Companion of Sir John Falstaff
2612	M4M	Barnardine
2314	Ham	Barnardo, courtier/soldier
1007	MoV	Bassanio, a Venetian merchant
0421	H61	Bassett, a Lancastrian
0802	Tan	Bassianus, son of the late emperor
0429	H61	Bastard of Orléans (in France)

No	Play	Character
3716	2NK	Bavian (fool in the Morris-dance)
3215	PPT	Bawd
1807	MAN	Beatrice, Niece of the Governor of Sicily
0404	H61	Bedford, King Henry's Uncle
1903	KHV	Bedford, King's Brother (English side)
3606	Cym	Belarius: a lord banished to Wales by King Cymbeline
1802	MAN	Benedick, Lord
1707	R&J	Benvolio, Romeo's Cousin
1312	RII	Berkeley
0934	RIII	Berkeley, Attendant
1202	LLL	Berowne, Lord of Ferdinand
2804	AWW	Bertram, son of the countess of Roussillon
0523	H62	Bevis, George, follower of Jack Cade
2506	OMV	Bianca, Cassio's Mistress
0203	ToS	Bianca, Daughter of Baptista
0211	ToS	Biondello, Servant
1321	RII	Bishop of Carlisle
0915	RIII	Bishop of Ely
1912	KHV	Bishop of Ely (English side)
3815	KH8	Bishop of Lincoln
0405	H61	Bishop of Winchester
3814	KH8	Bishop of Winchester
0722	LDJ	Blanch, John's Niece, Princess of Castille
1514	H42	Blunt
1405	H41	Blunt, At court
1505	H42	Blunt, At court
1531	H42	Blunt, Rebel
3513	TEM	Boatswain
1307	RII	Bolingbroke, Henry, Gaunt's Son
0531	H62	Bolingbroke, Roger, conjurer (*ie* medium)
0631	H63	Bona, sister of the Queen of France
1810	MAN	Borachio, Don John's Henchmen
1117	MND	Bottom, Nick, Weaver
3216	PPT	Boult, Servant
3712	2NK	Boy
1926	KHV	Boy (Robin) (English side)
2509	OMV	Brabantio, Desdemona's Father
2110	JlC	Brutus, Decius, Conspirator
2106	JlC	Brutus, Marcus, Conspirator
3110	COR	Brutus, tribune

1547	H42	Bullcalf, recruit – in Gloucestershire
3803	KH8	Bullen, Anne, Queen Katherine's maid of honour
2708	KLr	Burgundy, Cordelia's Husband
1318	RII	Bushy
0522	H62	Cade, Jack, Rebel
2101	JlC	Caesar, Julius
3002	A&C	Caesar, Octavius, Joint Ruler of Rome
2912	Mac	Caithness, Nobleman of Scotland
0816	Tan	Caius, Noble Roman
2421	T&C	Calchas, a priest who has defected to the Greeks
3508	TEM	Caliban, a savage and deformed slave
2102	JlC	Calpurnia, Wife of Julius Caesar
3414	WnT	Camillo, Lord
3006	A&C	Canidius, Follower of Antony
1915	KHV	Captain Fluellen (English side)
1916	KHV	Captain Gower (English side)
1917	KHV	Captain Jamy (English side)
1918	KHV	Captain Macmorris (English side)
3806	KH8	Capucius, French Ambassador
0505	H62	Cardinal Beaufort, Bishop of Winchester
3805	KH8	Cardinal Campeius
3804	KH8	Cardinal Wolsey
2108	JlC	Casca, Conspirator
2418	T&C	Cassandra, Daughter of King Priam, a prophetess
2503	OMV	Cassio, Othello's Lieutenant
2107	JlC	Cassius, Caius, Conspirator
2121	JlC	Cato, Young, Friend and Supporter of Brutus and Cassius
2004	AYL	Celia, Daughter of Frederick
3212	PPT	Cerimon (of Ephesus), Lord
1422	H41	Chamberlain – from the Boar's Head Tavern
2014	AYL	Charles, wrestler
3027	A&C	Charmian, Maid of Cleopatra
0718	LDJ	Chatillon, French Ambassador
0812	Tan	Chiron, son of Tamora
0938	RIII	Christopher Urswick, Priest
2115	JlC	Cicero, Senator
2112	JlC	Cimber, Metellus, Conspirator
2109	JlC	Cinna, Conspirator
2120	JlC	Cinna, The Poet
1515	H42	Clarence

No	Play	Character
2603	M4M	Claudio
1803	MAN	Claudio, Lord
2126	JlC	Claudius, Brutus' Servant
2302	Ham	Claudius, The King, Hamlet's Uncle
3415	WnT	Cleomenes, Lord
3209	PPT	Cleon, governor of Tarsus
3026	A&C	Cleopatra
0536	H62	Clerk of Chatham
2127	JlC	Clitus, Brutus' Servant
3604	Cym	Cloten: son of Cymbeline
0820	Tan	Clown
2513	OMV	Clown
3034	A&C	Clown
3411	WnT	Clown, Son of Shepherd
1113	MND	Cobweb, Fairy
1529	H42	Coleville, Rebel
3107	COR	Cominius, consul
1811	MAN	Conrad, Don John's Henchmen
1812	MAN	Constable Dogberry
2609	M4M	Constable Elbow
1931	KHV	Constable of France (French side)
0705	LDJ	Constance, Mother of Arthur
2702	KLr	Cordelia, Daughter of King Lear
2009	AYL	Corin, Shepherd
2315	Ham	Cornelius, courtier/soldier
3614	Cym	Cornelius: a doctor
2705	KLr	Cornwall, Regan's Husband
1214	LLL	Costard, a Rustic
0434	H61	Countess of Auvergne (in France)
2803	AWW	Countess of Roussillon
2202	12N	Countess Olivia
3713	2NK	Countrymen (Morris-Dancers)
3807	KH8	Cranmer, Archbishop of Canterbury
2422	T&C	Cressida, Daughter of Calchas
3821	KH8	Cromwell, Servant
3312	ToA	Cupid
2715	KLr	Curan
2212	12N	Curio, Lord
0212	ToS	Curtis, Servant
3601	Cym	Cymbeline: King of Britain

2128	JlC	Dardanius, Brutus' Servant
0422	H61	Dauphin, Charles (Later King) (in France)
1930	KHV	Dauphine, The (Lewis) (French side)
1546	H42	Davy – in Gloucestershire
1209	LLL	de Armado, Don Adriano
0709	LDJ	de Burgh, Hubert
2412	T&C	Deiphobus, Son of King Priam
1106	MND	Demetrius (in love with Hermia)
3007	A&C	Demetrius, Follower of Antony
0813	Tan	Demetrius, son of Tamora
2016	AYL	Denis, Oliver's Servant
3817	KH8	Denny, Knight
3008	A&C	Dercetas, Follower of Antony
2502	OMV	Desdemona, Wife of Othello
2812	AWW	Diana, Daughter of the Widow of Florence
3217	PPT	Diana, goddess of chastity
0525	H62	Dick the Butcher, follower of Jack Cade
3030	A&C	Diomedes
2406	T&C	Diomedes, Commander
3416	WnT	Dion, Lord
3210	PPT	Dionyza, Wife of Cleon
3714	2NK	Doctor
1616	MWW	Doctor Caius, French physician
3015	A&C	Dolabella, Follower of Caesar
2903	Mac	Donalbain, son of Duncan King of Scotland
3408	WnT	Dorcas, Shepherdess
0908	RIII	Dorset, Son of Elizabeth
1411	H41	Douglas
0304	CoE	Dromio, of Syracuse, Servant of Antipholus of Syracuse
0305	CoE	Dromio, Twin with Dromio, Servant of Antipholus of Syracuse
0504	H62	Duchess of Gloucester
1306	RII	Duchess of Gloucester
1305	RII	Duchess of York
0904	RIII	Duchess of York, Mother of King Edward IV, Richard III and George Duke of Clarence
2003	AYL	Duke Frederick
0427	H61	Duke of Alençon (in France)
1308	RII	Duke of Aumerle, York's Son
1932	KHV	Duke of Berri (French side)

No	Play	Character
1933	KHV	Duke of Bourbon (French side)
1934	KHV	Duke of Bretagne (French side)
0509	H62	Duke of Buckingham
0916	RIII	Duke of Buckingham
3808	KH8	Duke of Buckingham
0428	H61	Duke of Burgundy (in France)
1935	KHV	Duke of Burgundy (French side)
0605	H63	Duke of Exeter
2802	AWW	Duke of Florence
0503	H62	Duke of Gloucester
0109	TGV	Duke of Milan, Father of Silvia
0606	H63	Duke of Norfolk
0917	RIII	Duke of Norfolk
1309	RII	Duke of Norfolk
3809	KH8	Duke of Norfolk
1936	KHV	Duke of Orléans (French side)
0511	H62	Duke of Somerset
0607	H63	Duke of Somerset
0510	H62	Duke of Suffolk
3810	KH8	Duke of Suffolk
3811	KH8	Duke of Surrey
1005	MoV	Duke of Venice
2508	OMV	Duke of Venice
0406	H61	Duke of York
0506	H62	Duke of York
0608	H63	Duke of York
1304	RII	Duke of York, Gaunt's Brother
2201	12N	Duke Orsino of Illyria
2001	AYL	Duke Senior
2601	M4M	Duke Vincentio
1213	LLL	Dull, a Constable
2807	AWW	Dumain, French Captain
1203	LLL	Dumain, Lord of Ferdinand
2901	Mac	Duncan, King of Scotland
0407	H61	Earl of Cambridge
0918	RIII	Earl of Derby
0710	LDJ	Earl of Essex
2709	KLr	Earl of Gloucester
0609	H63	Earl of Hastings
2710	KLr	Earl of Kent

0408	H61	Earl of March
1406	H41	Earl of Northumberland, Rebel
1506	H42	Earl of Northumberland, Rebel
1522	H42	Earl of Northumberland, Rebel
0611	H63	Earl of Northumberland
1310	RII	Earl of Northumberland
0610	H63	Earl of Oxford
0919	RIII	Earl of Oxford
0612	H63	Earl of Pembroke
0711	LDJ	Earl of Pembroke
0613	H63	Earl of Richmond
0912	RIII	Earl of Richmond, Later Henry VII
0409	H61	Earl of Salisbury
0514	H62	Earl of Salisbury
0712	LDJ	Earl of Salisbury
0410	H61	Earl of Somerset
0920	RIII	Earl of Surrey
0411	H61	Earl of Warwick
0614	H63	Earl of Warwick
0515	H62	Earl of Warwick, son of the Earl of Salisbury
0615	H63	Earl of Westmoreland
2711	KLr	Edgar, Gloucester's Son
0620	H63	Edmund
2712	KLr	Edmund, Gloucester's Son
0932	RIII	Edward, Clarence's Child
0930	RIII	Edward, Prince of the Tower
0603	H63	Edward, Prince of Wales
0507	H62	Edward, son of the Duke of York
0619	H63	Edward, York's son (Later Edward IV)
0302	CoE	Egeon, a merchant from Syracuse
1107	MND	Egeus, Hermia's Father
0905	RIII	Elizabeth, Queen of Edward IV
3418	WnT	Emilia, Attendant
2505	OMV	Emilia, Iago's wife
3705	2NK	Emilia, Sister of Hippolyta
2322	Ham	English Ambassadors
3005	A&C	Enobarbus, Dominitus, Antony's second-in-command
3009	A&C	Eros, Follower of Antony
2614	M4M	Escalus
1701	R&J	Escalus, Prince of Verona
3213	PPT	Escanes (of Tyre), Lord

No	Play	Character
3024	A&C	Euphronius, an ambassador
3715	2NK	Executioner
0402	H61	Exeter, King Henry's Great Uncle
1904	KHV	Exeter, King's Uncle (English side)
2208	12N	Fabian, an upper servant
1530	H42	Falconbridge, Rebel
1543	H42	Falstaff's page – from the Boar's Head Tavern
0633	H63	Father that has killed his son
0707	LDJ	Faulconbridge, Lady, Mother of The Bastard
0706	LDJ	Faulconbridge, Philip, The Bastard Son of Richard the Lionheart
0708	LDJ	Faulconbridge, Robert, Half Brother of the Bastard
1548	H42	Feeble, recruit – in Gloucestershire
1612	MWW	Fenton, In love with Anne Page
1201	LLL	Ferdinand, King of Navarre
3503	TEM	Ferdinand, son of Sebastian
2206	12N	Feste, Jester of Countess Olivia
1313	RII	Fitzwater
3310	ToA	Flavius, Timon's steward
2118	JlC	Flavius, Tribune
2917	Mac	Fleance, Banquo's Son
3406	WnT	Florizel, Son of Polixenes
1118	MND	Flute, Francis, Bellows-Mender
2713	KLr	Fool
3313	ToA	Fool
1606	MWW	Ford, Frank, citizen of Windsor
1607	MWW	Ford, Mistress Alice
2312	Ham	Fortinbras, Prince of Norway
1421	H41	Francis, the drawer – from the Boar's Head Tavern
1540	H42	Francis, the drawer – from the Boar's Head Tavern
2618	M4M	Francisca, a nun
3514	TEM	Francisco, a Lord
2316	Ham	Francisco, courtier/soldier
1814	MAN	Friar Francis
1714	R&J	Friar John Abram
1713	R&J	Friar Lawrence
2617	M4M	Friar Peter
2616	M4M	Friar Thomas
2610	M4M	Froth
1423	H41	Gadshill – from the Boar's Head Tavern

3016	A&C	Gallus, Follower of Caesar
0313	CoE	Gaoler
3419	WnT	Gaoler
3708	2NK	Gaoler
3709	2NK	Gaoler, Daughter of the
3718	2NK	Gaoler's Brother
0433	H61	General, at Bordeaux (in France)
2815	AWW	Gentle Astringer
0621	H63	George (Later Duke of Clarence)
0903	RIII	George Duke of Clarence, Brother of King Edward IV and Richard III
2303	Ham	Gertrude, The Queen, Hamlet's Mother
2304	Ham	Ghost of Hamlet's Father
1412	H41	Glendower, Owen
1415	H41	Glendower's Wife
1516	H42	Gloucester
0403	H61	Gloucester, King Henry's Uncle
1902	KHV	Gloucester, King's brother (English side)
1013	MoV	Gobbo, Launcelot, Shylock's servant
1014	MoV	Gobbo, Old, father of Launcelot
2703	KLr	Goneril, Daughter of King Lear
3507	TEM	Gonzalo, an old honest counsellor
0540	H62	Gough, Matthew
1942	KHV	Governor of Harfleur (French side)
0430	H61	Governor of Paris (in France)
3201	PPT	Gower, as Chorus
2510	OMV	Gratiano, Brabantio's brother
2313	Ham	Gravediggers
1319	RII	Green
1716	R&J	Gregory, Servant
0207	ToS	Gremio, Bianca's Suitor
0909	RIII	Grey, Son of Elizabeth
3822	KH8	Griffith, Servant
0213	ToS	Grumio, Servant
3608	Cym	Guiderius known as Cadwal son of Belarius banished to Wales by K Cymbeline, but actually the latter's long-lost son
2309	Ham	Guildenstern, courtier
3818	KH8	Guilford, Knight
0720	LDJ	Gurney, Servant of Lady Faulconbridge
0215	ToS	Haberdasher

No	Play	Character
2301	Ham	Hamlet, Prince of Denmark
1521	H42	Harcourt
2920	Mac	Hecate
2413	T&C	Hector, Son of King Priam
2403	T&C	Helen, Menelaus' wife
3612	Cym	Helen: a servant
1104	MND	Helena (loves Demetrius)
2805	AWW	Helena, Protégée of the countess of Roussillon
2414	T&C	Helenus, Son of King Priam
3214	PPT	Helicanus (of Tyre), Lord
1511	H42	Henry, Prince of Wales
1402	H41	Henry, Prince of Wales, At court
1502	H42	Henry, Prince of Wales, At court
0702	LDJ	Henry, Son of King John
3717	2NK	Herald
1103	MND	Hermia (loves Lysander)
3402	WnT	Hermione, Queen of Sicilia
1806	MAN	Hero, Daughter of the Governor of Sicily
1102	MND	Hippolyta
3704	2NK	Hippolyta, Bride of Theseus
0524	H62	Holland, John, follower of Jack Cade
1211	LLL	Holofernes, Schoolmaster
1721	R&J	Horatio
2308	Ham	Horatio, Hamlet's friend
0208	ToS	Hortensio, Bianca's Suitor
1617	MWW	Host, of the Garter inn
0538	H62	Hume, John, Priest
2021	AYL	Hymen
3711	2NK	Hymen, God of weddings
3609	Cym	Iachimo: Italian friend of Posthumus
2504	OMV	Iago, Othello's Ancient
0528	H62	Iden, Alexander, Kentish Gentlemen
3602	Cym	Imogen: Cymbeline's daughter
3028	A&C	Iras, Maid of Cleopatra
2604	M4M	Isabella, Sister of Claudio
2018	AYL	Jacques, Brother of Oliver and Orlando
1215	LLL	Jaquenetta, a Rustic
2007	AYL	Jaques
1011	MoV	Jessica, Shylock's daughter
3314	ToA	Jeweller

1303	RII	John of Gaunt, Richard II's Uncle
0413	H61	John Talbot, Lord Talbot's son
1804	MAN	John, Don, Don Pedro's Brother
0530	H62	Jourdain, Margery, witch
0106	TGV	Julia, Loved by Proteus
1710	R&J	Juliet
1712	R&J	Juliet's Nurse
3616	Cym	Jupiter: in Posthumus's vision
1544	H42	Justice Shallow – in Gloucestershire
1545	H42	Justice Silence – in Gloucestershire
0204	ToS	Katharina (Kate), Daughter of Baptista
1206	LLL	Katharine, Lady of the Princess of France
0936	RIII	Keeper of the Tower of London
1518	H42	Kent
1927	KHV	King Charles (French side)
0901	RIII	King Edward IV
1510	H42	King Henry IV
1401	H41	King Henry IV, At court
1501	H42	King Henry IV, At court
1901	KHV	King Henry V (English side)
0401	H61	King Henry VI
0501	H62	King Henry VI
0601	H63	King Henry VI
3801	KH8	King Henry VIII
0701	LDJ	King John
2701	KLr	King Lear
0604	H63	King Louis XIV of France
2716	KLr	King of France
2801	AWW	King of France
2411	T&C	King Priam
0423	H61	la Pucelle, Joan (in France)
0910	RIII	Lady Anne
1709	R&J	Lady Capulet
0629	H63	Lady Grey, later Edward's Queen
1705	R&J	Lady Montague
1532	H42	Lady Northumberland, Rebel
2306	Ham	Laertes, Polonius' son
2808	AWW	Lafeu, an old Lord
0105	TGV	Lance, Servant of Proteus
3108	COR	Lartius, General
2810	AWW	Lavache, a clown

No	Play	Character
0805	Tan	Lavinia, daughter of Titus Andronicus
2020	AYL	Le Beau
1940	KHV	Le Fer (French side)
2116	JlC	Lena, Popilius, Senator
2908	Mac	Lennox, Nobleman of Scotland
1017	MoV	Leonardo, a servant
1805	MAN	Leonato, Governor of Sicily
3605	Cym	Leonatus, Posthumus: secretly married to Imogen, King Cymbeline's daughter
3218	PPT	Leonine, Servant
3401	WnT	Leontes, King of Sicilia
3003	A&C	Lepidus, M. Ameilius, Joint Ruler of Rome
2105	JlC	Lepidus, triumvir with Antony and Octavius
0715	LDJ	Lewis, Son of Phillip II
0634	H63	Lieutenant of the Tower
2111	JlC	Ligarius, Conspirator
2511	OMV	Lodovico, Brabantio and Gratiano's cousin
1204	LLL	Longaville, Lord of Ferdinand
1526	H42	Lord Bardolph, Rebel
0713	LDJ	Lord Bigot
1216	LLL	Lord Boyet
1906	KHV	Lord Cambridge (English side)
3812	KH8	Lord Chamberlain
3813	KH8	Lord Chancellor
1520	H42	Lord Chief Justice Gower
0512	H62	Lord Clifford
0616	H63	Lord Clifford
1938	KHV	Lord Grandpré (French side)
0617	H63	Lord Hastings
0921	RIII	Lord Hastings
1527	H42	Lord Hastings, Rebel
0922	RIII	Lord Lovel
1217	LLL	Lord Marcade
0418	H61	Lord Mayor of London
0937	RIII	Lord Mayor of London
1528	H42	Lord Mowbray, Rebel
1937	KHV	Lord Rambures (French side)
0630	H63	Lord Rivers
1907	KHV	Lord Salisbury (English side)
3816	KH8	Lord Sands

0516	H62	Lord Say
0517	H62	Lord Scales
1908	KHV	Lord Scroop (English side)
0618	H63	Lord Stafford
0412	H61	Lord Talbot
1909	KHV	Lord Warwick (English side)
1910	KHV	Lord Westmoreland (English side)
1012	MoV	Lorenzo, in love with Jessica
3819	KH8	Lovell, Knight
0308	CoE	Luce, Adriana's Servant
0206	ToS	Lucentio, son of Vincentio, in love with Bianca
0107	TGV	Lucetta, Servant of Julia
0307	CoE	Luciana, Sister of Adriana
2122	JlC	Lucilius, Friend and Supporter of Brutus and Cassius
2606	M4M	Lucio
2129	JlC	Lucius, Brutus' Servant
3611	Cym	Lucius, Caius: a Roman general
3304	ToA	Lucius, Flatterer
0806	Tan	Lucius, Son of Titus Andronicus
3305	ToA	Lucullus, Flatterer
3219	PPT	Lychorida, Marina's Nurse
1105	MND	Lysander (in love with Hermia)
3211	PPT	Lysimachus, governor of Mytilene
2904	Mac	Macbeth
2905	Mac	Macbeth, Lady
2913	Mac	Macduff, Lady
2907	Mac	Macduff, Nobleman of Scotland
2914	Mac	Macduff, Son of Lady
3017	A&C	Maecenas, Follower of Caesar
2902	Mac	Malcolm, son of Duncan King of Scotland
2203	12N	Malvolio, Steward of Countess Olivia
2317	Ham	Marcellus, courtier/soldier
2119	JlC	Marcellus, Tribune
3101	COR	Marcius, Caius, later Coriolanus
3105	COR	Marcius, Young, Coriolanus's son
0804	Tan	Marcus, brother of Titus Andronicus
3031	A&C	Mardian
2415	T&C	Margarelon, Son of King Priam
0933	RIII	Margaret, Clarence's Child
0426	H61	Margaret, Daughter of Duke of Anjou (in France)
1808	MAN	Margaret, Hero's Maid

No	Play	Character
0911	RIII	Margaret, Widow of Henry VI
2207	12N	Maria, Chambermaid of Countess Olivia
1207	LLL	Maria, Lady of the Princess of France
2605	M4M	Mariana
2814	AWW	Mariana, Neighbour of the Widow of the Florence
3205	PPT	Marina, Daughter of Pericles and Thaisa
0623	H63	Marquess of Montague
3220	PPT	Marshal
0807	Tan	Martius, Son of Titus Andronicus
0431	H61	Master-Gunner of Orléans (in France)
0432	H61	Master-Gunner of Orléans' son (in France)
3404	WnT	Maximillius, Son of the King and Queen of Sicilia
0537	H62	Mayor of St Albans
0635	H63	Mayor of York
0721	LDJ	Melun, a French Lord
3021	A&C	Menas, Follower of Pompey
3022	A&C	Menecrates, Follower of Pompey
2402	T&C	Menelaus, Brother of Agamemnon
2910	Mac	Menteith, Nobleman of Scotland
3316	ToA	Mercer (fabric merchant)
3315	ToA	Merchant
1702	R&J	Mercutio, Kinsmen of Escalus
2123	JlC	Messala, Friend and Supporter of Brutus and Cassius
0527	H62	Michael, follower of Jack Cade
3505	TEM	Miranda, Daughter of Prospero
2607	M4M	Mistress Overdone
1417	H41	Mistress Quickly – from the Boar's Head Tavern
1536	H42	Mistress Quickly – from the Boar's Head Tavern
1922	KHV	Mistress Quickly (English side)
1618	MWW	Mistress Quickly, Servant
2512	OMV	Montano, former Governor of Cyprus
3409	WnT	Mopsa, Shepherdess
1413	H41	Mortimer (Earl of March)
1534	H42	Morton, Rebel
1114	MND	Moth, Fairy
1210	LLL	Moth, Page of Adriano de Armado
1549	H42	Mouldy, recruit – in Gloucestershire
1939	KHV	Mountjoy, a herald (French side)
1115	MND	Mustardseed, Fairy
0808	Tan	Mutius, Son of Titus Andronicus

1002	MoV	Nerissa, Gentlewoman to Portia
2407	T&C	Nestor, Commander
3111	COR	Nicanor
2320	Ham	Norwegian captain
2321	Ham	Norwegian captain's soldiers
1924	KHV	Nym (English side)
1603	MWW	Nym, Companion of Sir John Falstaff
1109	MND	Oberon, Fairy King
3025	A&C	Octavia, Octavius' sister, married to Antony
2104	JlC	Octavius, Nephew of Marcus Antonius
1708	R&J	Old Capulet, Juliet's Father
3823	KH8	Old Lady, Servant
1704	R&J	Old Montague, Romeo's Father
2005	AYL	Oliver, Brother of Orlando
2307	Ham	Ophelia, Polonius' daughter
2006	AYL	Orlando, Brother of Oliver
2310	Ham	Osric, a courtier
2714	KLr	Oswald, Goneril's steward
2501	OMV	Othello
1610	MWW	Page, Anne, Daughter of George and Margaret Page
1608	MWW	Page, George, citizen of Windsor
1609	MWW	Page, Mistress Margaret
1611	MWW	Page, William, the young son of George and Margaret Page
3701	2NK	Palamon, Nephew of the King Creon of Thebes
3221	PPT	Pandar
2423	T&C	Pandarus, Uncle of Cressida
0717	LDJ	Pandulph, Cardinal
0111	TGV	Panthino, servant
1703	R&J	Paris, Kinsmen of Escalus
2416	T&C	Paris, Son of King Priam
2806	AWW	Parolles, a follower of Bertram
3824	KH8	Patience, Servant
2408	T&C	Patroclus, Commander
3417	WnT	Paulina, Antigonus' Wife
1112	MND	Peaseblossom, Fairy
1801	MAN	Pedro, Don, Prince of Aragon
0216	ToS	Pendant
1407	H41	Percy, Harry ('Hotspur'), Rebel
1507	H42	Percy, Harry ('Hotspur'), Rebel
1523	H42	Percy, Harry ('Hotspur'), Rebel

No	Play	Character
1311	RII	Percy, Henry, Son of Earl of Northumberland, nicknamed 'Hotspur'
1409	H41	Percy, Lady, Hotspur's wife, Rebel
1509	H42	Percy, Lady, Hotspur's wife, Rebel
1525	H42	Percy, Lady, Hotspur's wife, Rebel
3403	WnT	Perdita, Daughter of the King and Queen of Sicilia
3202	PPT	Pericles, Prince of Tyre
0719	LDJ	Peter of Pomfret, mad Yorkshire prophet
1717	R&J	Peter, Servant
0535	H62	Peter, Thomas Horner's man
1419	H41	Peto – from the Boar's Head Tavern
1538	H42	Peto – from the Boar's Head Tavern
1722	R&J	Petruchio
0210	ToS	Petruchio, Katharina's Suitor
2011	AYL	Phebe, Shepherd
3610	Cym	Philario: Italian friend of Posthumus
3222	PPT	Philemon (Servant)
3615	Cym	Philharmonus: a soothsayer
0714	LDJ	Philip II, King of France
3010	A&C	Philo, Follower of Antony
1108	MND	Philostrate, master of the revels
3308	ToA	Phrynia, whore
0311	CoE	Pinch, A quack doctor
2132	JlC	Pindarus, Cassius' Servant
3706	2NK	Pirithous, Theseus' Friend
3613	Cym	Pisanio: a servant
1541	H42	Pistol – from the Boar's Head Tavern
1925	KHV	Pistol (English side)
1604	MWW	Pistol, Companion of Sir John Falstaff
1420	H41	Poins – from the Boar's Head Tavern
1539	H42	Poins – from the Boar's Head Tavern
3405	WnT	Polixenes, King of Bohemia
2305	Ham	Polonius, Lord Chamberlain
3004	A&C	Pompeius, Sextus
2608	M4M	Pompey
2921	Mac	Porter
1001	MoV	Portia, Heiress of Belmont
2114	JlC	Portia, Wife of Brutus
1718	R&J	Potpan, Servant
1512	H42	Prince John of Lancaster

1403	H41	Prince John of Lancaster, At court
1503	H42	Prince John of Lancaster, At court
1004	MoV	Prince of Aragon, Suitor to Nerissa
1003	MoV	Prince of Morocco, Suitor to Nerissa
1929	KHV	Princess Katharine (French side)
1205	LLL	Princess of France
1919	KHV	Private Bates (English side)
1920	KHV	Private Court (English side)
1921	KHV	Private Williams (English side)
3018	A&C	Proculeius, Follower of Caesar
2425	T&C	Prologue
3504	TEM	Prospero, the rightful Duke of Milan
0103	TGV	Proteus
2613	M4M	Provost
0817	Tan	Publius, Noble Roman
2117	JlC	Publius, Senator
1111	MND	Puck, Fairy
0939	RIII	Pursuivant, Messenger
0703	LDJ	Queen Elinor, Mother of King John
1928	KHV	Queen Isabel (French side)
3802	KH8	Queen Katharine
0602	H63	Queen Margaret
0502	H62	Queen Margaret of Henry VI
1302	RII	Queen of Richard II
3603	Cym	Queen: Cymbeline's 2nd wife
1116	MND	Quince, Peter, Carpenter
0809	Tan	Quintus, Son of Titus Andronicus
2704	KLr	Regan, Daughter of King Lear
0425	H61	Reignier, Duke of Anjou (in France)
2809	AWW	Reynaldo, a steward
2318	Ham	Reynaldo, courtier/soldier
0622	H63	Richard (Later Duke of Gloucester and Richard III)
1301	RII	Richard II
0902	RIII	Richard of Gloucester, Brother of King Edward IV, later Richard III
0931	RIII	Richard, Prince of the Tower
0508	H62	Richard, son of the Duke of York
0907	RIII	Rivers, Brother of Elizabeth
1605	MWW	Robin, Companion of Sir John Falstaff
2507	OMV	Roderigo, In love with Desdemona
1706	R&J	Romeo

No	Play	Character
2002	AYL	Rosalind, Daughter of Duke Senior
1208	LLL	Rosaline, Lady of the Princess of France
2311	Ham	Rosencrantz, a courtier
1314	RII	Ross
2909	Mac	Ross, Nobleman of Scotland
1619	MWW	Rugby, Servant
1552	H42	Rumour as prologue
1008	MoV	Salerio, a Venetian merchant
1315	RII	Salisbury
1719	R&J	Sampson, Servant
0801	Tan	Saturninus, son of the late emperor
3011	A&C	Scarus, Follower of Antony
3502	TEM	Sebastian, Brother of Alonso
2210	12N	Sebastian, Twin brother of Viola
3032	A&C	Seleucus
3306	ToA	Sempronius, Flatterer
0818	Tan	Sempronius, Noble Roman
2918	Mac	Seyton
1550	H42	Shadow, recruit – in Gloucestershire
1613	MWW	Shallow, Robert, Country Justice
0424	H61	Shepherd, father of Joan la Pucelle (in France)
3410	WnT	Shepherd, Thought to be Perdita's Father
0940	RIII	Sheriff of Wiltshire
1010	MoV	Shylock, a Jewish moneylender
3109	COR	Sicinius, tribune
3012	A&C	Silius, Follower of Antony
0108	TGV	Silvia, Loved by valentine
2010	AYL	Silvius, Shepherd
3203	PPT	Simonides, King of Pentapolis
0533	H62	Simpcox, Mistress, wife of Saunder Simpcox
0532	H62	Simpcox, Saunder, impostor (ie con-man)
1620	MWW	Simple, Servant
2205	12N	Sir Andrew Aguecheek, Suitor of Countess Olivia
1615	MWW	Sir Hugh Evans, Welsh Parson
0626	H63	Sir Hugh Mortimer
0923	RIII	Sir James Blount, Knight
0928	RIII	Sir James Tyrell, Knight
1601	MWW	Sir John Falstaff
1416	H41	Sir John Falstaff – from the Boar's Head Tavern
1535	H42	Sir John Falstaff – from the Boar's Head Tavern

0414	H61	Sir John Fastolfe
0624	H63	Sir John Montgomery
0625	H63	Sir John Mortimer
0627	H63	Sir John Somerville
0112	TGV	Sir Knight Eglamour
1212	LLL	Sir Nathaniel, Curate
2013	AYL	Sir Oliver Martext
1323	RII	Sir Piers Exton
0927	RIII	Sir Richard Ratcliff, Knight
0924	RIII	Sir Robert Brakenbury, Knight
1324	RII	Sir Stephen Scroop
1914	KHV	Sir Thomas Erpingham (English side)
0417	H61	Sir Thomas Gargrave
1913	KHV	Sir Thomas Gray (English side)
0929	RIII	Sir Thomas Vaughan, Knight
2204	12N	Sir Toby Belch, Uncle of Countess Olivia
0926	RIII	Sir Walter Herbert, Knight
0925	RIII	Sir William Catesby, Knight
0416	H61	Sir William Glansdale
0415	H61	Sir William Lucy
0628	H63	Sir William Stanley
2915	Mac	Siward, Earl of Nothumberland
2916	Mac	Siward, Young, Son of Siward
3719	2NK	Six Knights
1614	MWW	Slender, Abraham, Cousin of Robert Shallow
0201	ToS	Sly, Christopher a tinker
0526	H62	Smith the Weaver, follower of Jack Cade
1119	MND	Snout, Tom, Tinker
1120	MND	Snug, Joiner
1009	MoV	Solanio, a Venetian merchant
0301	CoE	Solinus, Duke of Ephesus
0632	H63	Son that has killed his father
3033	A&C	Soothsayer
0539	H62	Southwell, John, Priest
0102	TGV	Speed, Servant of Valentine
0518	H62	Stafford, Sir Humphrey
0519	H62	Stafford, William, Brother of Sir Humphrey Stafford
0520	H62	Stanley, Sir John
1121	MND	Starveling, Robin, Tailor
3511	TEM	Stephano, a drunken butler
1018	MoV	Stephano, a servant

No	Play	Character
2130	JlC	Strato, Brutus' Servant
1316	RII	Surrey
1519	H42	Surrey
3720	2NK	Taborer (drummer)
0810	Tan	Tamora, queen of the Goths
3019	A&C	Taurus, Follower of Caesar
1542	H42	Tearsheet, Doll– from the Boar's Head Tavern
3204	PPT	Thaisa, Daughter of Simonides, King of Pentapolis
3208	PPT	Thaliard, Antiochus' dastardly servant
2410	T&C	Thersites, a deformed and scurrilous soldier
1101	MND	Theseus
3703	2NK	Theseus, Duke of Athens
0534	H62	Thomas Horner, armourer
3721	2NK	Three Queens
3317	ToA	Three Strangers
0110	TGV	Thurio, also in love with Silvia
3020	A&C	Thyreus, Follower of Caesar
3309	ToA	Timandra, whore
3420	WnT	Time (as Chorus)
3301	ToA	Timon
1110	MND	Titania, Fairy Queen
2124	JlC	Titinius, Friend and Supporter of Brutus and Cassius
0803	Tan	Titus Andronicus
2008	AYL	Touchstone, jester
0214	ToS	Tranio, Servant
1533	H42	Travers, Rebel
2113	JlC	Trebonius, Conspirator
0935	RIII	Tressel, Attendant
3510	TEM	Trinculo, a jester
2417	T&C	Troilus, Son of King Priam
1015	MoV	Tubal, Shylock's friend
1711	R&J	Tybalt, Juliet's Cousin
2409	T&C	Ulysses, Commander
1809	MAN	Ursula, Hero's Maid
0101	TGV	Valentine
2213	12N	Valentine, Lord
0819	Tan	Valentine, Noble Roman
3104	COR	Valeria, Friend of Virgilia
3707	2NK	Valerius, a Theban
3023	A&C	Varrius, Follower of Pompey

2615	M4M	Varrius, Servant to the Duke
2131	JlC	Varro, Brutus' Servant
3820	KH8	Vaux, Knight
0521	H62	Vaux, Sir William
3013	A&C	Ventidius, Follower of Antony
3303	ToA	Ventidius, Timon's false friend
1414	H41	Vernon
0420	H61	Vernon, a Yorkist
0205	ToS	Vincentio, an old Gentleman
0209	ToS	Vincentio, Bianca's Suitor
2209	12N	Viola
2813	AWW	Violenta, Neighbour of the Widow of Florence
3103	COR	Virgilia, Wife of Caius Marcius
2319	Ham	Voltemand, courtier/soldier
3102	COR	Volumnia, Mother of Caius Marcius
2125	JlC	Volumnius, Friend and Supporter of Brutus and Cassius
1551	H42	Wart, recruit – in Gloucestershire
1517	H42	Warwick
1723	R&J	Watchmen
1513	H42	Westmoreland
1404	H41	Westmoreland, At court
1504	H42	Westmoreland, At court
0529	H62	Whitmore, a Pirate
2811	AWW	Widow of Florence
2015	AYL	William
1317	RII	Willoughby
2919	Mac	Witches
0906	RIII	Woodville, Brother of Elizabeth
0419	H61	Woodville, lieutenant of the Tower
3710	2NK	Wooer of the Daughter of Gaoler
1410	H41	Worcester
1905	KHV	York, King's Cousin (English side)
0513	H62	Young Clifford, son of Lord Clifford

Film

Oscars – multiple winners

The Oscars (first awarded in 1928) are more properly the annual awards of the American Academy of Motion Picture Arts and Sciences (AMPAS) which has about 5,000 members who by and large are fair-minded and take their responsibilities seriously. They vote in a secret ballot to award outstanding performances and creative and technical achievements in the films released the previous year. The statuette itself is thirteen and a half inches high and made of gold-plated bronze. At nearly nine pounds it is heavy enough to brain a jealous rival. The original was created by the sculptor George Stanley based on a drawing by the art director Cedric Gibbons, and legend has it that the name stuck after Margaret Herrick, a librarian at the Academy (later its executive director), said it reminded her of her uncle Oscar (ie Oscar Pierce, an American wheat and fruit grower).

Since 1952 the award ceremony has been televised, and over the years it has grown in pomp, extravagance and commercial importance. Couturiers compete for the privilege of designing the actresses' gowns which attract as much attention as any political event. Massive displays of jewellery and cleavage are obligatory. Well-toned, cosmetically adjusted faces smile with practised insincerity when a rival wins, and the delicious embarrassments of the acceptance speech are subject to serious analysis in all the media. Dustin Hoffman thanked his parents for not practising birth control. Gwyneth Paltrow cried. Sally Anne Field cried for two days. Jane Fonda made the audience cringe when she was nominated in 1970 for *They Shoot Horses, Don't They?* by giving the Black Panther salute, and Vanessa Redgrave offended many by thanking the Academy for her 1977 Supporting Actress Award 'despite the threats of a small bunch of Zionist hoodlums'. The great Marlon Brando (*d* 2004) refused his Oscar in 1973 and sent instead a Native American Indian called Littlefeather to make a rambling speech on his behalf about the violation of Indian rights. In keeping with the spirit of the occasion, Littlefeather turned out to be an actress. This tradition of exploiting the podium with its gigantic audience continues to this day – most recently in 2003 with Michael Moore's speech thanking the Academy for his Documentary Award for *Bowling for Columbine* when 'we live in fictitious times with a fictitious President'.

Despite – or possibly because of – these dangers, the spectacle is always watchable. Sometimes cruel, usually sentimental and always over the top, The Oscars, now with an audience of over a billion people, have become a global event in which the world's richest entertainment industry struts upon its own stage and mythologises itself.

Some multiple winners

Name	Nominations	Category of award	Comment
Katherine Hepburn	12	**Four Oscars** Actress (1932/33); Supporting Actress (1967, 1968,1981)	Angular face, clear diction, she thought actors should not compete with each other.
Ingrid Bergman	7	**Three Oscars** Actress (1944, 1956); Supporting Actress (1974)	Beautiful, independent Swede. Wonderful in *Casablanca*.
Walter Brennan	4	Supporting Actor (1936, 1938, 1940)	America's most successful character actor.

Remaining artists have two Oscars each

Name	Nominations	Category of award	Comment
Jack Nicholson	12	Actor (1975, 1997); Supporting Actor (1983)	Writes, directs, acts. Strong screen presence.
Marlon Brando	8	Two Oscars Actor (1954, 1973)	Brought Lee Strasberg's Method to Hollywood.
Michael Caine	6	Supporting Actor (1986, 1999)	Technically expert Brit, played many a hard case.
Gary Cooper	5	Actor (1941, 1952) (Also Honorary Award – 1960)	Leading man, often played Mr Decent small-town virtues.
Bette Davis	10	Actress (1935, 1938)	'no one but her mother could have loved her at the height of her career'.*
Olivia de Havilland	5	Actress (1946, 1949)	Old Hollywood glamour – immensely stylish.
Robert De Niro	6	Supporting Actor (1974); Actor (1980)	Finest of his generation? Can do sensitive or psycho.
Melvyn Douglas	3	Supporting Actor (1963, 1979)	Familiar face, unfamiliar name, also won the Tony and Emmy.

Sally Field	2	Actress (1979, 1984)	Esp. roles of the emotionally fragile.
Jane Fonda	7	Actress (1971, 1978)	Politically radical, from Hollywood dynasty.
Jodie Foster	4	Actress (1988, 1991)	Directs too, a child star – the complete professional.
Gene Hackman	5	Actor (1971); Supporting Actor (1992)	Superbly versatile from moist to macho.
Tom Hanks	5	Actor (1993, 1994)	Also producer. Fine actor with slight tendency to soppy.
Helen Hayes	2	Actress (1931/32); Supporting Actress (1970)	Also radio, TV, and theatre from childhood.
Dustin Hoffman	7	Actor (1979, 1988)	Intense, small, clever – the ultimate Method mumbler.
Glenda Jackson	4	Actress (1970, 1973)	Clear-speaking Brit, now earnest Labour MP.
Jessica Lange	6	Supporting Actress (1982); Actress (1994)	Blonde, handsome rather than glam, plays real people.
Vivien Leigh	2	Actress (1939, 1951)	Very beautiful English actress, m. Olivier, fragile.
Jack Lemmon	8	Supporting Actor (1952, 1956)	Subtle, quick-talking American character actor.
Frederic March	5	Actor (1931/32, 1946)	Cerebral stage and film actor, good in *Dr Jekyll and Mr Hyde*.
Anthony Quinn	4	Supporting Actor (1952, 1956)	Theatrically-trained Brit who could do tough for films.
Luise Rainer	2	Actress (1936, 1937)	Beautiful, non-conformist German actress, m. Clifford Odets.
Jason Robards	3	Supporting Actor (1976, 1977)	Gunfighters to executives – brought gravitas to all roles.
Maggie Smith	6	Actress (1969); Supporting Actress (1978)	Grande Dame of English theatre.
Kevin Spacey	2	Supporting Actor (1995), Actor (1999)	Controlled, good at creepy, Artistic Dir. Old Vic, London.

Meryl Streep	13	Supporting Actress (1979); Actress (1982)	Brainy, large-range character actress, can do accents.
Elizabeth Taylor	5	Actress (1960, 1966)	Sex-symbol star on old model, m. x 8 (Burton x2).
Spencer Tracy	9	Actor (1957, 1938)	Chunky, esp. tough guys, long time companion to Hepburn.
Peter Ustinov	3 (+1 writing)	Supporting Actor (1960, 1964)	Russian-born Brit, also witty raconteur and novelist.
Denzel Washington	5	Supporting Actor (1986); Actor (2001)	Good-looking black actor, mainly action roles.
Dianne Wiest	3	Supporting Actress (1986, 1994)	Consistent character actress, the DA in TV's *Law and Order*.
Shelley Winters	4	Supporting Actress (1959, 1965)	Too plump for romantic leads, but consistently good.

* By 1937 Bette Davis was an actress who exercised a lot of power. She gave a hard time to those who had been less than kind to her on the way up. This famous quote is from Brian Aherne, once her co-star – though his fame has now faded.

Useful arts

Architects

Some important twentieth-century architects

Alvar Aalto (1898–1976), Finnish, is one of the founding fathers of modern architecture. His buildings, such as the Paimio Sanatorium in Finland, are uncompromisingly modern in their use of concrete and machine-made components, yet beautifully detailed and sensitive to natural forms.

Ove Arup (1895–1988) Danish engineer who pioneered methods of using concrete in London in the 1930s. The engineering consultancy he founded is hugely respected and the company is often used in complex structural designs.

Le Corbusier (Charles-Edouard Jeanneret, 1887–1965), French–Swiss, the city planner and modernist architect of many projects and unrivalled influence. He started off as a cubist painter, and that can be seen in his white, geometrical early buildings, but he became more sculptural as in the famous chapel at Ronchamp. His huge blocks of flats for workers in Marseilles, the Unités d'Habitation, were beautifully made and worked well under the smiting sun of the south of France. Much copied but with less care over execution, they could be pretty grim in other parts of the world.

Charles Eames (1907–78) and **Ray Eames** (1916–88), an American husband and wife team, made beautiful and comfortable modern houses, often with a double height area full of light. They also designed furniture, and the classic Eames chair is still available at a cheeky price.

Norman Foster (*b* 1935), evangelically futurist and influential British exponent of high-tech ingenuity and elegance. His terminal at Stansted Airport, UK, is much admired but it palls into insignificance compared to the enormous plane-shaped terminal he designed for Chep Lap Kok airport in China. He also designed the central glass dome for the remodelled Reichstag in Berlin.

Buckminster Fuller (1895–1983), American inventor and architect, an ebullient exponent of modernism, always tried to use the least material to contain the maximum space – thus his Dymaxion House is very much ahead of its time. It was, however, expensive and not easy to live in. He is also associated with the geodesic dome and his evangelism on the subject meant that a class of carbon molecules that show a similar structure are named Fullerenes in his honour.

Antonio Gaudi (1852–1926), Catalan–Spanish, whose designs are famously curvy, decorated and organic as if they had grown rather than been built. His famous cathedral in Barcelona is still being constructed.

Frank Gehry *(b* 1929), American, an architectural iconoclast, who plays with form – especially with wild, swooping roof structures. His remarkable Guggenheim Museum in Bilbao, Spain, clad in titanium, has changed the art of the possible.

Walter Gropius (1883–1969) born in Germany but naturalised American, the grand old man of the Bauhaus school. His housing for workers in Siemenstadt, Berlin, was often copied though seldom as well. He became Professor of Architecture at Harvard (1938–52) and designed the Harvard Graduate Center (1949) and the US Embassy in Athens (1960).

Zaha Hadid *(b* 1951) Iraqi, an exponent of the dynamic, bold and angular, she won a competition to build the Opera House in Cardiff, Wales, but her design proved to be too innovative for the men in suits and was blocked. The museum she designed for Cincinnati, Ohio, was completed and has been a huge success.

Arne Jacobsen (1902–1988), Danish rationalist architect and furniture designer of the international school. The clean-lined elegance of Danish houses and municipal buildings owes a lot to Jacobsen.

Edwin Lutyens (1869–1944), a very English classical architect capable of the domestic and the very grand. He designed much of New Delhi, India, including the Viceroy's House. Dining with King George V on some catering fish, Lutyens is reported to have said: 'Your Majesty, this is the piece of cod that passeth all understanding ... '

Charles Rennie Mackintosh (1862–1928), Scottish architect and decorative artist who integrated his designs into a coherent art nouveau vision. His Glasgow School of Art building is his best known. His furniture designs are still popular.

Oscar Niemeyer *(b* 1907), Visionary Brazilian and chief architect of Brasilia, the spectacular but artificial capital city that never quite overcame its social and economic problems.

I M Pei (*b* 1917) Chinese–American, creator of elegant post-modernist architecture such as the extension to the National Gallery of Art in Washington and the glass pyramid and subterranean space for controlling the flow of tourists at the Louvre, Paris. The locals protested vehemently against the latter though it has now become much loved.

Cesar Pelli (*b* 1926), Argentine, a post-modernist on a grand scale responsible for the huge but blocky Canary Wharf Tower in London's Docklands and also for the gigantic, spectacular but undeniably kitsch Petronas Towers in Kuala Lumpur, Malaysia.

Auguste Perret (1874–1954), important French architect of apartment blocks who combined concrete construction with art nouveau details. He was one of the first to leave concrete structural members exposed as part of the design.

Renzo Piano (*b* 1937), Italian engineer architect who worked with Richard Rogers on the Pompidou Centre in Paris. Both romantic and high tech, Piano's greatest achievement is Kansai Airport, Osaka Bay, Japan, which is constructed on an artificial island.

Richard Rogers (*b* 1933), British post-modernist high-tech architect. His Lloyd's Building, with its vast internal space and silent escalators, is very innovative and the technique of putting the services outside the shell of the building in order to leave the interior uncluttered has been much followed.

Mies van der Rohe (1886–1969), German architect of the Bauhaus who became hugely influential as head of the Illinois Institute of Technology whose campus he designed in the late 30s. The clean lines of his Seagram Building in New York inspired many a monumental corporate HQ.

Eero Saarinen (1910–61), Finnish architect of the international school, but less blocky and more expressionistic than others. His TWA terminal at JFK airport is striking.

Skidmore Owings and Merrill (SOM), a huge American practice, was founded in 1936 and soon had branches in Chicago, San Francisco and New York. It has always eschewed the prima donna in favour of team work. SOM created many skyscrapers and slab-sided office blocks (of which the Lever Building in New York is a good example). In 1982 it showed its versatility by designing the Haj Air Terminal in Saudi Arabia using a high-tech Arabian tent motif to great effect.

James Stirling (1926–92), internationally famous British architect whose uncompromising approach to form and function was close to Brutalism. His History Faculty building in Cambridge (UK) is characteristic.

Louis Henry Sullivan (1856–1924), Chicago-based architect who designed the early and revolutionary steel-framed skyscrapers.

Kenzo Tange (b 1913), Japanese architect and town-planner known for his work in Japanese cities in the 1950s. He managed to combine Brutalist Le Corbusier-influenced structures with traditional Japanese elements. He also designed Nigeria's crescent-shaped capital, Abuja.

Vladimir Tatlin (1885–1953), Russian, abstract painter and designer, was associated with the idea of constructivism. He designed colossal, heroic projects to celebrate the Third International (1919); the model was exhibited, but the Monument was never built

Jørn Utzon (b 1918), is the Danish architect famous for the Sydney Harbour Opera House, the result of an international competition which he won in 1956. He fell out with the powers that be and left the project in 1966 – which may account for why the inside of the building does not quite live up to the excitement of the spectacular shell-shape roof line.

Frank Lloyd Wright (1869–1959), influential American architect who introduced a new era of the modern planar look. His Robie House in Chicago with its dramatic flat roof and built-in garage epitomised the modernist times. Ayn Rand was said to have based the hero of her bombastic novel *The Fountainhead* on Frank Lloyd Wright.

The first Channel swimmers

The English Channel between France and England ('La Manche') has always had a fascination for long-distance swimmers, particularly since the 1920s when a certain nationalism informed the contest. The shortest route from Dover to Calais is just under 22 miles (35 kilometres), but there are treacherous off-shore currents near the coasts of England and France. As anybody knows who has enjoyed a holiday at one of England's seaside resorts, the local tourist office has to fall back on weasel words such as 'bracing' to describe the temperature of the water. This is turbid, grey and always cold, even in the height of the summer, and quite polluted with debris jettisoned from ships and washed down the rivers. The Channel is one the busiest waterways in the world.

The very first man to succeed in swimming across the channel – a feat that had been regarded as impossible – was the massively strong Captain Matthew Webb (1843–83). He took to the water liberally smeared in porpoise oil to protect against the cold and was further fortified by beef tea, beer, coffee and an omelette. In the last few hours nearing France he was badly stung by perfidious French jelly fish and had to struggle against rising seas and a running tide. However, he made it and became a national hero. Unfortunately he over-reached himself trying to swim the rapids and whirlpools below the Niagara Falls and was drowned in 1883.

The Channel has been swum dozens of times since by long-distance swimmers of many nationalities and once by a twelve-year-old, Marcus Hooper, in 1979. Several competing bodies offer their services as observers and time keepers, and this has led to some argument about official and unofficial times. Lists are maintained that differentiate between the route from France to England as opposed to that from England to France. The current record for the fastest time is held by a prize-winning long-distance swimmer, the American Chad Hundeby, who managed it in the extraordinary time of only 7 hours 17 minutes in September 1994.

Swimmer	Nationality	Date	Time
Matthew Webb	British	24/25 August 1875	21.45
Thomas Burgess	British	5/6 September 1911	22.35
Henry Sullivan	American	5/6 August 1923	26.50
Enrico Tiraboschi	Italian	12 August 1923	16.33
Charles Toth	American	8/9 September 1923	16.58
Gertrude Ederle	American	6 August 1926	14.39
Millie Corson	American	27/28 August 1926	15.29
Arnst Vierkotter	German	30 August 1926	12.40
Edward Temme	British	5 August 1927	14.29
Mercedes Gleitze	British	7 October 1927	15.15

Collectors and their collectables

Arranged by collector

Collector	Objects collected
Aerophilatelist	Airmail stamps
Arctophilist / Arctophile	Teddy bears
Audiophile	Music
Bestiarist	Medieval books on animals

Bibliophile	Books
Brandophilist	Cigar bands
Cactophile	Cactus and Succulent plants
Cameist	Cameos
Conchologist	Shells
Copoclephilist	Keyrings
Deltiologist	Postcards
Discophile	Records or CDs
Ephemologist	Ephemera
Errinophilist	Revenue or tax stamps
Ex-librist	Book plates
Exonumist	Numismatic material other than coins or notes
Fusilatelist	Phone cards
Helixophile	Corkscrews
Heortologist	Religious calendars
Iconophile	Prints and engravings
Labeorphilist	Beer bottles
Lepidopterist	Butterflies
Notaphilist	Paper money
Numismatist	Money and medals
Oologist	Birds' eggs
Philatelist	Postage stamps
Phillumenist	Matchbook covers
Philographist	Autographs
Phonophile	Phonograph records
Plangonologist	Dolls
Receptarist	Recipes
Sinistrophilist	Left-handed objects
Sucrologist	Sugar packets
Tegestologist	Beer mats
Telegerist	Telephone calling cards
Vecturist	Transport tokens
Vexillologist	Flags
Xylographer	Woodcuts / engraving

Arranged by object

Objects collected	*Collector*
Airmail stamps	Aerophilatelist
Autographs	Philographist
Beer bottles	Labeorphilist
Beer mats	Tegestologist
Birds' eggs	Oologist
Book plates	Ex-librist
Books	Bibliophile
Butterflies	Lepidopterist
Cactus	Cactophile
Cameos	Cameist
Cigar bands	Brandophilist
Corkscrews	Helixophile
Dolls	Plangonologist
Flags	Vexillologist
Keyrings	Copoclephilist
Left handed objects	Sinistrophilist
Matchbook covers	Phillumenist
Medieval books on animals	Bestiarist
Money and medals	Numismatist
Music	Audiophile
Numismatic material other than coins or notes	Exonumist
Paper money	Notaphilist
Phone cards	Fusilatelist
Phonograph records	Phonophile
Postage stamps	Philatelist
Postcards	Deltiologist
Prints and engravings	Iconophile
Recipes	Receptarist
Records or CDs	Discophile
Religious calendars	Heortologist
Revenue or tax stamps	Errinophilist
Shells	Conchologist
Sugar packets	Sucrologist
Teddy bears	Arctophilist / Arctophile
Telephone calling cards	Telegerist
Transport tokens	Vecturist
Woodcuts / engraving	Xylographer

Classical cooks and commentators on cookery

Marcus Gabius Apicius (1st century CE) A Roman epicure reputed to have spent the equivalent of hundreds of thousands of pounds on gourmandising. When his income was down to its last few tens of thousands he killed himself rather than cut back on his foodie career. Juvenal, Martial, Pliny and Seneca all credited him with influence on Roman cooking.

Wynkyn de Worde Publisher and printer, pupil of Caxton, whose contribution to writings on cookery features a *Book of Kerving* (1508). The precision of terms used in carving reflects the high status of this job in grand households of the time:

'The termes of a Kerver be as here followeth:

'Breke that dere'
'rere that goose'
'lyfte that swan'
'sauce that capon'
'spoyle that hen'
'unbrace that mallarde'
'dismembre that heron'
'display that crayn'
'disfigure that peacock'
'untache that curlewe'
'wyng that quayle'
'myne that plover'
'thye that pigeon'
'strynge that lampreye'
'tymbre that fyere'
'tyere that egg'
'chynne that samon'
'splat that pyke'
'tuske that barbell'
'culpon that troute'
'trassene that ele'
'trance that sturgion'
'under trance that porpose'
'tayme that crabbe'
'barbe that lopster'

Gervase Markham *The English Hus-wife* (1615); also *The Compleat Cook* (1655), giving the earliest recipe for Batalia pye, whose ingredients are: 4 game pigeons, 4 ox palates, 6 lamb's stones, 6 veal sweetbreads, 20 cockscombs, 4 artichoke bottoms, 1 pint oysters, marrow of 3 bones, butter, gravy, mace and seasoning.

Francois La Varenne Chef to the sister of the King of France, Henry IV, and author of the first books on cookery to be planned according to a proper system: *Le Cuisinier francais* (1651), *Le Patissier francais* (1653), *Le Confiseur francais* (1664).

Robert May *The Accomplish't Cook, or The Art and Mystery of Cookery* (1660) From an era that produced several dishes whose names are now just an oddity, i.e. whim-wham, flummery, kickshaw, subtlety, this book's recipe for the latter concoction deserves some kind of respect:

> 'Made the likeness of a ship in paste-board and cover it with paste, with Flags and streamers, the guns belonging to it of Kickses [usually a kind of marzipan] with such holes and trains of powder that they may all take Fire; place your ship firm in a great Charger; then make a salt round about it, and stick therein egg shells filled with rose water.
>
> Then in another Charger have the proportion of a stag made of course [sic] paste, with a bread arrow in the side of him and his body filled with claret wine.
>
> In another Charger have the proportion of a Castle with Battlements, Percullises, Gates and Drawbridges made of paste-board, the guns of Kickses, and covered with course paste as the former; place it at a distance from the Ship, to fire at each other, the Stag being placed between them ... At each end of the Charger, wherein is the Stag, place a pie made of course paste in one of which there be live Frogs, in the other live Birds. Make these Pies of course paste filled with Bran, and yellowed over with Saffron or Yolks of Eggs, gild them over in spots, as also the Stag, the Ship and the Castle; bake them and place them with gilt pay-leaves on the turrets and tunnels of the Castle and Pies; being baked, make a hole in the bottom, take out the bran, put in your Frogs and Birds and close up with course paste.
>
> Fire the trains of powder, order it so that some of the Ladies may be persuaded to pluck the Arrow out of the Stag, then will the claret follow as blood running from a wound. This being done with admiration to the beholders, after some short pause, fire the train of the Castle, that the pieces all of one side may go off; then fire the trains of one side of the Ship, as in a battle, and by degrees fire the trains of each other side as before. This done, to sweeten the stink of the powder, let the ladies take the egg-shells full of sweet waters and throw them at each other. All dangers being over, by this time you

may suppose they will desire to see what is in the pies; where, lifting off the lid of one pie, out skips some Frogs, which makes the Ladies to skip and shreek; next after the other Pie, whence comes out the Birds, who by a natural instinct flying at the light, will put out the Candles, so that what with the flying Birds and skipping Frogs, the one above, the other beneath, will cause much delight and pleasure to the company: at length the candles are lighted and a banquet brought in, the music sounds and everyone with much delighrt and content rehearses their actions in the former passages. There were formerly the delights of the Nobility, before good-housekeeping had left England, and the sword really acted that which was only counterfeited in such honest and laudable Exercises as these.'

Elisabeth Smith *The Compleat Housewife or Accomplish'd Gentlewoman's Companion* (1727) Some of her recipes were archaic even in her own time, i.e. potted swan; some others are laborious by the standards of our own, as with her pulpatoon or pupton of pigeons.

Hannah Glasse *The Art of Cookery Made Plain and Easy* (1747), featuring instructions on the making of potted cheese, comfrey leaf fritters, fricassee of mushrooms, Cheshire pork and apple pie, goose pie; compote of Bonchretien pears. This work also describes how to turn a 60-lb live turtle into a series of different soups, from a thick stew made with minced turtle veal, down to a clear soup based on stock from the head and bones.

John Farley *The London Art of Cookery* (1783) Supremely popular work of its time; characteristic recipes include leg of lamb stuffed with crab, and John Farley's fine cheesecake.

Mme Marie Harel Unlike most innovators in the realm of traditional food, this farmer's wife, the principal creator of Camembert cheese, is not lost to history. Indeed, the small village of that name features a statue of Mme Harel, shown as she would have appeared, c.1790, in cap, shawl and clogs.

Jean-Anthelme de Brillat-Savarin (1755–1826) Author of *Physiologie du gout*, translated into English as *A Handbook of Gastronomy*. Its preface included the following maxims:

'The destiny of nations depends on their manner of eating ...
'Tell me what you eat, and I shall tell you what you are ...
'The table is the only place where one is never bored during the first hour.
'The discovery of a new dish does more for the happiness of mankind than the discovery of a star ...

'The correct order of foods is starting with the heaviest and ending with the lightest.
'The correct order of beverages is starting with the most temperate and ending with the most heady ...
'A dessert without cheese is like a beautiful woman with one eye.'

Elsewhere:

'Man's palate, by the delicacy of its texture and of the various membranes which surround it, gives sufficient proof of the sublimity of functions for which it is intended ...
'Thinness is not a great drawback for men, but it is a dreadful misfortune for women ...
'We were not satisfied with the qualities which nature gave to poultry; art stepped in, and under the pretext of improving fowls, has made martyrs of them.'

Mrs A. Rundle *A New System of Domestic Cookery* (1807) gives such typically English recipes as partridge pie, Benton [horseradish] sauce, roast cheese, almond puddings made with snow, and Cambridge burnt cream.

Antoine Careme (1784–1833) Described as 'the Cook of kings and the King of cooks'; self-made genius abandoned in infancy by a destitute family with twenty-five children; defined the fine arts as 'five in number, to whit: painting, sculpture, poetry, music, architecture – whose main branch is confectionery' – supreme creator of architectural structures in pastry. His books include *Le Patissier royal parisien* and *Le Patissier pittoresque*.

Richard Dolby *Cook's Dictionary* (1830) Head cook at the celebrated Thatched House Tavern in St James's Street, known for such dishes as cream omelette, stewed cheese with red wine, bubble and squeak, quaking pudding, jumbles [a biscuit] and rich rice soufflé.

Eliza Acton *Modern Cookery in all its branches reduced to an easy practice* (1845): typical recipes include apple soup, and John Bull's pudding (steak and oyster).

Alexis Soyer *The Gastronomic Regenerator* (1846) Chef to the Reform Club. Also an energetic reorganiser of hospital catering during the war in the Crimea, where his banquet to mark the ensuing peace was dominated by a giant centrepiece salad, or Salamongundy, inscribed 'Soyer's Culinary Emblem of peace ... ' and famously representing a triumph of war-zone improvisation.

Isabella Beeton (1836–65) Author of the best-selling *Household Management*. Some of the world it catered to can be deduced from the following menu, characteristic of an upper-middle-class dinner party of the time.

Ox-tail Soup	Soup a la Jardinière
Turbot and Lobster Sauce	Crimped Cod and Oyster Sauce
Stewed Eels	Soles a la Normandie
Pike and Cream Sauce	Fried Filleted Soles
Filet de Boeuf a la Jardiniere	Croquettes of Game aux Champignons
Chicken Cutlets	Mutton Cutlets and Tomato Sauce
Lobster Rissoles	Oyster Patties
Roast Beef –	Haunch of Mutton
Poulet aux Cressons	Roast Turkey
Boiled Turkey and Celery Sauce	Ham
Grouse	Pheasants
Hare	Salad
Artichokes	Stewed Celery
Italian Cream	Charlotte aux Pommes
Compote of Pears	Croûtes madrées
Fruits	Pastry
Punch Jelly	Iced Pudding
Dessert and Ices	

Auguste Escoffier (1847–1935) His 62-year career included, in 1871 during the Franco-Prussian War, the job of *chef de cuisine* to the general staff of the Rhine army; later employed by Mr Ritz, notably at the Savoy Hotel, London. Invented such dishes as the *bombe Nero*, made of flaming ice, and the *peche Melba*.

Fashion eponyms

Albert A watch chain fastened to a waistcoat, as worn by Albert, Prince Consort, after one was presented to him on a visit to the city of Birmingham in 1849.

Apollo knot Widely *de rigeur* for women of fashion throughout most of the 1820s, it consisted of a wired loop of false hair arranged to stand vertically upright and was mostly regarded as evening wear.

Bloomers These were invented by an American, Mrs Amelia Bloomer, who sought an escape from the extravagant fashions of the 1850s. In place of the vast, fire-hazardous crinoline, much lampooned by cartoonists, she proposed the wearing of bloomers, a pair of loose trousers gathered at the ankles. Despite their modesty and obvious convenience, as a fashion they were almost instantly killed by the forces of public ridicule.

Cardigan This style of knitted jacket, usually buttoned down the front, was named after James Thomas Brudenell, 7th Earl of Cardigan. The earl is otherwise known to history for his role during the Crimean War in leading the disastrous charge of the Light Brigade, which took place near the village of Balaclava on 25 October 1854.

Chesterfield Within the world of fashion this name was given to a style of man's overcoat; one that was immensely popular during late C19. The chesterfield had braid edging, a velvet collar and hidden fastenings, and was initially knee-length but grew longer by degrees. It was named after an Earl of Chesterfield – which one is uncertain – from the time of Queen Victoria.

Derby Throughout Canada and the US this is the name given to the form of hat known in Britain as a bowler. It is thought to refer to Edward Stanley, 12th Earl of Derby (1752–1834), founder of the far-famed horse race. Bowlers, later part of the British businessman's standard wardrobe, originated as sporting wear, largely in the hunting field. In North America the name changed to derby in response to advertisements describing them as 'hats like the English wear at the Derby' (pronounced as Derby).

Dolly Varden This style of dress, popular in the early 1870s, was something of an historical hybrid. In reality it reflected current fashion; in theory, however, it was supposed to resurrect a look of ninety years before. Only the wide-brimmed hat, tilted steeply forward as part of the whole period ensemble, differed much from most outfits of the time. Its name referred to a character in Charles Dickens' *Barnaby Rudge*, set at the time of the Gordon Riots in 1780.

Garibaldi Of the names honouring the Italian patriot Giuseppe Garibaldi, the one used in fashion describes a type of woman's loose blouse with long sleeves. This style was so called because it resembled a garment worn by Garibaldi and his Redshirt volunteers, with whom he conquered Sicily and Naples in 1860–61, thus achieving the unification of Italy.

Gladstone A name given after the British prime minister William Ewart Gladstone (1809–98). It's commonly used to describe a Victorian type of hand luggage, but it also refers to a style of short, caped overcoat, also from late C19.

Havelock This is a cover for a military cap, featuring a long flap of cloth designed to keep off the sun. Though it had previously been used for many generations, it takes its name from the British soldier Sir Henry Havelock, whose decades of service in India included his command during the five-month siege of Lucknow (1857).

Knickerbockers This style of trouser developed in the nineteenth century from the breeches worn by sportsmen; they were loose, and gathered into a band fastened just below the knee. In the first part of twentieth-century they often took the form of plus-fours, popular with golfers. The term knickerbockers refers to part of the costume associated with early Dutch settlers in America; it was as 'Dietrich Knickerbocker' that the American writer Washington Irving penned his *History of New York from the Beginning of the World to the End of the Dutch Dynasty* (1809).

Leotard A leotard is a figure-hugging one-piece garment designed for such indoor physical exercise as ballet or acrobatics. It was designed by the French acrobat Jules Leotard, who died of smallpox in 1870, aged twenty-eight. His career had been a triumph: it was he who invented the flying trapeze and developed the mid-air somersault; and in 1860 he became known to the world, through the song by George Leybourne, as 'That Daring Young Man on the Flying Trapeze'.

Mackintosh Nowadays this word is given to any waterproof coat. It originally described a raincoat made of rubberised cloth, patented by the Scots chemist Charles Macintosh, whose Glasgow company started production in 1830. The fashion persisted despite the fact that early mackintosh wearers complained of the smell they gave off.

Mae West An inflatable life jacket, worn by airmen in WW2. It got its name from its likeness to an enormous bust, *ie* that of the extravagant-mannered film star Mae West (1892–1980).

Marcel A marcelled hairstyle consists of a series of waves made with a curling iron according to a process devised in 1875 by the French hair-dresser Marcel Grateau (1852–1936). The procedure itself was in use for many years, through several changes of fashion. Grateau himself was able to retire early on the proceeds, having become prodigiously wealthy while still in his twenties.

Petersham This is the name given to a tough, ribbed kind of ribbon used on belts, outer garments and hats. It was designed by the British soldier

Charles Stanhope, Viscount Petersham, 4th Earl of Harrington (1780–1851).

Plimsoll A canvas, rubber-soled lace-up sports shoe. It takes its name indirectly from the English reformer Samuel Plimsoll, whose efforts led to the use of the Plimsoll line as a marking on sea-going vessels, to prevent them being loaded beyond a certain point, as 'coffin ships' sent out to founder for the sake of an insurance payment. On the shoes of the same name, the upper edge of the rubber sole has been seen as looking like the Plimsoll line on a ship.

Pompadour The Marquise de Pompadour, born Jeanne Antoinette Poisson (1721–64), was the *maitresse en titre* of the French king Louis XV, a position in which she made a great show of wealth, taste and influence. It would have been unlikely if no fashion had taken its name from her; in the event, a pompadour was initially a hairstyle for women, one in which the hair was contrived into rolls around the face, having been drawn back, usually over pieces of padding known as 'rats' and 'mice'. A similar combed-back style was later adopted by both sexes.

Raglan A style of overcoat evolved, like the cardigan and the balaclava, in the course of the Crimean War (1854–6). It was loose fitting, with sleeves that joined the collar without any shoulder seams; in C21 the fashion survives, mostly as worn by older people. The raglan coat was named after the British field marshal Fitzroy James Henry Somerset, 1st Baron Raglan (1788–1855), whose record in the Crimea was uneven, despite (or perhaps because of) the fact that his military experience extended back to the time of Napoleon.

Spencer From 1790 the spencer was a fashion for men, in the form of a short-waisted jacket worn out of doors. For elderly wearers it survived until about 1850. It is said that this style was invented by the British politician George John Spencer, 2nd Earl of Spencer, who bet that he could make it popular merely by being seen wearing it in public.

Stetson A style of hat designed and manufactured by John Batterson Stetson (1830–1906). It was produced in response to a journey made by Stetson in the western part of America in the 1860s, where it appeared to him that some type of high, broad-brimmed hat would meet the needs of the local cowboys, providing both shade and a means of carrying water.

Trilby This style of hat, brimmed, and with indentations in the front of the crown, was a male fashion for much of twentieth-century. It was first worn, however, by a woman, the actress in the role of the heroine, Trilby

O'Ferrall, when the novel of that name by the Englishman George du Maurier (1834–96) was dramatised for the stage (1895).

Wellington The name of Arthur Wellesley, 1st Duke of Wellington (1769–1852), is commemorated in several ways. Best known of these is probably the type of boot the duke is said to have worn both on campaign and in later years. Initially, a Wellington boot was made of leather and cut away at the back of the knee, an apt response to spending any amount of time in the saddle. Currently, it's made of rubber (fashionably green) and reaches all round to the same height. The width of its sole, together with its looseness and lack of a heel, now make it supremely inappropriate for wearing on horseback.

Gardeners and gardening writers of yesteryear – with some of their works

Leon Battista Alberti (1404–72) *De Re Aedificatoria*

Andre Lenotre (1613–1700) Versailles; St James's Park, London

John Evelyn (1620–1706) *Sylva, or a discourse of Forest-trees*

Sir John Vanbrugh (1664–1726) Castle Howard, Yorkshire; Blenheim, Oxfordshire

William Kent (1684–1748) Stowe, Buckinghamshire; Holkham, Norfolk

Charles Bridgeman (c.1690–1738) Rousham, Oxfordshire; Stowe, Buckinghamshire

Lancelot 'Capability' Brown (1715–1783) Blenheim Palace, Oxfordshire; Petworth, Sussex; Botanical Gardens, Kew, Surrey

Sir William Chambers (1726–96) Botanical Gardens, Kew, Surrey; *A Dissertation on Oriental Gardening*

Humphry Repton (1752–1818) *Observations in the Theory and Practice of Landscape Gardening*; Sheringham Hall, Norfolk; Harleston Hall, Northants

John Claudius Loudon (1783–1843) *An Encyclopaedia of Gardening; An Encyclopaedia of Plants*

Sir Joseph Paxton (1801–65) Chatsworth House, Derbyshire; *The Magazine of Botany*

Frederick Law Olmsted (1822–1903) Central Park, New York

William Robinson (1838–1932) Gravetye Manor, Sussex; Nymans, Sussex

Gertrude Jekyll (1843–1932) Munstead, Surrey; *Roses for English Gardens*

Victoria Sackville-West (1892–1962) Sissinghurst Castle, Kent

Pub names

Some (mostly) common pub names

References to figures from English myth or legend include names such as the *Adam and Eve*, *Britannia*, *Robin Hood*, *Friar Tuck*, *George and Dragon*, *Dick Whittington* and *Dick Turpin*. They also feature types: *The Man of Kent*, *The Saracen's Head* or *Turk's Head*, *The Honest Lawyer*.

Many pub names refer to members of a local occupation or trade: *The Woodman*, *Hop-picker*, *Gunmaker's Arms*, *Grenadier*, *Volunteer*, *Chelsea Potter*, *Bricklayer's Arms*, *Weaver's Arms*, *Cooper's Arms*, *Jolly Collier*, *Cricketer's Arms*, *Shepherd and Dog*, *Saddler's Arms*, *Bowlturner's Arms*, *Lifeboatman*. *The London Apprentice* was once a Thames-side resort of apprentices from the City's Guilds; in Kent *The Cat and Cracker*, patronised by oil workers on the Isle of Sheppey, is named – approximately – after the catalytic cracker in the refinery.

Some historical figures appear on signboards nationwide, as at many instances of *The Shakespeare's Head*, and *The Duke of Wellington*, who often features instead as *The Iron Duke*. *The Lord Nelson* is also a common name, though pubs in the county of his birth tend to call him *The Norfolk Hero*. Rhyming slang, originally from London, is responsible in several areas for the growing number of pubs called *Brahms and Liszt*.

Other nationally famous people seem more likely to have pubs named for them because of a local association: among London examples are *The Samuel Pepys* and *The Dickens Inn*.

Royalty is perhaps the most conspicuous source of pub names. Some crop up all over England; others, like *The William the Conqueror*, near the Sussex coast, advertise a nearby piece of history. Not all monarchs and their kin are popular in this way; the ones most often seen include: *The Old Queen's Head*, referring to Elizabeth I, and *The William IV*, *Queen Victoria*, and *Prince Albert*.

Government

English/British monarchs

Regnal year In England, or Britian, a year beginning with the date of a monarch's accession, used until fairly recently (1962) for dating statutes and for other legal purposes. In earlier times, the use of the regnal year was the normal way of expressing a given year – but the way that the passage of time was then viewed was different from ours. The following table shows the year of accession of English monarchs from 802–1066, and then the regnal years of the monarchs to the present day.

Years of reign	Monarch	Year of accession
	House of Wessex	
37	Egbert	802
16	Æthelwulf	839
15	Æthelbald	855
6	Æthelbert	860
5	Æthelred	866
28	Alfred the Great	871
26	Edward the Elder	899
15	Athelstan	925
6	Edmund the Magnificent	940
9	Eadred	946
4	Eadwig (Edwy) All-Fair	955
16	Edgar the Peaceable	959
3	Edward the Martyr	975
38	Æthelred the Unready	978
1	Edmund Ironside	1016
	Danish Line	
2	Svein Forkbeard	1014
19	Canute the Great	1016
5	Harald Harefoot	1035
2	Hardicanute	1040

Years of reign	Monarch	Year of accession		
	House of Wessex, restored			
24	Edward the Confessor	1042		
1	Harold II	1066		
	Norman Line			
1	William I the Conqueror	25 December 1066	24 December 1067	A
21	William I	25 December 1086	9 September 1087	
1	William II Rufus	26 September 1087	25 September 1088	A
13	William II	26 September 1099	2 August 1100	
1	Henry I Beauclerc	5 August 1100	4 August 1101	A
36	Henry I	5 August 1135	1 December 1135	
1	Stephen	22 December 1135	21 December 1136	B
19	Stephen	22 December 1153	25 October 1154	
	Plantagenet, Angevin line			
1	Henry II Curtmantle	19 December 1154	18 December 1155	A
35	Henry II	19 December 1188	6 July 1189	
1	Richard I the Lionheart	3 September 1189	2 September 1190	A
10	Richard I	3 September 1198	6 April 1199	
1	John Lackland	27 May 1199	17 May 1200	C
2	John	18 May 1200	2 May 1201	
3	John	3 May 1201	22 May 1202	
4	John	23 May 1202	14 May 1203	
5	John	15 May 1203	2 June 1204	
6	John	3 June 1204	18 May 1205	
7	John	19 May 1205	10 May 1206	
8	John	11 May 1206	30 May 1207	
9	John	31 May 1207	14 May 1208	
10	John	15 May 1208	6 May 1209	
11	John	7 May 1209	26 May 1210	
12	John	27 May 1210	11 May 1211	
13	John	12 May 1211	2 May 1212	
14	John	3 May 1212	22 May 1213	
15	John	23 May 1213	7 May 1214	
16	John	8 May 1214	27 May 1215	
17	John	28 May 1215	18 May 1216	
18	John	19 May 1216	19 October 1216	
1	Henry III	28 October 1216	27 October 1217	A
57	Henry III	28 October 1272	16 November 1272	

1	Edward I Longshanks	20 November 1272	19 November 1273	A
35	Edward I	20 November 1306	7 July 1307	
1	Edward II	8 July 1307	7 July 1308	
20	Edward II	8 July 1326	20 January 1327	D
1	Edward III	25 January 1327	24 January 1328	A
13	Edward III	25 January 1339	24 January 1340	
14/1	Edward III	25 January 1340	24 January 1341	E
34/21	Edward III	25 January 1360	8 May 1360	E
34	Edward III	9 May 1360	24 January 1361	
43	Edward III	25 January 1369	10 June 1369	E
43/30	Edward III	11 June 1369	24 January 1370	
51/38	Edward III	25 January 1377	21 June 1377	
1	Richard II	22 June 1377	21 June 1378	
23	Richard II	22 June 1399	29 September 1399	
	Plantagenet, Lancastrian line			
1	Henry IV	30 September 1399	29 September 1400	
14	Henry IV	30 September 1412	20 March 1413	
1	Henry V	21 March 1413	20 March 1414	
10	Henry V	21 March 1422	31 August 1423	
1	Henry VI	1 September 1422	31 August 1422	
39	Henry VI	1 September 1460	4 March 1461	F
	Plantagenet, Yorkist line			
1	Edward IV	4 March 1461	3 March 1462	
39	Edward IV	1 September 1460	4 March 1461	
10	Edward IV	4 March 1470	3 March 1471	
49/1	Henry VI	9 October 1470	14 April 1471	G
11	Edward IV	4 March 1471	3 March 1472	
23	Edward IV	4 March 1483	9 April 1483	
1	Edward V	9 April 1483	25 June 1483	
1	Richard III	26 June 1483	25 June 1484	
3	Richard III	26 June 1485	22 August 1485	
	House of Tudor			
1	Henry VII Tudor	22 August 1485	21 August 1486	
24	Henry VII	22 August 1508	21 April 1509	
1	Henry VIII	22 April 1509	21 April 1510	
38	Henry VIII	22 April 1546	28 January 1547	
1	Edward VI	28 January 1547	27 Jan 1548	
7	Edward VI	28 January 1553	6 July 1553	
1	Lady Jane Grey	6 July 1553	19 July 1553	
1	Mary I Tudor	19 July 1553	5 July 1554	H
2	Mary I	6 July 1554	24 July 1554	

Years of reign	Monarch	Year of accession		
1/2	Philip & Mary	25 July 1554	5 July 1555	I
1/3	Philip & Mary	6 July 1555	24 July 1555	
2/3	Philip & Mary	25 July 1555	5 July 1556	
2/4	Philip & Mary	6 July 1556	24 July 1556	
3/4	Philip & Mary	25 July 1556	5 July 1557	
3/5	Philip & Mary	6 July 1557	24 July 1557	
4/5	Philip & Mary	25 July 1557	5 July 1558	
4/6	Philip & Mary	6 July 1558	24 July 1558	
5/6	Philip & Mary	25 July 1558	17 November 1558	
1	Elizabeth I	17 November 1558	16 November 1559	
45	Elizabeth I	17 November 1602	23 March 1603	

Monarch of Great Britain

House of Stuart

1/36	James I	24 March 1603	23 July 1603	J
1/37	James I	24 July 1603	23 March 1604	
23/58	James I	24 March 1625	27 March 1625	
1	Charles I	27 March 1625	26 March 1626	
24	Charles I	27 March 1648	30 January 1649	K
1	Charles II	30 January 1649	29 January 1650	
	Commonwealth	*30 January 1649*	*29 May 1660*	L

House of Stuart, restored

37	Charles II	30 January 1685	6 February 1685	
1	James II	6 February 1685	4 February 1686	
4	James II	6 February 1688	11 December 1688	
	Interregnum	12 December 1688	12 February 1689	

House of Orange and Stuart

1	William & Mary	13 February 1689	12 February 1690	
6	William & Mary	13 February 1694	27 December 1694	M
6	William III	28 December 1694	12 February 1695	
14	William III	13 February 1702	8 March 1702	

House of Stuart

1	Anne	8 March 1702	7 March 1703	
13	Anne	8 March 1714	1 August 1714	

House of Brunswick, Hanover line

1	George I	1 August 1714	31 July 1715	
13	George I	1 August 1726	11 June 1727	
1	George II	11 June 1727	10 June 1728	
25	George II	11 June 1751	10 June 1752	
26	George II	11 June 1752	21 June 1753	N

34	George II	22 June 1760	25 October 1760	
1	George III	25 October 1760	24 October 1761	
60	George III	25 October 1819	29 January 1820	
1	George IV	29 January 1820	28 January 1821	
11	George IV	29 January 1830	26 June 1830	
1	William IV	26 June 1830	25 June 1831	
7	William IV	26 June 1836	20 June 1837	
1	Victoria	20 June 1837	19 June 1838	
64	Victoria	20 June 1900	22 January 1901	
	House of Saxe-Coburg-Gotha			
1	Edward VII	22 January 1901	21 January 1902	
10	Edward VII	22 January 1910	6 May 1910	
	House of Windsor			
1	George V	6 May 1910	5 May 1911	
26	George V	6 May 1935	20 January 1936	
1	Edward VIII	20 January 1936	11 December 1936	O
1	George VI	11 December 1936	10 December 1937	
16	George VI	11 December 1951	16 February 1952	
1	Elizabeth II	6 February 1952	5 February 1953	
10	Elizabeth II	6 February 1961	5 February 1962	P

A   Date of coronation.
B   Date of coronation according to William of Malmesbury.
C   John was crowned on Ascension Day, and his regnal years follow that movable date.
D   Edward II deposed.
E   In 1340, Edward III asserted his claim to the crown of France, and added his French regnal years to his English ones. He renounced his claim to the crown of France in 1360, and re-asserted it in 1369.
F   Henry VI deposed; Edward IV accepted.
G   Short-lived restoration of Henry VI.
H   Mary ignored Jane and backdated the start of her reign to 6 July.
I   Mary married Philip of Naples and Jerusalem, and later Spain; he was never crowned king of England.
J   James (1st and Sixth) acceded to the Scottish throne on 24 July 1567.
K   Charles I was beheaded on 30 January 1649; it was assumed that Charles II succeeded on that date.
L   Oliver Cromwell took over until his death on 3 September 1658; his heir Richard Cromwell abdicated on 24 May 1659; Parliament and the Army then governed until Charles II was restored to the throne on 29 May 1660.
M   Queen Mary died during the night of 27–28 December 1694.
N   The year from which the eleven days 3–13 September were omitted.
O   Edward VIII abdicated on 11 December 1936.
P   Since 1962, Acts of Parliament have been dated by calendar years. However, the anniversary of the accession of a monarch is still clearly of interest during that monarch's reign.

Kings and Queens of Scots 1016–1603

Name	Reign	Name	Reign
Kenneth I	843–85	William I	1165–1214
Donald I	858–62	Alexander II	1214–49
Constantine I	863–77	Alexander III	1249–86
Aed	877–78	Margaret	1286–90
Giric and Echiad	878–89	*Interregnum*	
Donald II	889–900	John (Balliol)	1292–96
Constantine II	900–943	*Interregnum*	
Malcom I	943–54	Robert I	1306–29
Indulf	954–62	David II	1329–71
Dubh	962–67	Robert II	1371–90
Culen	967–71	Robert III	1390–1406
Kenneth II	971–95	James I	1406–37
Constantine III	995–97	James II	1437–60
Kenneth III	997–1005	James III	1460–88
Malcolm II	1016–34	James IV	1488–1513
Duncan I	1034–40	James V	1513–42
Macbeth	1040–57	Mary Queen of Scots	1542–67
Lulach	1057–58		
Malcolm III	1058–93	James VI	1567–1625
Donald III	1093–97	Charles I	1625–49
Duncan II	1094	Charles II	1649–85
Edgar	1097–1107	James VII	1685–89
Alexander I	1107–24	William II	1689–1702
David I	1124–53	and Mary	1689–94
Malcolm IV	1153–65	Anne	1702–7

Monarchs of Wales

Name	Reign
Gwynedd	
Rhodir Mawhr (Rhodri the Great)	844–78
Anarawad ap Rhodri	878–916
Idwal the Bald	916–42
Hywel Dda (Hywel the Good)	942–50
Ieuaf ad Idwal; Iago ap Idwal	950–69; 950–79
Hywel ap Ieuaf	979–85
Cadwallon ap Ieuaf	985–86
Maredudd ap Owain	986–99
Cynan ap Hywel	999–1005
Llewlyn ap Seisyll	1005–23
Iago ap Idwal ap Meurig	1023–39
Gruffydd ap Llwelyn	1039–63
Rhiwallon ap Cynfyn; Bleddyn ap Cyfyn	1063–70; 1063–75
Trahaern ap Caradog	1075–81
Gruffydd ap Cynan	1081–1137
Owain Gwynedd	1137–70
East Gwynedd	
Dafydd ab Owain	1170–95
West Gwynedd	
Rhodri ab Owain	1170–90
Gwynedd, Restored	
Llwelyn ap Iorwerth	1195–1240
Dafydd ap Llywelyn	1240–46
Owain Goch; Llywelyn ap Gruffydd	1246–55; 1246–82
Dafydd ap Gruffydd	1282–83
Deheubarth	
Hywel Dda (Hywel the Good)	920–950
Interregnun	
Owain ap Hywel	954–86
Maredudd ap Owain	986–99
Cynan ap Hywel	999–1005
Edwin and Cadell ap Einion	1005–18
Llywelyn ap Seisyll	1018–23
Rhydderch ab Iestyn	1023–33
Hywel ap Edwin	1033–44
Interregnum	
Gruffydd ap Rhydderch	1047–55

Gruffydd ap Llywelyn	1055–63
Maredudd ap Owain	1063–72
Rhys ap Owain	1072–78
Rhys ap Tewdwr	1078–93
Interregnum (Norman possession)	
Gruffydd ap Rhys	1116–36
Anarawd ap Gruffydd	1136–43
Cadell ap Gruffydd	1143–51
Maredudd ap Gruffydd	1151–55
Rhys ap Gruffydd	1155–97
Gruffydd ap Rhys	1197–1201
Powys	
Bleddyn ap Cynfy	1063–75
Maredudd ap Bleddyn	1116–32
Madog ap Maredudd	1132–60
Southern Powys	
Owain Cyfeiliog	1160–95
Gwenwynwyn	1195–1216
Gruffydd ap Gwenwynwyn	1240–57; r 1263–74; r 1277–86
Northern Powys	
Gruffudd Maelor I	1160–91
Madog ap Gruffudd	1191–1236
Gruffydd Maelor II	1236–69

British royal posts

Lord Paramount of Holdernesse (first appointed in 1071)

The duties of this position include – according to legend – the firing of arrows bearing symbolic gold coins into the North Sea to ward off Danish invaders.

Lord High Almoner (1103)

Once the organiser of many different court ceremonies. The High Almoner's role is now limited to supervising the Queen's handing out of specially minted Maundy Money, on the Thursday before Easter, to a group of people numbering the years of her life so far.

Lord of the Isles, Prince and Great Steward of Scotland

This title, partly derived from the 1130s, is now given to the royal heir apparent.

Lord Warden of the Cinque Ports, Constable of Dover Castle, and Admiral of the Cinque Ports

A title made official in 1268. It entailed responsibility for defence of the towns, once major ports, of Hythe, Dover, Hastings, Romney and Sandwich.

Hereditary Master of the Royal Household, High Justiciar of Argyll, Admiral of the Western Isles, High Sheriff of Argyll and Keeper of the Royal Castles of Carrick, Dunoon, Dunstaffnage, Sween and Tarbert

These titles effectively became combined over a period of time from the C13 to C18.

Governor of the Military Knights and the Military Knights of Windsor (1348)

Down several centuries the Military Knights have had a variety of names; throughout, they have been paid to observe the chivalric rituals of the College of St George, at Windsor Castle.

Speaker to the House of Commons (1376)

The Speaker's duties include keeping order during debates. By tradition each new Speaker is brought into the Commons by force – a reflection of the job's earlier hazards in facing down powerful monarchs.

Dam de Rosel and Butler to the Duke of Normandy

From 1376 this hereditary post used to demand that the holder carried any visiting English ruler, who was also Duke or Duchess of Normandy, through the waves from ship to shore whenever the monarch visited the Channel Island of Jersey. Nowadays the Dam de Rosel merely has to greet the Queen on the arrival of the royal aircraft.

Resident Governor of the Tower of London and Keeper of the Crown Jewels

The first 'Keper of ye Kinges Jewells' was appointed in 1378; after an eventful history this role was combined with that of Resident Governor in 1967.

Provost of Eton (1440)

Originally the Provost was appointed to run Eton College as a school for poor boys only.

Master of the Corporation of Trinity House (1514)

The corporation's roles include supervising all navigation around the coasts of Britain, and guiding the monarch's vessel in home waters.

The Royal Watermen and the Queen's Bargemaster

Royal bargemasters were extant in medieval times; the Watermen are members of the Worshipful Company of Watermen and Lightermen established by Act of Parliament in 1555.

Marshall of the Diplomatic Corps

As Master of Ceremonies, from the early years of James I's reign this official has overseen the monarch's encounters with visiting diplomats.

Poet Laureate (1668)

A position whose responsibilities continue to evolve, away from the court and towards the country as a whole.

Gold Stick in Waiting

Following the 'Popish Plot' of 1678 alleged against Charles II, a personal bodyguard to the king was appointed under this title. It is traditionally held by a colonel of the Life Guards, whose potential replacement would stand in as Silver Stick.

Painter and Limner in Ordinary (1702)

Portraitist to the monarch and other members of the royal family.

Knight Grand Cross of the Most Honourable Order of the Bath (1725)

This title revived a medieval name, established when bathing was strongly symbolic because unusual.

Piper to Her Majesty/Page of the Presence (1843)

One of several court titles combining more than one function. There are three Pages of the Presence, who oversee the royal reception of visitors.

Prelate to the Order of St John (1888)

Leader of a revived order – in full the Most Venerable Order of the Hospital of St John of Jerusalem – whose history stretches back to the eleventh-century Knights Hospitaller, and which has connections to several first-aid organisations.

Registrar of the Imperial Society of Knights Bachelor (1908)
The foundation of this organisation formalised a tradition of Knights Bachelor dating from the reign of Henry III (1216–72).

Counsellors of State
Laws governing the Council of State were last modernised in 1953; if the monarch becomes incapable, this body, made up from members of the royal family, is responsible for any Regency.

First Minister and Keeper of the Scottish Seal (1999)
Appointed on the establishment of the Scottish Parliament.

Harpist to the Prince of Wales (2000)
This post revives a tradition created in the early seventeenth century by James I.

Prime Ministers of Britain

Name	Date	
Sir Robert Walpole	1721–42	W
Sir Spencer Compton, Earl of Wilmington	1742–43	W
Henry Pelham	1743–46	W
Sir William Pulteney, Earl of Bath	1746	W
Henry Pelham	1746–54	W
Sir Thomas Pelham-Holles, Duke of Newcastle upon Tyne	1754–56	W
Sir William Cavendish, Duke of Devonshire	1756–57	W
James Waldegrave, Earl of Waldegrave	1757	W
Sir Thomas Pelham-Holles, Duke of Newcastle upon Tyne	1757–62	W
Sir John Stuart, Earl of Bute	1762–63	T
George Grenville	1763–65	W
Lord Charles Watson-Wentworth, Marquess of Rockingham	1765–66	W
William Pitt (the Elder), Earl of Chatham	1766–68	W
Sir Augustus Henry FitzRoy, Duke of Grafton	1768–70	W
Lord North	1770–82	T
Lord Charles Watson-Wentworth, Marquess of Rockingham	1782	W
Sir William Petty, Earl of Shelburne	1782–83	Coal

Name	Date	
Sir William Henry Cavendish Bentnick, Duke of Portland	1783	T
William Pitt (the Younger)	1783–01	T
Henry Addington	1801–04	T
William Pitt	1804–06	T
William Wyndham Grenville, Baron Grenville	1806–07	W
Sir William Henry Cavendish Bentinck, Duke of Portland	1807–09	T
Spencer Perceval	1809–12	T
Sir Robert Banks Jenkinson, Earl of Liverpool	1812–27	T
George Canning	1827	T
Frederick John Robinson, Viscount Goderich	1827–28	T
Sir Arthur Wellesley, Duke of Wellington	1828–30	T
Sir Charles Grey, Earl Grey	1830–34	W
Sir William Lamb, Viscount Melbourne	1834	W
Sir Robert Peel	1834–35	T
Sir William Lamb, Viscount Melbounre	1835–41	W
Sir Robert Peel	1841–46	T
Lord John Russell	1846–52	W
Sir Edward Geoffrey Smith-Stanley, Earl of Derby	1852	T
Sir George Hamilton Gordon, Earl of Aberdeen	1852–55	P
Sir Henry John Temple, Viscount Palmerston	1855–58	L
Sir Edward Geoffrey Smith-Stanley, Earl of Derby	1858–59	C
Sir Henry John Temple, Viscount Palmerston	1859–65	L
Lord John Russell	1865–66	L
Sir Edward Smith-Stanley, Earl of Derby	1866–68	C
Benjamin Disraeli, Lord Beaconsfield	1868	C
William Ewart Gladstone	1868–74	L
Benjamin Disraeli	1874–80	C
William Ewart Gladstone	1880–85	L
Robert Arthur Talbot Gascoyne-Cecil, Marquess of Salisbury	1885–86	C
William Ewart Gladstone	1886	L
Robert Arthur Talbot Gascoyne-Cecil,	1886–92	C
William Ewart Gladstone	1892–94	L
Sir Archibald Philip Primrose, Earl of Rosebery	1894–95	L

Robert Arthur Talbot Gascoyne-Cecil, Marquess of Salisbury	1895–02	C
Arthur James Balfour	1902–05	C
Sir Henry Campbell-Bannerman	1905–08	L
Herbert Henry Asquith	1908–15	L
Herbert Henry Asquith	1915–16	Coal
David Lloyd George	1916–22	Coal
Andrew Bonar Law	1922–23	C
Stanley Baldwin	1923–24	C
James Ramsay MacDonald	1924	S
Stanley Baldwin	1924–29	C
James Ramsay MacDonald	1929–31	S
James Ramsay MacDonald	1931–35	NC
Stanley Baldwin	1935–37	NC
Neville Chamberlain	1937–40	NC
Sir Winston Churchill	1940–45	Coal
Sir Winston Churchill	1945	C
Clement Attlee	1945–51	S
Sir Winston Churchill	1951–55	C
Anthony Eden	1955–57	C
Harold Macmillan	1957–63	C
Sir Alexander Douglas-Home	1963–64	C
Sir Harold Wilson	1964–70	S
Sir Edward Heath	1970–74	C
Sir Harold Wilson	1974–76	S
Sir James Callaghan	1976–79	S
Margaret Thatcher	1979–90	C
John Major	1990–97	C
Tony Blair	1997	S

Key to political affiliations:
Coal = Coalition, C = Conservative, L = Liberal, NC = National Coalition, P = Peelite, S = Socialist, T = Tory, W = Whig

Speakers of the British House of Commons

The speaker is the presiding officer of a legislative body, and is so called in, for example, the House of Representatives in the US and Australia, or the House of Commons in Britain and Canada. There have been a hundred and fifty-six Speakers so far in the British House of Commons; those named below have held this office during or after the year when the current direct line of British monarchs was established, with the first Hanoverian, George I. The date given in each case is that of the Speaker's election.

Sir Thomas Hanmer, 16 February 1714
Spencer Compton (Earl of Wilmington), 17 March 1715
Arthur Onslow, 23 January 1728
Sir John Cust, 3 November 1761
Sir Fletcher Norton, 22 January 1770
Charles Cornwall, 31 October 1780
Hon William Grenville, 5 January 1789
Henry Addington, 8 June 1789
Sir John Mitford (Lord Redesdale), 11 February 1801
Charles Abbot (Lord Colchester), 10 February 1802
Charles Manners-Sutton (Viscount Canterbury), 2 June 1817
James Abercromby (Lord Dunfermline), 19 February 1835
Charles Shaw-Lefevre (Viscount Eversley), 27 May 1839
J Evelyn Denison (Viscount Ossington), 30 April 1857
Sir Henry Brand (Viscount Hampden), 9 February 1872
Arthur Wellesley Peel (Viscount Peel), 26 February 1884
William Gully (Viscount Selby), 10 April 1895
James Lowther (Viscount Ullswater), 8 June 1905
John Whitley, 27 April 1921
Hon Edward Fitzroy, 20 June 1928
Douglas Clifton-Brown, 2 March 1943
William Morrison, 31 October 1951
Sir Harry Hylton-Foster, 20 October 1959
Horace King (Lord Maybray-King), 26 October 1965
Selwyn Lloyd (Lord Selwyn-Lloyd), 12 January 1971
George Thomas (Viscount Tonypandy), 2 February 1976
Bernard Weatherill (Lord Weatherill), 15 June 1983
Betty Boothroyd, 27 April 1992
Michael Martin, 23 October 2000

Presidents of the United States of America

No	Name	b–d	President	
1	George Washington	1732–1799	1789–1797	
2	John Adams	1735–1826	1797–1801	F
3	Thomas Jefferson	1743–1826	1801–1809	DR
4	James Madison	1751–1836	1809–1817	DR
5	James Monroe	1758–1831	1817–1825	DR
6	John Quincy Adams	1767–1848	1825–1829	DR
7	Andrew Jackson	1767–1845	1829–1837	D

8	Martin Van Buren	1782–1862	1837–1841	D
9	William Henry Harrison	1773–1841	1841	W
10	John Tyler	1790–1862	1841–184	W
11	James Knox Polk	1795–1849	1845–1849	D
12	Zachary Taylor	1784–1850	1849–1850	W
13	Millard Fillmore	1800–1874	1850–1853	W
14	Franklin Pierce	1804–1869	1853–1857	D
15	James Buchanan	1791–1868	1857–1861	D
16	Abraham Lincoln	1809–1865	1861–1865	R
17	Andrew Johnson	1808–1875	1865–1869	NU
18	Ulysses Simpson Grant	1822–1885	1869–1877	R
19	Rutherford Birchard Hayes	1822–1893	1877–1881	R
20	James Abram Garfield	1831–1881	1881	R
21	Chester Alan Arthur	1830–1886	1881–1885	R
22	Stephen Grover Cleveland	1837–1908	1885–1889	D
23	Benjamin Harrison	1833–1901	1889–1893	R
24	Stephen Grover Cleveland	1837–1908	1893–1897	D
25	William McKinley	1843–1901	1897–1901	R
26	Theodore Roosevelt	1858–1919	1901–1909	R
27	William Howard Taft	1857–1930	1909–1913	R
28	Thomas Woodrow Wilson	1856–1924	1913–1921	D
29	Warren Gamaliel Harding	1865–1923	1921–1923	R
30	John Calvin Coolidge	1872–1933	1923–1929	R
31	Herbert Clark Hoover	1874–1964	1929–1933	R
32	Franklin Delano Roosevelt	1874–1964	1933–1945	D
33	Harry S Truman	1884–1972	1945–1953	D
34	Dwight David Eisenhower	1890–1969	1953–1961	R
35	John Fitzgerald Kennedy	1917–1963	1961–1963	D
36	Lyndon Baines Johnson	1908–1973	1963–1969	D
37	Richard Milhous Nixon	1913–1994	1969–1974	R
38	Gerald Rudolph Ford	1913–	1974–1977	R
39	James Earl Carter	1924–	1977–1981	D
40	Ronald Wilson Reagan	1911–2004	1981–1989	R
41	George Herbert Walker Bush	1924–	1989–1993	R
42	William Jefferson Clinton	1946–	1993–2001	D
43	George W Bush	1946–	2001–	R

Key to political affiliations:
D = Democratic, DR = Democratic Republican, F = Federalist, N = National Union, W = Whig

US Presidential elections are held on the First Monday of November, normally every four years. Election is by a majority of votes in the Electoral College, which comprises 538 electors divided between the states: one for each of the 100 Senators and 435 Representatives – plus, since 1964, three Electors for the District of Columbia. The victorious candidate thus receives at least 270 votes.

Nobel Peace Prizewinners

A quarter of a century of the Nobel Peace Prize

Alfred Bernhard Nobel (1833–96) was a Swedish industrial chemist chiefly remembered for inventing dynamite (1867) and leaving money to award prizes for excellence in various fields. Most of the prizewinners are chosen by Swedish academics; the Peace Prizewinners are chosen by a committee elected by the Norwegian Parliament, and the Prize for Economics, in memory of Alfred Nobel, has been financed by the Swedish National Ban since 1969.

The Peace prize was initiated in 1901 but has not been awarded every year. The Committee has not always been able to find a worthy candidate, and sometimes the world has been in such a convulsion of war that awarding the prize was clearly impossible. The years in which it has not been awarded are 1914–16, 1918, 1923–4, 1928, 1932, 1939–43, 1955–6, 1966–7, 1972. The Peace Prize may be awarded to organisations as well as individuals and not infrequently given as a joint award if, for instance, two leaders in a negotiation have both taken exceptional personal and political risks. In addition to immense prestige there is also a financial benefit to the winner which can be considerable. Médicins Sans Frontières, for example, were given $1.4 million with their prize.

With the clarity of hindsight we can see that some of the solutions for which prizes were granted did not last for long (as in the Middle East). Cynicism is too easy. The prize has been won by many dogged and courageous individuals who have devoted their lives to peace or human rights in perilous circumstances. Organisations such as Amnesty International or Médicins sans Frontières are also hugely deserving. However, there have been winners who in retrospect seem less appropriate. The sardonic American singer/mathematician, Tom Lehrer, maintains that he stopped writing songs after Secretary of State Henry Kissinger (author of a secret policy to bomb Cambodia) won the prize in 1973. Lehrer said that the world had become too much of an ironic parody of itself to be satirised any further.

2003 Shirin Ebadi (1947–), the first Iranian woman judge, for her efforts for democracy and human rights

2002 Jimmy Carter Jr, (1924–), former President of the United States of America, for his decades of effort since his presidency to find peaceful solutions to international conflicts and to promote economic and social development.

2001 United Nations and Kofi Annan (*b* Ghana 1939), United Nations Secretary General Kofi Annan is regarded as the best Secretary-General for a generation; he has raised the profile of the UN and used its prestige to advantage in many conflicts. The organisation remains handicapped by the chronic inability of some of its members to pay their dues (the USA being the worst offender), but for all its many problems it is a vital international forum that has become more strategically important in the new millennium.

2000 Kim Dae Jung (1925–) for his work for democracy and human rights in South Korea and in East Asia in general, and for his efforts to seek reconciliation with North Korea.

1999 Doctors Without Borders (Médecins Sans Frontières), is based in Brussels, Belgium. This organisation was founded in France in 1971 and now recruits medical staff from all over the world. Wherever there is a humanitarian crisis, exhausted-looking MSF doctors can be found doing their best for people, independently of any political interest.

1998 John Hume (1937–, leader of the Social Democratic and Labour Party – the SDLP) and David Trimble (1944–, the leader of the Ulster Unionists) for their efforts to find a peaceful solution to the conflict in Northern Ireland. Peace in Northern Ireland is still fragile but, after decades of fighting and bombing since the latest round of Troubles began in the 1970s, it seems to be holding.

1997 International Campaign to Ban Landmines (ICBL) and Jody Williams for their work for the banning and clearing of anti-personnel mines. The world's conflict zones are littered with millions of landmines that continue to kill and maim (especially children) for years after placement. Diana, Princess of Wales, was associated with this cause, but American academic Jody Williams is the passionate, clever and determined person behind the organisation.

1996 Carlos Felipe Ximenes Belo (1949–, a Catholic Bishop) and Jose Ramos-Horta (1949–) for their work towards a peaceful solution to the conflict in East Timor, a disputed area whose independence was brutally resisted by Indonesia.

1995 Joseph Rotblat and to the Pugwash Conferences on Science and World Affairs for their efforts to diminish the part played by nuclear arms in international politics. Joseph Rotblat (*b* Poland 1908) is the veteran physicist who worked on the Manhattan Project and thereafter devoted his life to medical physics and nuclear disarmament. The

Pugwash conferences are meetings of scientists who want to use science and technology in the interests of all mankind; they started in Pugwash, Canada in 1957.

1994 Yasser Arafat, Chairman of the Executive Committee of the PLO, President of the Palestinian National Authority; **Shimon Peres**, Foreign Minister of Israel; **Yitzhak Rabin**, Prime Minister of Israel. All three shared the prize for their efforts to create peace in the Middle East. Rabin, Israeli Prime Minister twice (1974–77 and 1992–95), was assassinated in 1995 by a right-wing zealot. Peres (*b* 1923 in Poland) then became Prime Minister until 1996. Yasser Arafat is still Chairman of the PLO. The Palestine/Israel conflict shows no sign of solution.

1993 Nelson Mandela, Leader of the African National Congress (ANC), and **Fredrik Willem De Klerk**, President of the Republic of South Africa, shared the prize for their success in dismantling apartheid in South Africa. Mandela (1918–) spent 26 years in jail before being released in 1990. He became president (1994–99). In 1990 F.W. de Klerk had suspended executions, unbanned the ANC and removed restrictions on political groups.

1992 Rigoberta Menchu Tum won the prize for her courageous campaign for human rights, especially for indigenous peoples, in Guatemala.

1991 Aung San Suu Kyi (1945–) was awarded the prize for human rights advocacy in Burma (Myanmar). She has led the opposition against the military regime for many years at great personal cost, much of that time under house arrest.

1990 Mikhail Sergeyevich Gorbachev, President of the USSR, helped to bring the Cold War to an end. Gorbachev (1931–) introduced *perestroika* (restructuring) into the creaky Soviet economy and allowed a greater degree of civil liberty by a policy of openness (*glasnost*). He changed the world but, as is often the case, he was regarded more highly abroad than at home.

1989 The 14th Dalai Lama (Tenzin Gyatso, 1935–), the religious and political leader of the Tibetan people, was given the prize for his commitment to non-violence. He is a spiritual leader with enormous moral prestige.

1988 The United Nations Peace-Keeping Forces. UN soldiers with their characteristic blue berets have contributed to peace-keeping missions for fifty years. Some 500,000 have been deployed and 731 have been killed on active service. The UN has no standing army and has to rely on forces supplied by its members.

1987 Oscar Arias Sanchez (1941–) President of Costa Rica, was awarded as the initiator of complex peace negotiations with Honduras, Nicaragua, Guatemala and El Salvador. Dr Arias is a lawyer who has studied in the USA and Britain.

1986 Elie Wiesel, naturalised American, Chairman of 'The President's Commission on the Holocaust'. Wiesel (1928–) survived the holocaust and became an international lawyer, author and humanitarian.

1985 International Physicians for the Prevention of Nuclear War. This organisation is based in Boston, MA, and lobbies the powerful.

1984 Desmond Mpilo Tutu, South Africa, Bishop of Johannesburg (1985–6) and Archbishop of Cape Town (1986–96), former Secretary General South African Council of Churches (SACC) for his work against apartheid. Bishop Tutu (1931–) has an extrovert and forgiving nature; the force of his personality has been deployed to advantage in the post-apartheid government's Commission for Truth and Reconciliation.

1983 Lech Walesa (1943–), Polish founder of Solidarity, won the prize as a campaigner for human rights. Solidarity broke the military government of Poland and helped to create the climate for the final collapse of the Soviet communist system in 1989. He became president of Poland in their first post-Soviet election, but was not regarded as all that effective.

1982 Alva Myrdal, former Cabinet Minister, diplomat, delegate to United Nations General Assembly on Disarmament, and **Alfonso García Robles,** diplomat, delegate to the United Nations General Assembly on Disarmament, former Secretary for Foreign Affairs, were jointly awarded the prize for their work on disarmament. Alva Myrdal (1902–86) was a Swedish writer and diplomat who fought tirelessly for disarmament. Robles (1911–91), a Mexican diplomat, was also a committed campaigner.

1981 Office of the United Nations High Commissioner for Refugees or UNHCR as it is normally called, is based in Geneva, Switzerland. It was established in 1951 and it works with refugees, mainly co-ordinating the efforts of other agencies though sometimes funding help for the most needy. The tide of desperate humanity displaced by wars and natural disasters has not abated since the Second World War.

1980 Adolfo Perez Esquivel, an Argentine architect and sculptor (1931–), was awarded the prize for his perilous work defending human rights under a military government.

1979 Mother Teresa, leader of the Order of the Missionaries of Charity, was given the prize for herself and her Order for their work with the poor and damaged children of Calcutta. She was born in Skopje, Macedonia, in 1910 and died in Calcutta in 1997.

1978 The prize was a joint award to Mohamed Anwar Al-Sadat, President of the Arab Republic of Egypt, and Menachem Begin, Prime Minister of Israel, for jointly negotiating peace between Egypt and Israel. Sadat was bitterly criticised by other Arab statesmen and was assassinated by extremists in Cairo in 1981. Begin (*b* Belarus 1913 – *d* Israel 1992) was a former leader of the Irgun Zvai Leumi resistance group in British-mandated Palestine. In 1973 he led the Likud front, a right-of-centre nationalist party.

Modes of address

Membership of the British peerage ranks as follows:

Royal Dukes, Dukes, Marquesses, Earls, Countesses in their own right, Viscounts, Barons, Baronesses in their own right. For convenience the titles listed here are given alphabetically.

Baron

The Right Hon Lord – (envelope, formal)
The Lord – (envelope, social)
My Lord (letter, formal)
Dear Lord – (letter, social)
Lord – (spoken)

Baron's wife

The Right Hon Lady —— (envelope, formal)
The Lady —— (envelope, social)
My Lady (letter, formal)
Dear Lady —— (letter, social)
Lady —— (spoken)

Baron's children

The Hon [forename surname] —— (envelope)
Dear Mr/Miss/Mrs —— [surname] (letter)
Mr/Miss/Mrs —— [surname] (spoken)

Baroness in own right

The Right Hon Lady/The Right Hon the Baroness —— (envelope, formal)
The Baroness/The Lady —— (envelope, social)
My Lady (letter, formal)
Dear Lady —— (letter, social)
Lady —— (spoken)

Baronet

Sir [forename surname] Bt (envelope)
Dear Sir —— (letter, formal)
Dear Sir [forename] (letter, social)
Sir [forename] (spoken)

Baronet's wife

Lady [surname] (envelope)
Dear Madam (letter, formal)
Dear Lady [surname] (letter, social)
Lady [surname] (spoken)

Countess in own right

The Right Hon the Countess [of] —— (envelope, formal)
The Countess [of] —— (envelope, social)
Madam (letter, formal)
Lady —— (letter, social)
Madam (spoken, formal)
Lady —— (spoken, social)

Dame

Dame [forename surname] (plus any post-nominal letters) (envelope)
Dear Madam (letter, formal)
Dear Dame [forename] (letter, social)
Dame [forename] (spoken)

Duke

His Grace the Duke of —— (envelope, formal)
The Duke of —— (envelope, social)

My Lord Duke (letter, formal)
Dear Duke —— (letter, social)
Your Grace (spoken, formal)
Duke —— (spoken, social)

Duke's wife
Her Grace the Duchess of —— (envelope, formal)
The Duchess of —— (envelope, social)
Dear Madam (letter, formal)
Dear Duchess (letter, social)
Duchess (spoken)

Duke's eldest son
As a courtesy title a Duke's heir apparent uses the highest of his father's other titles. Being holder of a courtesy title, he is not addressed as 'The Most Hon.' or 'The Right Hon'; in correspondence 'The' is left out before the title. The heir apparent to a Scottish title may be styled 'Master' (see below).

Duke's younger sons
Lord [forename surname] (envelope)
My Lord (letter, formal)
Dear Lord [forename] (letter, social)
My Lord (spoken, formal)
Lord [forename] (spoken, social)

Duke's daughter
Lady [forename surname] (envelope)
Dear Madam (letter, formal)
Dear Lady [forename] (letter, social)
Lady [forename] (spoken)

Earl
The Right Hon the Earl of —— (envelope, formal)
The Earl of —— (envelope, social)
My Lord (letter, formal)
Dear Lord —— (letter, social)
My Lord (spoken, formal)
Lord —— (spoken, social)

Earl's wife

The Right Hon the Countess [of] —— (envelope, formal)
The Countess [of] —— (envelope, social)
Madam (letter, formal)
Lady —— (letter, social)
Madam (spoken, formal)
Lady —— (spoken, social)

Earl's children

Eldest son: As a courtesy title an Earl's heir apparent uses the highest of his father's other titles. Being holder of a courtesy title, he is not addressed as 'The Most Hon' or 'The Right Hon'; in correspondence 'The' is left out before the title. The heir apparent to a Scottish title may be styled 'Master' (see below).
Younger sons: The Hon [forename surname] (envelope)
Dear Mr [surname] (letter)
Mr [surname] (spoken)
Daughters: Lady [forename surname] (envelope)
Dear Madam (letter, formal)
Dear Lady [forename] (letter, social)
Lady [forename] (spoken)

Knight (Bachelor)

Sir [forename surname] (envelope)
Dear Sir (letter, formal)
Dear Sir [forename] (letter, social)
Sir [forename] (spoken)

Knight (Orders of Chivalry)

Sir [forename surname] (plus any post-nominal letters) (envelope)
Dear Sir (letter, formal)
Dear Sir [forename] (letter, social)
Sir [forename] (spoken)

Knight's wife

Lady [surname] (envelope)
Dear Madam (letter, formal)
Dear Lady [surname] (letter, social)
Lady [surname] (spoken)

Marquess

The Most Hon the Marquess of —— (envelope, formal)
The Marquess of —— (envelope, social)
My Lord (letter, formal)
Dear Lord —— (letter, social)
My Lord (spoken, formal)
Lord —— (spoken, social)

Marquess's wife

The Most Hon the Marchioness of —— (envelope, formal)
The Marchioness of —— (envelope, social)
Madam (letter, formal)
Dear Lady —— (letter, social)
Lady —— (spoken)

Marquess's children

Eldest son: As a courtesy title a Marquess's heir apparent uses the highest of his father's other titles. Being holder of a courtesy title, he is not addressed as 'The Most Hon' or 'The Right Hon'; in correspondence 'The' is left out before the title. The heir apparent to a Scottish title may be styled 'Master' (see below).
Younger sons: Lord [forename surname] (envelope)
My Lord (letter, formal)
Dear Lord [forename] (letter, social)
My Lord —— (spoken, formal)
Lord [forename] (spoken, social)
Daughters: Lady [forename surname] (envelope)
Dear Madam (letter, formal)
Dear Lady [forename] (letter, social)
Lady [forename] (spoken)

Master

This title is used by the heir apparent to a Scottish peerage; mostly, however, the heir apparent to a Duke, Marquess or Earl will be styled instead by his courtesy title.
The Master of —— (envelope)
Dear Sir (letter, formal)
Dear Master of —— (letter, social)
Master, or Sir (spoken, formal)
Master, or Mr [surname] (spoken, social)

Master's wife

As for the appropriate form of peerage; otherwise as Mrs [surname]

Privy Counsellor

The Right (or Rt) Hon [forename surname] (envelope)
Dear Mr/Miss/Mrs [surname] (letter)
After the name the letters PC are not used, except when the Privy Counsellor is a peer below the rank of Marquess. In this case he or she will be styled 'The Right Hon', with the prefix 'The Right Hon' used together with any post-nominal letters.

Viscount

The Right Hon the Viscount ——— (envelope, formal)
The Viscount ——— (envelope, social)
My Lord (letter, formal)
Dear Lord ——— (letter, social)
Lord (spoken)

Viscount's wife

The Right Hon the Viscountess of ——— (envelope, formal)
The Viscountess ——— (envelope, social)
Madam (letter, formal)
Dear Lady ——— (letter, social)
Lady ——— (spoken)

Viscount's children

The Hon [forename surname] (envelope)
Dear Mr/Miss/Mrs [surname] (letter)
Mr/Miss/Mrs [surname] (spoken)

Some political scandals – a sample ...

'To be governed is to be watched, inspected, directed, indoctrinated, numbered, estimated, regulated, commanded, controlled, law-driven, preached at, spied upon, censored, checked, valued, enrolled – and by creatures who have neither the right, nor the wisdom, nor the virtue to do so.'

Pierre-Joseph Proudhon

Sir John Trevor (1637–1717) was Speaker of the House of Commons in the late C17 and one of the ugliest and most corrupt parliamentarians of all time. He had a lecherous squint which often caused confusion as he appeared to be looking at one Honourable Member while calling on another to speak. He took bribes from the City of London Corporation to ensure the passage of a measure to compensate them for debts incurred discharging their responsibility for orphans. He also received money from the East India Company for legislation helpful to their interests. Finally his corruption was so manifest that the other Members were embarrassed enough to draft a resolution condemning their own Speaker for 'high crime and misdemeanour'. It was the Speaker's duty to place the business of the day before the House, so it would have fallen to Sir Trevor to read his own indictment. However, he sent the House a sick note on the day in question, in 1694, followed by another when that particular item was postponed. He never returned to Parliament.

John Wilkes MP (1727–97) was a brilliant orator, a champion of liberty and an upholder of press freedom. He was also a compulsive womaniser and one of the most debauched men who ever lived. Although fearsomely ugly, he was very witty and boasted that 'he could talk away his face in half an hour'. He was famously quick with a put-down. When Lord Sandwich said he would die either upon the gallows or of the pox, Wilkes replied that it would depend on whether he embraced his Lordship's principles or his mistress. Wilkes bribed his way into Parliament spending £7,000 – a fortune in those days – on the voters of Aylesbury. Honourable Members could not be arrested for debt. He was a founder member of the Hellfire Club, a society of privileged rakes devoted to inventive depravities. Despite his awesome and unrelenting sexual appetite, he was an anti-royalist radical and in many ways politically admirable.

George Washington (1732–97), the first President of the United States, was a slave-owner and a competent soldier with service in the French and Indian wars as well as in the struggle for independence. But Bill Clinton is only the latest in a long line of philanderers. While the father of the nation was fighting the British he made sure he had a congressman procuring for him so that he never had to waste time on finding his own women when he returned from the front. The first of many hand-picked comforts was an Indian squaw, but the best-known – for it was picked up by the *Boston Weekly News Letter* – was Kate, the washerwoman's daughter. His reputation as a womaniser was such that the daughters of any house where he was billeted had to take care. This aspect of his nature is seldom emphasised in the school textbooks.

William Ewart Gladstone (1808–98), leader of the Liberal Party and four times British Prime Minister, was the Grand Old Man of British Politics who fought for Irish Home Rule and laid the foundations for universal (though male) suffrage with his Reform Bill of 1884. He was also a fierce moralist who had a compulsion to save London prostitutes, especially the younger ones. His colleagues begged him to stop. Nobody is sure if Gladstone had sex with these unfortunates, though he admitted to terrible carnal temptation. It seems more likely that he enjoyed the self-chastisement and the whipping that he inflicted upon himself in order to curb his desires. It was said that before his expeditions to rescue fallen women, he would have his trousers sewn up.

Robert Boothby (1900–86), Conservative MP, was a brilliant parliamentarian, brought down by financial scandal in 1940. He was a delinquent charmer, outgoing and boisterous. He had a long affair with Harold Macmillan's wife, Dorothy, and nurtured a general liking for other men's wives. But it was an undeclared conflict of interest that expelled him from politics. Boothby had a weakness for gambling and always needed money. Just before the outbreak of war he agreed (for a commission) to help a friend try and unfreeze his wife's assets held in a bank in Czechoslovakia. When Germany invaded Czechoslavakia in March 1939, a formal Committee was established to represent the interests of all the claimants of Czech assets in Britain. Boothby was appointed chairman, but failed to mention that he already had a private interest in one of the larger claims. When this was discovered, he resigned. After the war he had a successful career in television and was forgiven by the Establishment with a peerage.

John Profumo (1918–) was Secretary of State for War in Harold Macmillan's Conservative government. The 1960s, in the swinging tabloid sense, were going well. Viscount Astor, a lavish host, threw famously naughty weekend parties for the good and the great at his country seat in Cliveden, and it was there that Profumo met a beautiful young woman called Christine Keeler and embarked upon a surreptitious affair. Married to Valerie Hobson, a fine actress and independently wealthy, he was also a minister in the government so discretion was essential. However, word soon got out. Keeler was enjoying a passionate relationship with Colonel Yevgeny Ivanov, the Russian naval attaché, who was already the target of a possible sexual 'honey trap' set by MI5. It was the height of the Cold War so the government minister in charge of defence sharing a young woman with a Russian embassy official and putative spy was clearly a security risk. Stephen Ward, an urbane and cultured osteopath with a society practice, was the centre of a group of the privileged who enjoyed the access that he offered to pretty girls like Christine Keeler and her friend, Mandy Rice-Davis. The Profumo story broke in March 1963 and continued for several months with ever more salacious revelations. Profumo lied in the House of Commons, was found out, and had to resign. Stories of high-level sexual shenanigans involving other ministers, including a naked man in a mask, continued to circulate. The scandal rocked the government, leaving Prime Minister Harold Macmillan wounded, and he soon resigned 'for health reasons'. Stephen Ward was vilified for his part in the business and was convicted of living on immoral earnings, but on 3 July 1963, before serving his sentence, he committed suicide. Lord Denning wrote a report on the whole affair which was supposed to concentrate on the security aspect, though he found time to dwell in considerable detail on who did what and to whom.

Reginald Maudling and John Poulson were linked in an extraordinary scandal that should have made Britons wake up to the corruption endemic in local government. Maudling was Chancellor of the Exchequer in the Conservative government that was voted out in 1964. After he lost the battle for the leadership of the party to Ted Heath in 1965, he must have decided to make some money. Using expertise and inside knowledge gained in the Treasury, he hugely increased his earnings by taking on many well-paid directorships. He also became a consultant for a company called Peachey Properties; there he met John Poulson, who ran a large architectural practice doing a great deal of work for local authorities. This was unsurprising given the methods Poulson used to secure contracts. These including bribery and the building of houses for strategically placed civil servants and dodgy local politicians like T. Dan Smith, a prominent Labour Party fixer in the North of England. Paying tax was also something that Peachey Properties found rather alien. In 1970 the Conservatives were returned to power and Maudling was appointed Home Secretary, a job whose responsibilities included the police. By 1972 Poulson was paying out so much cash by front-loading his contracts that the company went into bankruptcy; soon it attracted the attention of The Metropolitan Police Fraud Squad. Poulson went to jail – though not for long – and Maudling resigned, though he stayed on as a backbench MP until he died, in 1979. Prime Minister Heath maintained that Maudling was 'an honourable man'.

President Richard Milhous Nixon (1913–94) caused the Watergate scandal, the biggest of the century. Nixon, born in small-town California, saw himself as an outsider and always distrusted the liberal East Coast élite, which he saw as out to do him down. He certainly inspired dislike after the McCarthy House Un-American Activities Committee hearings, in which he appeared as a prosecuting lawyer with a mission to bring about the downfall of Alger Hiss. Twice Vice-President, Nixon was narrowly defeated for the presidency in 1960 by Democrat John F Kennedy in an election which was retrospectively revealed to have employed some vote-stuffing in key marginals in Chicago. Kennedy was everything Nixon hated: East Coast, Catholic, glamorous, rich and a Harvard man. Finally, in 1968, Nixon was elected by a wide margin as the 37th President of the USA, partly because of the public backlash against the Vietnam War and partly because his opponent, Hubert Humphrey, was decent but unexciting. Nixon distrusted the CIA and wanted a small intelligence department to report to him directly. Haldeman was his Chief of Staff, John Ehrlichman the Assistant for Domestic Affairs, and Charles Colson, Nixon's own special counsel. They established a unit of 50 people who became known as 'the plumbers' to do the President's dirty work. E Howard Hunt (ex–CIA) and Gordon Liddy (ex–FBI) were two of the action men. Nixon was re-elected in 1972, but felt he needed the advantage of knowing the Democrats' strategy. To this end he commissioned the plumbers to bug the Democrats' HQ, which was based in the ugly Watergate Hotel in Washington. The Committee to Re-elect the President (the apt acronym was CREEP) and the plumbers sub-contracted this work, but on 16 June 1972 an alert nightwatchman at the hotel heard them and called the police. On the sixth floor, five burglars were caught with eavesdropping kit and wads of money. It wasn't long before the chain of command led back to CREEP. Woodward and Bernstein, two reporters on the *Washington Post*, managed to link the break-in to Colson, perilously close to Nixon himself. Slowly more and more detail emerged. In May 1973 the Senate appointed a Special Investigator, Archibald Cox who, live on television, pieced together a pattern of wrong-doing that went back before Watergate to the break-in to the office of the psychiatrist who had been treating Daniel Ellsberg, the intelligence analyst who had leaked the Pentagon Papers (with their revelations about illegal bombing in Cambodia) back in 1971. Cox was patient and shrewd. Soon Nixon had to reveal that all his conversations in the White House were recorded, and when these tapes were subpoenaed a grim tale of paranoia and bilious trickery emerged. Many Americans were also dismayed by the profanity, and 'expletive deleted' from the transcripts became a euphemism for more robust language. The American people had always held the office of President in some reverence; their anguish continued for another year while the world looked on with palsied fascination and some *Schadenfreude*. On 8 August 1974, facing impeachment, Nixon resigned and was replaced by Gerry Ford, the only President never to be elected in any capacity. Lyndon Johnson said of him that he had played too much football without his helmet on. Ford pardoned Nixon a month later. Some have argued that the scandal marked the moment when we forever lost our innocence about our leaders.

Laurent Fabius and **President Mitterand** were in power for the scandal of the *Rainbow Warrior*. In France politicians have the legal right to a *vie privée* or private life. Besides, they take a Gallic view of sexual indiscretions and regard the excitable writhing of their anglophone neighbours on the subject as hypocrisy. This scandal, however, has to do with French dreams of being a major power in the world. In pursuit of this aim France has developed its own *force de frappe*, a nuclear deterrent on which it is very keen. The French technological base is well able to provide the expertise, and the supply of fissile material is no problem for a country which supplies the world's highest percentage of its electricity from nuclear power stations. In 1985 the French conducted a series of bomb tests near Mururoa Atoll in French Polynesia. Greenpeace was determined to stop the tests, or at least inconvenience the French amid a blaze of publicity, by repeatedly sailing into the test zone. But on 10 July 1985, as their boat the *Rainbow Warrior* was moored in Auckland Harbour, it was sunk by a bomb which killed a crew member. The New Zealand authorities soon arrested Alain and Sophie Turenge, who purported to be Swiss tourists but who were uncovered as French secret service agents called Alain Mafart and Dominique Prieur. There were three other French agents in the team in New Zealand who had returned to France. The French prime minister Fabius held an inquiry that inculpated the intelligence services and offered compensation to the family of the murdered Greenpeace photographer, but he still refused to extradite the other members of the secret service team back to New Zealand. Prieur and Mafart were tried in New Zealand, but the French – nothing if not *pratique* – applied a lot of pressure, threatening to boycott New Zealand butter from the EC. The compromise was that Prieur and Dominique would serve a shorter sentence on a French Polynesian island. The French reneged even on that and repatriated their agents as soon as possible. The relations between France and New Zealand have been cool ever since.

Roberto Calvi (1918–1980) was 'God's Banker'. Italian political scandals often involved the Mafia and the Catholic Church; this one had the extra ingredient of Freemasonry. In the 1970s Italy had been plagued by acts of violent Marxist terrorism, but the masonic lodge 'P–2' represented a threat from the right. In the welter of conspiracy theorising, it is hard to assess whether P–2 was ever the 'creeping coup' that Prime Minister Spadolini feared. Perhaps it was just slightly more sinister business as usual with well connected businessmen using its network to obtain contracts or cut through Italy's rococo bureaucratic procedures. P–2 was revealed to the world in 1981 when investigating magistrates in Milan were looking into affairs of a Sicilian financier called Michele Sindona who had exploited his P–2 connections to build a financial empire that excelled in money laundering. Calvi picked up the remnants of this operation and soon his Banco Ambrosiano was the largest private bank in Italy. Among its clients was the Vatican Bank, the Instituto per le Opere di Religione (the IOR) which, under the leadership of Archbishop Marcinkus, placed huge sums with Calvi whose expertise in moving money around the world discreetly enabled him, for example, to channel money to Solidarity, the anti-communist Polish trade union. However, Banco Ambrosiano had also lent the best part of a billion dollars to other banks and strange-looking front companies around the world. The head of P–2, Licio Gelli, was arrested in Switzerland trying to withdraw $55 million in cash from a bank, but he escaped custody after being spirited over the border to France and a waiting private jet. On 10 June 1980 Calvi disappeared in London, and was found on 18 June hanging from some scaffolding under Blackfriars Bridge, his pockets full of large sums of cash – and some bricks. Blackfriars Bridge is a location fraught with masonic symbolism.

Colonel Oliver North was the right-wing ultra-patriot behind the Iran-Contra affair, the complexity of which bored the public and obscured the importance of the scandal. President Ronald Reagan had been elected in 1980 partly as the result of President Carter's humiliating defeats over the Iran hostage crisis. Iran was a pariah, a 'terrorist state' with which the USA would not do business. It was therefore hugely compromising when in November 1986 Colonel Oliver North, an official of the National Security Council, and his associate, Major-General Secord, were revealed to have been actively selling arms to Iran. The National Security Advisor, Vice-Admiral Poindexter, was also in on the transactions. Why? Oliver North, a Vietnam veteran with an uneasy liking for uniform, was applying the money (though some of it stayed at home) to the supply of weapons and other material to the Contras in Nicaragua. This unfortunate small country in Central America had been under the despotic rule of General Samoza until he was overthrown by the radical socialist forces of the Sandinista National Liberation Front in 1979. Changes in US law prohibited the CIA from meddling in the affairs of other countries with the abandon they once enjoyed, so the only way of helping the counter-revolutionary forces in Nicaragua, the Contras, was by means of a subterfuge such as the one employed by Oliver North. In the subsequent inquiry Oliver North wrapped himself in the flag. Despite being revealed as something of a fantasist, he was only sentenced to community service. President Reagan, smiling affably if alarmingly, maintained that he just could not remember if he had authorised such an action, but as he was later revealed as suffering from the early stages of Alzheimer's Disease this may well be credible.

Margaret Thatcher (1925–) became leader of the Conservative party in 1975 and was Prime Minister from 1979–90. Many scandals occurred during her long stay in power, but few can be laid at her door personally with the exception of her blind spot about her boorish son, Mark, who was allowed to accompany her on a visit to the Middle East. There he shamelessly traded on her name for financial advantage. Her regime was characterised by a vengeful attitude to anybody who caused embarrassment. Thames Television was believed to have lost its valuable TV franchise to the egregiously bland Carlton because of a World in Action program about the shooting of three IRA men in Gibraltar. The pursuit of the former spy, Peter Wright, was a telling example of her approach. Wright had written a book, *Spycatcher*, in which he alleged that former MI5 director, Sir Roger Hollis, was a Soviet agent and that a ginger group inside the intelligence services had plotted to remove Labour Prime Minister Harold Wilson. Publication in the UK was prevented by the Official Secrets Act, but the book was published in the USA and also Australia where the British government obtained an injunction against it. The matter came to court, and the government lost, appealed and lost again. Injunctions were also obtained against many British newspapers. From

1986–88 Thatcher's dogged pursuit of this sour and not entirely convincing book acted as a huge promotional campaign in its favour – one funded by the British taxpayer.

Kamitaka Kuze, head of the Financial Commission in Japan, was forced to step down in August 2000 following the news that he had accepted over $2million from the Mitsubishi Trust and Banking Corporation. The links between the ruling coalition (the Liberal Democratic Party and several smaller parties) and big business in Japan are multitudinous and generally accepted as long as the economy is booming and nobody does anything too overt or triumphalist. Prime Minister Yoshiro Mori took what in the West would be an unusual step of publicly apologising for the fact that one of his appointees had been forced to resign. This scandal was one of many that involved politicians taking bribes from large corporations. Hatoyama, the leader of the opposition Democratic Party, said that the incident was only the tip of an iceberg of systematic corruption in the ruling coalition. Recently there are signs, according to Professor Iwai of Tokiwa University, that the Japanese voters are less forgiving than they used to be.

Marta Andreasen is the honest Argentine-born former Chief Accountant to the European Union which has an annual budget of over 100 billion euros (about the same number of US dollars). In 1999 all twenty Commissioners resigned following a corruption scandal. Commissioner Neil Kinnock, former leader of Britain's Labour Party, was going to drive hard for reform, but somehow the Commissioners are back and reform remains some way off. Marta Andreasen is a whistle-blower on a vast scale. She refused to sign off the 2001 European Commission accounts on the grounds that nepotism, corruption and sloppy accounting practices allowed huge sums to vanish without a paper trail. According to the auditors Deloittes some 8 billion euros have simply vanished. Though there are many decent MEPs, the structure of the EU with its relatively less powerful parliament and its appointed Commission and Council of Ministers has left a democratic deficit in its heart. Scandals are too numerous to list, but Eurostat, a privately owned information service company that works for the EU, deserves a mention. It did not just overcharge for work; using a dual set of books it invoiced for millions of euros for doing no work at all. In 1999 Edith Cresson, former French Prime Minister, was also charged with misappropriating EU funds. Five years later, very quietly, all charges against her were dropped for lack of evidence. Meanwhile Marta Andreasen is suspended on full pay, but not allowed into any EU buildings or even to give out her business card.

Spiritual

Occult leaders

Jalal ad-Din ar-Rumi In Turkey during the thirteenth century CE this Persian poet established the 'whirling' dervishes of the Mawlawi order. The dervish fraternities of the time were part of Islam's mystical tradition, and sought the ecstatic 'remembering' of God via repetitive rituals, often musical and sometimes using hashish. The whirling dervishes are distinguished by tall conical hats, and wide black robes, signifying death, that they discard as they begin to dance, spinning rhythmically. Underneath, their garments are white, to stand for resurrection.

Emanuel Swedenborg Swedish visionary and polymath, had no experience of clairvoyance – until the relatively late age of fifty-seven. But following an industrious life as a scientist, economist and legislator, eventually he began to have strange, often predictive visions. These even included knowledge of the day of his own death, in 1772, aged eighty-four. He maintained that a correspondence existed between the whole of the physical world and everything spiritual; also that God had given him a preview of the afterlife, in which no one was sentenced to any particular fate, but gravitated spontaneously to heaven or hell. Though Swedenborg lived and died a Lutheran, he saw himself as having a mission to help bring about the Church of the New Jerusalem. After his death such a sect, also called the Swedenborgian church, was formed, and today has members in many countries.

Helena Petrovna Blavatsky Founder of the Theosophical Society, in New York (1875); Blavatsky's doctrine blended philosophy and religious ideas in search of a spiritual existence beyond the material world. Later she carried her message to India, where the Society's headquarters remain. She claimed that modern theosophy derived from an ancient mysticism predominating in the intellectual traditions of India; also that it was deeply rooted in the culture of the West. Her spiritual ancestry, so she and her followers alleged, included not only Hinduism and Buddha, but Pythagoras, Plato and the Neoplatonists, the Gnostics and, among figures of the late Renaissance, the philosopher Jakob Boehme.

For a time Blavatsky enjoyed huge acclaim for her alleged psychic powers, based, she said, on her ability to communicate with 'masters'. These were described as spirits that had achieved perfection but nonetheless remained on earth, following a protracted series of reincarnations.

Despite the movement's retreat from ideas based on the paranormal, Blavatsky's teachings have done much to bring Westerners closer to an awareness of Oriental religions.

Samuel Liddell MacGregor Mathers (*d* 1918). Translator/Author of the book *The Kabbalah Unveiled* (1887), he was also an eccentric founder of a magical society called the Hermetic Order of the Golden Dawn; at that time, magic was fashionable, the Golden Dawn had branches all over Britain, and many well-known people were members. New members to the society were accepted as novices, later to be promoted to higher grades once various rituals and initiation rites had taken place. The society had much in common with Freemasonry, Rosicrucianism, and Theosophy – all of which are secret/semi-secret societies in which members enjoy the feeling of belonging to an élite group. An efficient organiser, Mathers was very much responsible for the devising of rituals for the Golden Dawn, and *The Kabbalah Unveiled* provided much of the material for these magical rituals.

He adopted the name MacGregor as his 'true ancestral name', claiming that his family had been MacGregors until the outlawing of that Scottish clan in 1603 – although modern researchers concur that his family connections extend no further north than Bedford, England. He also called himself 'Comte MacGregor de Glenstrae', professing that he had inherited the Franco-Scottish title from his great-great-grandfather – a title that he doubtless put to use later when he went to live in Paris. He died there destitute in 1918 – some said as a result of a curse placed upon him by Aleister Crowley (see below) who had been expelled from the Golden Dawn. Others believe he died in the virulent influenza epidemic of that year.

Aleister Crowley (né Edward Alexander Crowley) An upbringing of extraordinary sectarian strictness was the background against which this British-born satanist developed his self-image as an anti-Christ. Sexual experimentation, to which he applied himself rigorously, was seen by him as a source of black magic; 'satyr' was a description given by many who knew him. He also held that his excrement, freely deposited, was sacred. Tantrism was an influence; so too his preoccupation with The Book of the Revelation's Scarlet Woman, Mother of Harlots. Crowley had learnt his craft from Mathers of the Golden Dawn (see above) but eventually they fell out and Crowley is said to have sent Beelzebub and 49 attendant demons to attack Mathers. (Whether or not the troupe arrived is not known.) Crowley's creed, heavily sadistic, was expressed through writings including *The Book of the Law*, which he claimed was dictated to him by a spirit named Aiwass, source of pagan societies' alleged solar–phallic worship. This work was centred on Crowley's creed of 'Do what thou wilt', according to which personal freedom from restraint would confer godlike status on mankind.

In the later decades of Crowley's life he used drugs including mescalin in search of an ecstatic condition of boundless unity with the universe. These substances, along with alcohol abuse, led to a state of addiction that eventually (1947) proved fatal.

Gerald Gardner a follower of Aleister Crowley, was a leading contributor to the witchcraft revival known as Wicca. This movement, whose essential creed dwells on unity with nature, was enormously boosted by Gardner's books *Witchcraft Today* (1954) and *The Meaning of Witchcraft* (1959). Gardner claimed that a number of witchcraft covens could claim direct descent from medieval equivalents – themselves practising a fertility religion that went back to north European Paleolithic societies. Doubtful though this was, it had a widespread influence on the formation of new covens.

Wicca does not hold to a complex system of theories; in addition to the mother goddess of fertility its followers believe in a horned god of death and the afterlife. Despite the enduring influence of Gardnerism, with its personal connection to Crowley, modern witches do not hold to devil worship, but see Satan as a fiction put about by Christianity. 'Sky clad' rituals, *ie*, rites performed when naked, are by no means the norm, and white magic predominates, often in the form of incantations to repel harm or sickness. Scourging is one of Gardner's more extreme practices that has been dropped; so too has the pursuit of ecstatic states.

Lafayette Ronald Hubbard was the founder, in the 1950s, of the internationally influential Church of Scientology. This movement evolved from the theory of dianetics, itself outlined by Hubbard, an American science fiction writer, as an introspective route to mental and physical health. Through dianetics, he claimed, the analytic part of the mind could make contact with the unconscious, reactive part, source of disruptive emotional responses known as engrams.

Subsequently Hubbard withdrew from the Dianetics Organization and embraced a religious approach to healing, via the Church of Scientology. In return for a fee of variable size, recruits, known as pre-Clears, might seek to free themselves of their engrams by use of dianetic processing. This involved holding two tin cans attached to a meter registering the electrical resistance of the skin. It was said that in this way levels of stress were measured, as the subject advanced towards the Clear stage of spiritual enlightenment. Beyond this condition lay the forever reincarnated self known as the Thetan. The success of scientology as a religion is shown by the fact that, whether or not its founder acquired great wealth, membership now stands at some millions.

Swami Prabhupada a Hindu monk and former Calcutta businessman, founded the Hare Krishna movement in New York in 1966. Its saffron-robed members now live a life of prayer and self-denial in ashrams throughout cities of many nations. They believe that, by chanting the Hare Krishna mantra two thousand times a day and renouncing meat, fish, alcohol, tobacco and extramarital sex, one can transcend the limitations of illness, old age and death. The movement is a revival of a sect first thought to have existed in Bengal about five hundred years ago. Swami Prabhupada himself has been seen by his followers as part of a reincarnated succession of divine leaders going back five millennia to Krishna. As the 'Supreme Personality of Godhead' Krishna is held to reside in every spirit, a being whose supernatural existence featured 16,000 wives, and who appeared to humankind as a young cowherd.

Reverend Sun Myung Moon In 1954 the Unification Church was founded by Moon, a Korean whose followers were taught to see him as a modern-day John the Baptist; some held that he was in fact a new Christ. The movement demands a life of austerity, fighting against communism and adhering to the notion of three historical stages towards a Second Coming: the successive ages of Judaism, Christianity, and the Moon church. It has prospered in many countries including the US, where it has large financial assets; members, living modestly in a communal way, mostly devote their time to fundraising. America and its government have been held in high regard by Moon, who once claimed that, if America repented its sins, it could surely save the soul of other nations, given its divinely ordained leadership by Richard Nixon.

Some important twentieth-century philosophers

Though this generalisation is too simple, twentieth-century philosophy is roughly divisible into two traditions. In the English-speaking world, exemplified by Oxford, Cambridge and the American universities, the emphasis was on Analytic Philosophy. This is concerned with argument, logic and clarity – especially the teasing out of fine distinctions from the linguistic mire of confusion. Some philosophers, such as Wittgenstein, despite coming from Vienna, can be placed in the Anglo–American camp.

Analytic Philosophy is never so pleased as when it can argue a case on a mathematical model. Using language to think about meaning is problematical, and this school of philosophy has developed a large technical vocabulary. Despite some great stylists, such as J L Austin, it can be tough going for the non-specialist.

The other tradition is called Continental Philosophy. It tends to be concerned with big questions about the meaning of existence and the freedom of individuals within a social context. The procedures of Continental Philosophy are more literary than analytic. This grand theoretical approach to the human situation can be appealing, but the actual writing is often desperately obscure. Icily courteous intellectual antagonism prevails between the different schools.

J L Austin (1911–60), British, a fine writer who analysed the subtleties of ordinary language.

A J Ayer (1910–89), British, studied with the Vienna Circle and was influential in bringing Logical Positivism to the English-speaking world. (*Language, Truth and Logic*, 1936). The key idea in logical positivism is that, for you to know that a proposition is the case, it must be verifiable. Unfortunately this renders whole classes of utterance meaningless.

Jean Baudrillard (1929–), French, a difficult social commentator who maintains that our perception of society (especially in the USA) has shifted. It is no longer real, but hyper-real, for we are conditioned by the simulation rather than representation.

Rudolf Carnap (1891–1970), German American, a brilliant logical positivist of great rigour who sought to exclude metaphysics from philosophical discussion.

Daniel Dennett (1942–), American, an explorer of consciousness, Dennett brings scientific and neurological research to theories of mind.

Jacques Derrida (1930–), French, fashionable purveyor of the idea of deconstruction. Meaning only emerges from an endless negotiation between the reader and the text. The subject/object distinction is ultimately untenable.

John Dewey (1859–1952), American, a problem-solving pragmatist and important educational reformer.

Kurt Gödel (1906–78), Czech, a mathematician. His famous 1931 proof (often called the Incompleteness Theorem) that any formal logical system will always be able to contain a grammatical proposition that cannot be proven to be true or false had a huge impact on a generation of thinkers.

Martin Heidegger (1889–1976), German, believed the human condition is only explicable by our interactions in the world (*Dasein* = being there – is a key concept). As a professor at the University of Freiburg he supported the Nazis in the 1930s, something which clouded his reputation.

Edmund Husserl (1859–1938), German, a phenomenologist interested in describing experience without assuming its causal connection to objects. He taught Heidegger.

G(eorge) E(dward) Moore (1873–1958), British, for many years the editor of the magazine *Mind*, his common-sense approach to philosophical problems was very influential.

William Van Orman Quine (1908–2000), American, a supreme logician who applied formal techniques of reasoning to language.

Bertrand Russell (1872–1970), British, a social commentator and crusading pacifist, his biggest contribution was *Principia Mathematica* with Whitehead which attempted to derive all of mathematics logically from just a few axioms. He also wrote the definitive *A History of Western Philosophy*.

Gilbert Ryle (1900–76), British, he developed many of the techniques of analytic philosophy. He was known as a philosopher of ordinary language.

Jean-Paul Sartre (1905–80), French, a prisoner during WW2 and then in the Resistance, he was a famous existentialist. There are many varieties of existentialism, but all hold that existence precedes essence – *ie* that human nature is not a universal given. Existence is all, and with it comes the anxiety of making decisions that define who we are. That anxiety is why so many live in bad faith by avoiding decisions through adhering to social rules of behaviour.

John Searle (1932–), American, is concerned with the whole social and physical context in which speech happens. His thought experiment – the Chinese Room – concerns the irreducible nature of consciousness and is often invoked in arguments about whether artificial intelligence (AI) could ever be truly conscious.

A N Whitehead (1861–1947), British, though based mainly at Harvard, sought to clarify philosophical methodology. Co-wrote the *Principia Mathematica* with Russell.

Ludwig Wittgenstein (1889–1951), Austrian, but he lived mostly in Cambridge, England. Tortured and brilliant, Wittgenstein was arguably the most important philosopher of the century. He tried to think about meaning beyond the confines of language that provides the categories into which we compress the world. His introduction of the concept of language games – the whole performative context in which words are uttered – transformed analytic attempts to discover meaning. His writing is often mysterious and seeks not to offer solutions but to stimulate thought in the reader.

Who's who in the major religions of the world

Judaism

Judaism, the world's oldest monotheistic religion, was founded by **Abraham**, from whom all the Jewish people are descended. It was first formalised after the Jews were taken into exile in Babylon in 586 BCE.

The near descendants of Abraham founded twelve tribes, each named after their ancestor among the sons of **Jacob**, as follows:

Reuben, **Simeon**, Levi, **Judah**, **Issachar**, **Zebulun**, **Dan**, **Napthali**, **Gad**, **Asher**, Joseph, and **Benjamin**. No tribe is named after **Joseph**; instead, two are each named after his sons, **Manasseh** and **Ephraim**. The tribe of **Levi** is not reckoned among the twelve, but has been associated with ceremonial functions.

The Bible records figures from both the legends and history of the Jewish people, or Hebrews, according to which the first man was **Adam**, father of all humanity. **David** (c1001–968 BCE), the first king of Israel, captured Jerusalem and made it his capital. **Deborah** was a prophetess, whose song of triumph on defeating the Canaanites (Judges, 5) is considered one of the finest pieces of early Hebrew literature. The prophet **Elijah** (C9 BCE) defended Judaism against the cult of the god Baal. **Esther**, queen of Persia, risked her life to save the Jews from massacre. **Eve**, the mother of humankind, was created by God from a rib taken from her husband Adam. **Gideon** saved Israel from an invasion by the Midianites, with an army of three hundred. **Herod** 'the Great', allied himself with the occupying Romans; he was the rebuilder of the Temple in Jerusalem. **Isaiah**, prophet and statesman, was a denunciator of the rich. **Jeremiah**, as a prophet of Israel, suffered many wrongs including persecution by his own people; as a result he is associated with the deepest pessimism. **Job** was assailed by God with all sorts of trouble as a test, and was rewarded in this life for not losing his faith. **Jonah**, having disobeyed God's instruction to become a missionary, survived being swallowed by a great fish and repented. **Joshua** was commanded by God to settle in the lands between the Mediterranean and the Euphrates river; he saw to it that the Promised Land was divided between the tribes of Israel. **Judith**, memorably recorded in paintings of the Renaissance, saved many of her fellow Jews by cutting off the head of the Babylonian general Holofernes while he slept. **Moses**, greatest of Hebrew prophets, led his people from slavery to the Promised Land. **Samson**, who came to be a personification of physical strength, was unmanned by Delilah, who found that he was made weak when his hair was cut off. **Zephaniah** (C7 BCE) was a prophet who led an impassioned denunciation of the Judean establishment.

Christianity

Christianity grew out of the teachings of **Jesus Christ**, who was put to death by the Romans in about 30 CE. His first followers, the Twelve Apostles, each has his own emblem:

Peter: the key to the Kingdom of Heaven; **Andrew**: a decussate or diagonal cross; **Thomas**: a spear or arrow; **James the Less**: a fuller's bat, as used in cloth manufacture; **John**: chalice and dragon; **Jude**: a club or cross or carpenter's square; **Matthew**: a purse or money box, or a spear or axe; **Matthias**: an axe, halberd, lance or a book; **Bartholomew**: a butcher's knife; **Philip**: a cross, or loaves and fishes; **James**: scallop shells; **Simon**: a saw, or sometimes fishes.

The Christian Church eventually divided into three main denominations: **Roman Catholic**, **Protestant**, and **Eastern Orthodox**. Of these in turn, Protestantism has shown most readiness to form flourishing sub-sects; its main groups, mostly active internationally, are:

Baptists, founded in England (1609) and Rhode Island (1638); **Church of England** (1534); **Episcopal Church** (1784), an American offshoot of the Church of England; **Presbyterian Church** (1557), founded in Scotland; **Quakers** (mid C17), first established in England; **Unitarians** (1560s), founded in northern and eastern Europe.

Within Christianity there are many orders of monks, friars, and nuns living in groups together under vows of poverty, chastity and obedience. Hermits – monks living in solitude – are an exception. The following orders are each given with their date of foundation.

Monks and friars

Pachomian monks: 318
Basilian monks: 360
Augustinian monks: 388
Benedictine monks: 529
Constitutions of Theodore: c 800
Camaldulian monks: c 970
Vallombrosan monks: c 1038
Augustinian canons: c 1060
Carthusian monks: 1080
Cluniac monks: 1090
Cistercian monks: 1098
Fontevrault monks: c 1100
Order of St Gilbert of Sempringham: 1148
Carmelite friars: c 1155
Trinitarian order: 1198
Premonstratensian canons: 1200
Franciscan friars: 1209
Dominican friars: 1215
Monks of Our Lady of Ransom: 1223
Silvestrine monks: 1231
Servite monks: 1233
Austinian hermits: 1256
Celestine monks: c 1260
Olivetan monks: 1319
Ambrosian monks: c 1370
Hieronoymite friars: 1374
Franciscan Observant friars: 1415
Minim brothers: 1435
Capuchin friars: 1525
Hospitaller friars of St John of God: 1537
Discalced Carmelite friars: 1562
Augustinian recollect friars: 1588
Trappist monks: 1664
Mekhitarist monks: 1702
Marist brothers: 1817
Society of St John the Evangelist: 1866
Priests of the Sacred Heart: 1878
The Taizé Community: 1948

Nuns

Benedictine nuns: 529

Fontevrault nuns: c 1100

Beguine nuns: c 1180

Poor Clare nuns: 1214

Carthusian nuns: 1229

Bridgettine nuns: 1344

Carmelite nuns: 1452

Ursuline nuns: 1535

Discalced Carmelite nuns: 1562

Theatine nuns: 1583

Sisters of the Institute of the Blessed Virgin Mary: 1609

Sisters of Charity of St Vincent de Paul: 1629

Servite nuns: 1640

Redemptorist nuns: 1750

Passionist nuns: 1770

Sisters of Mercy: 1827

Little Sisters of the Poor: 1840

Nuns of the Community of St Mary: 1865

Society of the Sacred Heart of Jesus: 1880

Sisters of Our Lady of Charity of the Good Shepherd: 1883

Sisterhood of St John the Divine: 1884

Poor Clares of Reparation: 1922

The Old Testament, in roughly the same form, is common to both Judaism and Christianity; only Christians acknowledge the New Testament as a sacred text. This part of the Bible covers the life of Christ, and the establishment of Christianity, up to about the year 125.

Within the New Testament, the Apostle **Matthew** figures largely, along with **Mark**, **Luke** and **John**, as the authors of the four Gospels making up most of this part of the Bible. **Barnabas**, who is also referred to as Joseph, was a Cypriot who worked with St Paul to spread Christianity. **Judas Iscariot**, originally one of the Apostles, became a byword for treachery of any kind following his betrayal of Jesus to the Roman authorities. **John the Baptist** initiated Jesus' life as a preacher by baptising him; later he was beheaded by King Herod of Galilee. **Joseph** was the husband of Jesus' mother Mary. He was a descendant of King David, and a carpenter from the village of Nazareth. **Mary**, as mother of Jesus, is described as the Virgin Mary, on account of the doctrine that Jesus was conceived by a miracle while she was still a virgin. She is revered, in particular among Roman Catholics, as a symbol of maternal virtues. **Mary**

Magdalene was a follower of Jesus, often seen as a figure of repentance. **Paul**, originally named Saul, was at first a persecutor of the early Christians. However, while on his way to Damascus one day he was temporarily struck blind and heard a message from God as a result of which he became a leading member of the infant Church. The Romans eventually beheaded him. As a Roman governor with responsibility for Judaea, **Pontius Pilate** is conspicuous in Christian doctrine for his part, however reluctant, in Jesus' crucifixion. Among religious groupings dominant in Judaea during the lifetime of Jesus, the **Pharisees** had both religious and political influence, exercised in support of an inflexible traditionalism much criticised by Jesus. Their enemies the **Sadducees** were also concerned with politics as well as religious belief, and were drawn largely from the local governing class. Strongly connected with the Pharisees were the **Scribes**, the traditional students and interpreters of the Torah.

Islam

The foundations of Islam lie in ancient times: the first Muslim, according to the Koran, was **Ibrahim**, the Abraham of the Jewish and Christian religions, who was divinely guided to see God as the only deity and to reject all pagan beliefs. Islam was established as an organised religion by **Muhammad**, whose name means 'Praised One'. Other spellings of Muhammad are Mohammed, Mahomet, and Mohomed. Muslims believe that he was the last of the prophets, completing the teachings of **Moses** and **Jesus**.

The anti-idolatry of Muhammad's teachings is reflected in the fact that the representation of people in art is forbidden; consequently most historical figures or movements within Islam are known mainly through written records. From within Muhammad's own lifetime, **Abu Bakr** was a wealthy follower of the Prophet who became the first leader or caliph to succeed him. **Abu Talib** was Muhammad's uncle and guardian. **Aisha** was the daughter of Abu Bakr and Muhammad's wife. **Fatima**, Muhammad's daughter, became the wife of Abu Talib's son **Ali**. **Ismail**, Ibrahim's son, was traditionally the ancestor of the Arab peoples. **Khadja**, Muhammad's first wife, was originally his employer and subsequently his earliest follower. **Omar**, or Umar Ibn al-Khattab, initially persecuted Muhammad, but became a convert and, after Muhammad's death, the second caliph to succeed him. Among the northern tribes of Arabia, the **Quraysh** was the one to which Muhammad belonged.

Muslim sects

Nearly thirty years after the death of Muhammad, the world of Islam divided into two main factions. Of these, the **Sunni** Muslims are the more conservative group and make up a large majority, who acknowledge leadership exercised by caliphs from Muhammad's own tribe. The **Shi'ites** consider the only lawful Muslim authority to come from **imams**, descendants of Muhammad through his daughter Fatima and Ali, her husband. They are a minority throughout Islam except in Iran.

Later schisms produced a number of smaller sects. The Baha'i faith, which grew out of the Shi'ite sect, was established by **Mirza Husaynali** in Iran in 1863; it believes in the unification of all faiths. **Wahhabis** predominate in Saudi Arabia and comprise a movement founded in C18 by **Muhammad bin' Abd al-Wahhab**, who sought a return to the simplicity of early Islam. Their influence currently means holding off such Western influences as the use of alcohol. **Sufis** represent the continuing search for closer contact with God, through mysticism and indifference to material wealth. **Black Muslims** are a movement generated in twentieth-century America. Under the name the Nation of Islam it was established by **Elijah Muhammad**, following on from the ideas of **Wallace D. Fard**, and was further developed by **Malcolm X**. One of its main objects was to declare black people as superior to any other; however some white people are now included among its members.

Hinduism

The earliest forms of Hinduism lie in prehistoric times, when they were already practised in the Indus Valley. There was no one founding figure, and Hindu gods are many and various. But the different forms of Hinduism share certain beliefs: in reincarnation, in rules of behaviour, in given forms of ceremony, and in the caste system. This last has been officially outlawed, but still has an influence. It determines the social standing of everyone from birth and divides them into four main classes: at the top, **brahmins**, or priests; then **kshatriyas**, warriors and rulers; **viasyas**, traders and minor officials; and unskilled workers, or **sudras**. Below all these is the **pariah** class, the 'untouchables'.

The numerous gods of Hinduism are seen as parts of one divine entity. This universal spirit is known as **Brahman**, whose most important aspects are the many-armed gods **Brahma**, **Vishnu** and **Shiva**.

The good side of Brahma, the creator, is Vishnu, who traditionally has appeared on earth so far in nine incarnations. These have been: **Matsya** – fish; **Kurma** – tortoise; **Varaha** – boar; **Narasimha** – man–lion; **Vamana** – dwarf; **Parashurama** – Rama with the axe; **Rama** – prince; **Krishna** – young hero and lover; and the **Buddha**. One incarnation, **Kalki**, is still to come. The attributes of Vishnu are: disk, mace, conch shell, lotus, seven-headed cobra, caste mark, and garland of forest flowers.

The other side of this 'trinity' is Brahma's destructive aspect, which takes the form of Shiva, also known as Nataraja, Lord of the Dance. In this form he is also shown with several typical features: as he dances, he crushes the demon of ignorance; he holds a drum and the flame of destruction; a surrounding arch of fire stands for the circle of life and death; a cobra represents fertility; a leopard skin signifies strength; he wears a look of concentration, and his several hands are raised in blessing.

There are few temples to Brahma himself, but he is depicted in many others, where he is shown to have: four faces, one for each part of the universe: a sacrificial ladle; prayer beads; four scriptures; a jar of water from the sacred Ganges river; and a lotus throne. Paradoxically, as the One and the All he tends not to be an object of worship.

Other gods

Aditi was the mother of all the gods; **Agni**, the god of fire and sacrifice. The Bhakta saints were members of the **Vaisnava Bhakti** movement, which flourished in the C11 and early C12. Though they considered God to be inaccessible to all understanding, they held him nonetheless to be the only reality. Their faith expressed itself in doing good, and in seeking God by chanting and singing. **Ganesha** is the elephant-headed deity, protector of scribes and traders. **Hanuman** is the monkey god. The black deity **Kali** is Shiva's bloodthirsty wife; as Uma or Parvati she is also the goddess of motherhood. Krishna, one of the incarnations of Vishnu, is worshipped as a lover and as a dragon-slayer. Vishnu's wife **Lakshmi** is the goddess of wealth, beauty, and good fortune. **Saravasti**, the wife of Brahma, is a river deity. As goddess of knowledge and truth, she is also protector of writers. **Sati** was the first wife of Shiva. By tradition it was through her that the practice of suttee was established whereby widows (without unborn or young children) died on their husband's funeral pyre; a practice forbidden in British India in 1829, though it continued in Nepal until 1877.

Buddhism

The founder of Buddhism, known as 'the **Buddha**', or 'the enlightened', was born Siddhartha Gautama, c 563 BCE in what is now the kingdom of Nepal. He grew up in the household of his father, **Prince Suddodhana**, rajah of the **Sakya** tribe, and subsequently married the beautiful **Princess Yasodhara**.

In about his thirtieth year Gautama had a succession of visions. These showed him an old man; a sick man; a dead body; and an encounter between himself and an itinerant holy man. The first three of these visions confirmed in him a view of life as governed by suffering; as a response to these, and to his perceived meeting with the holy man, he left a life of courtly luxury, together with his wife and his son **Rahula**, to seek enlightenment.

This he did by living a dismal life of self-denial as a wandering monk for six years, during which time his search met with no success. Coming to a village one day, he decided to stay, sitting beneath a bodhi tree until an answer to his quest might come to him. Here he was suddenly shown that the perfect way lay in a life of contemplation, based upon the fact that the route to avoidance of suffering lay through rejection of selfish desires. Much of Buddhism is a radical development of Hinduism, rather than an original religion. Its heritage includes the **sangha**, or order of Buddhist monks and nuns. This word is sometimes also used to describe an ideal community of those who have reached a higher state of spiritual awareness.

Buddha died c 483 BCE, having spent about forty years preaching his message of dharma, or the truth of salvation, throughout northern India. Subsequently Buddhism spread widely throughout southern and eastern Asia. In the middle years of the C3 BCE the Indian emperor **Ashoka** made it a national religion. During the C7 CE it became widely established in Japan; one large Buddhist sect, founded here by the dogmatically inclined **Nichiren** (1222–82), still flourishes. The C14 and C15 saw the rise of Tibetan Buddhism or Lamaism, whose current leader, the **Dalai Lama**, has lived in exile since 1959.

Confucianism

Confucius is the Latinised name by which the West usually refers to the Chinese philosopher K'ung-fu-tzu (551–479 BCE), a descendant through the dukes of **Sung** to the kings of the **Shang** dynasty. The code of belief and behaviour founded by him comprises a system of moral behaviour without religion; its most famous tenet was, 'What you do not wish done to yourself, do not do to others.' In 517 BCE he met **Lao-Tzu**, whose teachings were to lead much later to the development of Taoism. Confucius gained many followers over a lifetime in senior government and as a teacher. After his death the philosopher **Mencius**, properly Meng-tse (372–298 BCE), the Second Sage, strove to show officialdom how it should govern following practical rules derived from Confucianism. The rationalist **Hsun Tzu** (298–230 BCE) differed from Mencius' belief in man's innate virtue; he spread the doctrine that humankind was born without virtue, but that it can benefit from the right moral teaching. Over the following centuries the spread of Confucianism was accompanied by support from various rulers. In the second century BCE it became the Chinese state ideology; during this time it was the Confucians who educated the **Emperor Wu Ti** (140–87 BCE). The **Emperor Ming** decreed in 59 BCE that sacrifices should be made to Confucius in every public school. During the Sung dynasty, Neo-Confucianism developed as a reaction to Taoist and Buddhist doctrines. Some centuries after the spread of Confucius' teachings to Japan, it was Neo-Confucianism that became adopted by that country's **Tokugawa** shoguns.

Scientific and technical

Names of hurricanes

Hurricanes are given approved names, repeated every six years. The first hurricane of the year begins with A, the next with B, and so on. It is not expected that there will be more than 23 hurricanes in any year. To determine which set of names to be used, divide the year by six; the remainder (R) indicates the column to use.

R=0	R=1	R=2	R=3	R=4	R=5
1992, 1998, 2004	1993, 1999, 2005	1994, 2000, 2006	1995, 2001, 2007	1996, 2002, 2008	1997, 2003, 2009
Alex	Arlene	Alberto	Allison	Arthur	Ana
Bonnie	Bret	Beryl	Barry	Bertha	Bill
Charley	Cindy	Chris	Chantal	Cristobal	Claudette
Danielle	Dennis	Debby	Dean	Dolly	Danny
Earl	Emily	Ernesto	Erin	Edouard	Erika
Frances	Floyd	Florence	Felix	Fay	Fabian
Gaston	Gert	Gordon	Gabrielle	Gustav	Grace
Hermine	Harvey	Helene	Humberto	Hanna	Henri
Ivan	Irene	Isaac	Iris	Isidore	Isabel
Jeanne	Jose	Joyce	Jerry	Josephine	Juan
Karl	Katrina	Keith	Karen	Kyle	Kate
Lisa	Lenny	Leslie	Lorenzo	Lili	Larry
Matthew	Maria	Michael	Michelle	Marco	Mindy
Nicole	Nate	Nadine	Noel	Nana	Nicholas
Otto	Ophelia	Oscar	Olga	Omar	Odette
Paula	Philippe	Patty	Pablo	Paloma	Peter
Richard	Rita	Rafael	Rebekah	Rene	Rose
Shary	Stan	Sandy	Sebastien	Sally	Sam
Tomas	Tammy	Tony	Tanya	Teddy	Teresa
Virginie	Vince	Valerie	Van	Vicky	Victor
Walter	Wilma	William	Wendy	Wilfred	Wanda

Medical pioneers

Anaesthetics

Gardner Quincy Colton (1814–98), American chemist; employing nitrous oxide for tooth extraction (1844).

Robert Liston (1794–1847), Scots surgeon; first user of general anaesthetic in a public operation (1846).

Crawford Williamson Long (1815–78), American physician; first user of ether as an anaesthetic (1842).

Sir James Young Simpson (1811–70), Scots obstetrician; initiated the use of ether in childbirth (1847); became physician in Scotland to the frequently pregnant Queen Victoria.

Antibodies

Linus Carl Pauling (1901–94), American biochemist; prepared artificial antibodies.

Antiseptics

Joseph Lister (1827–1912), English surgeon; introduced the use of the antiseptic system (1860).

Eric Keightley Rideal (1890–1974), English chemist; invented a test for the germicidal power of disinfectants.

Antitoxins

Emil von Behring (1854–1917), German bacteriologist; discovered diphtheria and tetanus antitoxins; in 1901 he was awarded the first Nobel prize in medicine.

Appendicitis

James Parkinson (1755–1824), British physician; the first to describe appendicitis and the consequences of perforation.

Arsenic, test for

James Marsh (1789–1846), English chemist and an expert on poisons; he gave his name to the standard test for arsenic.

Artificial insemination

Lazaro Spallanzani (1729–99), Italian biologist; discoverer of the possibility of artificial insemination.

Artificial respiration

Edward Sharpey-Schafer (1850–1935), English physiologist; inventor of the method of prone-pressure for artificial respiration.

Bacteria, test for

Hans Christian Joachim Gram (1853–1938), Danish bacteriologist; devised a testing method for bacteria (1884).

Bacteriophage

Frederick William Twort (1877–1950), English bacteriologist; discoverer of the bacteriophage (1915), a virus capable of attacking certain bacteria.

Birth control clinics

Margaret Sanger (1883–1966), American member of the birth control movement; imprisoned for her work, which she subsequently extended to India.

Marie Carmichael Stopes (1880–1958), English advocate of birth control; founder of the first birth control clinic in North London.

Blood, circulation of

Erasistratus (304–c245 BCE), founded a medical school, and came close to anticipating Harvey's theory of the circulation of the blood.

William Harvey (1578–1657), English physician; discoverer of the circulation of the blood, which he published in 1628.

Blood, corpuscles

Jan Swammerdam (1637–80), Dutch naturalist; the first to observe the existence of red blood corpuscles (1658).

Blood, cross circulation

Corneille Heymans (1892–1968), French–Belgian physiologist; developer of the techique of 'cross-circulation' of blood.

Blood groups

Karl Landsteiner (1868–1943), Austrian pathologist; winner of the 1930 Nobel prize for physiology and medicine, largely on account of his discovering the four types of blood group and the Rh factor.

Bubonic plague

Shibasaburo Kitasato (1856–1931), Japanese bacteriologist who in 1894 discovered the bacillus of bubonic plague; he also isolated the bacilli of dysentery and tetanus and devised an antitoxin against diptheria.

Alexandre Emile John Yersin (1863–1943), Swiss–French bacteriologist; developed a serum against the plague bacillus, which he discovered in the same year as Kitasato.

Chemotherapy

Gerhard Domagk (1895–1964), German biochemist; discovered the use of sulphanilamide in chemotherapy; he turned down the 1939 Nobel prize for physiology and medicine on the orders of the German government.

Childbirth, natural

Grantly Dick-Read (1890–1959), English gynaecologist; caused initial controversy with his recommendation (*Natural Childbirth*, 1933) of prenatal exercises as opposed to anaesthetics in childbirth.

Cholera

Robert Koch (1843–1910), German bacteriologist; discoverer of the cholera bacillus.

Richard Friedrich Johannes Pfeiffer (1858–?1945), German bacteriologist; discoverer of a serum against cholera.

Cholesterol

Konrad Emil Bloch (1912–2000), American biochemist; shared the Nobel prize for medicine in 1964 for his work on the workings of cholesterol.

Feodor Lynen (1911–79), German biochemist; with Bloch, winner of the 1964 Nobel prize for medicine for work on the nature of the cholesterol molecule.

Cocaine

August Bier (1861–1949), German surgeon, a pioneer in the use of cocaine as an anaesthetic.

William Stewart Halsted (1852–1922), American surgeon; first deployed injections of cocaine as a local anaesthetic.

Coenzyme A

Fritz Albert Lipmann (1899–1986), German–American biochemist; awarded the Nobel prize for physiology and medicine in 1953 for his discovery of 'coenzyme A'.

Colour blindness

John Dalton (1766–1844), English chemist who first described colour blindness, or Daltonism, a condition he shared with his brother.

Cortisone

Philip Showalter Hench (1896–1965), American physician; discoverer of cortisone.

Digitalis

William Withering (1741–99), English naturalist and physician; the first to identify digitalis as a drug for the treatment of heart disease.

Diphtheria

Friedrich August Johann Löffler (1852–1915), German bacteriologist; first to culture the diphtheria bacillus (1884).

Pierre Émile Roux (1853–1933), French bacteriologist; assistant and successor to Pasteur; one of the discoverers of the antitoxic method for the treatment of diphtheria.

Dysentery

Shibasaburo Kitasato (1856–1931), Japanese bacteriologist who isolated the bacillus of dysentery, for which he devised an antitoxin.

Fritz Richard Schaudinn (1871–1906), German zoologist who demonstrated the amoebic nature of tropical dysentery.

Enzymes

Henry Drysdale Dakin (1880–1950), English chemist who developed 'Dakin's solution', which was used in WW1 for the treatment of wounds.

Otto Heinrich Warburg (1883–1970), German physiological chemist who won the 1931 Nobel prize for medicine on account of his research into enzymes.

Eugenics

Francis Galton (1822–1911), English scientist, cousin of Charles Darwin and grandson of Erasmus Darwin; founder of the science of eugenics and author of works including *Hereditary Genius* (1869), *English Men of Science: their Nature and Nurture* (1874) and *Natural Inheritance* (1889).

Eustachian tubes

Alcmaeon (*fl* 520 BCE), Greek physician; discoverer of the Eustachian tubes and an early advocate of experiment.

Homeopathy

Christian Friedrich Samuel Hahnemann (1755–1843), German physician and founder of homeopathy, whose procedures were based on the observation that in healthy people medicine provokes the same response that it cures in the sick.

Hormones

Ernest Henry Starling (1866–1927), English physiologist who devised the word 'hormones' to describe substances internally secreted by the ductless glands.

Hydrochloric acid

Johann Rudoph Glauber (c1603–68), German physician who discovered hydrochloric acid (1648).

William Prout (1785–1850), English chemist and physiologist; discoverer of the presence in the stomach of hydrochloric acid.

Inoculation

Edward Jenner (1749–1823), English physician, who discovered vaccination, following his investigation into the tradition that cowpox was a protection against smallpox.

William Boog Leishman (1865–1926), Scots bacteriologist, discoverer of a vaccine against typhoid.

Louis Pasteur (1822–95), French chemist whose discoveries are the foundation of modern bacteriology; his work revealed methods of preventing diphtheria, tubercular disease, cholera, yellow fever and plague.

Almroth Edward Wright (1861–1947), English bacteriologist, specializing in parasitic diseases and in blood as a protection against bacteria; devised a system of inoculation against typhoid.

Insulin

Frederick Grant Banting (1891–1941), Canadian physiologist; shared the Nobel prize with J J R Macleod in 1923 following their discovery of insulin.

John James Richard Macleod (1876–1935), Scots physiologist who shared the Nobel prize with Banting for his part in discovering insulin.

Intercellular spaces

Ludolf Christian Treviranus (1779–1864), German naturalist; known as the discoverer of intercellular spaces.

Kala-azar parasite

William Boog Leishman (1865–1926), Scots bacteriologist; the first to discover the parasite connected with the disease kala-azar.

Leprosy bacillus

Armauer Hansen (1841–1912), Norwegian bacteriologist; discoverer of the leprosy bacillus.

Lymphatic glands

Thomas Bartholinus (1616–80), one of a notable family of Danish physicians; he did much work on the lymphatic glands and confirmed the discovery of the thoracic duct.

Olof Rudbeck (1630–1702), Swedish zoologist and botanist; discovered the lymphatic glands.

Mercurial blood-pump

Karl Friedrich Wilhelm Ludwig (1816–95), German physiologist whose invention of the mercurial blood-gas pump uncovered the part played in the bloodstream by gases including oxygen.

Muscular contraction

Andrew Fielding Huxley (1917–), English physiologist, from a remarkable family of scientists and writers; his researches helped find an explanation of nerve transmission, and he devised the first substantial theory of muscular contraction.

Ophthalmoscope

Hermann von Helmholtz (1821–94), German physiologist who was also outstanding in mathematics and experimental physics; inventor of the ophthalmoscope (1850) independently of the English mathematician Charles Babbage.

Penicillin

Ernest Boris Chain (1906–79), German-born bio-chemist with Russian ancestry; fled from the Nazis to Britain in 1933; in 1945 shared the Nobel prize for medicine following his part in developing penicillin.

Alexander Fleming (1881–1955), Scots bacteriologist whose brilliant career featured various innovations, including the use of antityphoid vaccines. He is chiefly remembered for his part in producing penicillin together with Chain and Florey, eleven years after his initial discovery in 1928 of its antibiotic powers.

Howard Walter Florey (1898–1968), British pathologist, who shared the 1945 Nobel prize for medicine together with Chain and Fleming.

Plastic surgery

Harold Delf Gillies (1882–1960), British plastic surgeon, whose *Plastic Surgery of the Face* made this branch of medicine generally respected.
Archibald MacIndoe (1900–60) British plastic surgeon, foremost pupil of Harold Gillies; famous for his work during WW2 on injured airmen.
Gasparo Tagliacozzi (1546–99), Italian surgeon celebrated for his technique of mending noses by transplanting skin from the arm.

Polio

Jonas Edward Salk (1914–95), American virologist; in 1953 he discovered the vaccine against poliomyelitis, which he then tested successfully with his family as subjects.

Puerperal fever

Oliver Wendell Holmes (1809–94), American writer and physician, who discovered (1843) the contagious nature of puerperal fever.

Pulse

Galen (c 130–201CE), Greek physician otherwise known as Claudius Galenus, whose writings on current medical knowledge became the source for all his Greek and Roman successors; the first to attempt diagnosis by taking the patient's pulse.

Quinine

Joseph Bienaimé Caventou (1795–1878), French chemist, whose discoveries include quinine (in 1820), brucine, cinchonine and strychnine.
Pierre Joseph Pelletier (1788–1842), French chemist, who with Caventou achieved the naming of chlorophyll, along with the discovery of alkaloids including quinine and strychinine.

Radium

Marie and Pierre Curie (1867–1934 and 1859–1906), French physicists who worked together on radioactivity and discovered radium, sharing a Nobel prize with Becquerel in 1903. Marie Curie isolated radium in 1910; in 1911 she once more gained the Nobel prize.

Reflex actions

Marshall Hall (1790–1857), English physician and physiologist; made significant discoveries concerning the reflex action of the spinal system.

Ivan Petrovich Pavlov (1849–1936), Russian physiologist; the most famous aspect of his career was his researches into 'conditioned' reflexes, each of which was connected to some particular part of the brain cortex.

Charles Scott Sherrington (1857–1952), English physiologist, whose work *The Integrative Action of the Nervous System* (1906) is a benchmark.

Sleeping sickness

David Bruce (1855–1931), British physician, who identified the tsetse fly as the carrier of sleeping sickness.

Stethoscope

René Theophile Hyacinthe Laennec (1781–1826), French physician; inventor of the stethoscope.

Streptomycin

Selman Abraham Waksman (1888–1973), American biologist; his investigations into antibiotics and the effect of micro-organisms on organic substances led to him gaining the 1952 Nobel prize for medicine following his discovery of streptomycin.

Suture, surgical

Alexis Carrel (1873–1944), French biologist, discoverer of a way to suture blood vessels so that arteries could be replaced.

Thermometer

Thomas Clifford Allbutt (1836–1925), English physician; devised the short clinical thermometer (1867), superseding a version that had to be kept in place for twenty minutes.

Ismael Boulliau (fl. c1650); in 1659, the inventor of the mercury thermometer.

Gabriel Daniel Fahrenheit (1686–1736), German physicist; substituted quicksilver in his thermometers instead of spirits of wine, and devised a system of measuring temperatures that defined freezing point of water as 32° and its boiling point as 212°.

Sanctorius (1561–1636), or Santorio Santorio, Italian physician and inventor of various instruments including the clinical thermometer.

Tuberculosis

Albert Calmette (1863–1933), French bacteriologist; jointly with Guerin he discovered the vaccine for the prevention of tuberculosis, the Bacillus Calmette–Guerin or BCG.

Typhus

Charles Jules Henri Nicolle (1866–1936), French physician and bacteriologist; studied under Pasteur, and identified the body louse as a carrier of
typhus fever. He was awarded the 1928 Nobel prize for medicine.

X-rays

Charles Glover Barkla (1877–1944), English physicist, who did
outstanding research into short wave emissions including X-rays; he
gained the Nobel prize in 1917.

Arthur Holly Compton (1892–1962), American physicist and a foremost
authority on X-rays; Nobel prizewinner for physics in 1927.

Henry Gwyn Jeffreys Moseley (1887–1915), English physicist who
discovered the atomic numbers of the elements by means of X-ray
spectra; he was killed at Gallipoli.

Wilhelm Konrad von Röntgen (1845–1923), German physicist; in 1895
he discovered the phenomenon he named X-rays, in the form of electromagnetic radiation also known as Röntgen rays.

Yellow fever

James Carroll (1854–1907), English-born surgeon in the American army;
did strategic research on yellow fever, in the cause of which he deliber-
ately infected himself.

William Crawford Gorgas (1854–1920), American military doctor
whose career as an epidemiologist famously included the extermination
of yellow fever in Panama during the building of the Panama Canal.

Hideyo Noguchi (1876–1928), Japanese bacterologist, working from
1899 in the US; he made considerable discoveries concerning the origin
and treatment of yellow fever, a disease that caused his death.

Some modern astronomers, cosmologists and physicists

It may seem odd to bunch these categories together, but in fact they are
intimately connected. The way the universe behaves on the largest scale
turns out to be utterly contingent on atomic interactions on the smallest
scale. The physics of the Big Bang can only be teased out by a deep understanding of what happens in the sub-atomic world, though the singularity
itself is hidden by the Planck moment (about 10^{-43} s) when the universe
was so small that Heisenberg Uncertainty makes theory break down.

New models of the origins of the universe are now emerging that suggest that the question of what happened before the Big Bang need not be as meaningless as we once supposed. The Big Bang theory is beautiful and it successfully predicts the Hubble Red Shift, the microwave background and the hydrogen/helium ratio. On the other hand it is horribly incomplete. Its explanation of the universe cannot account for over 90% of it and to cover this embarrassing lacuna theorists have to posit undetectable cold dark matter and the mysterious 'dark energy'. String theory is one hope for a Theory of Everything, as is 'M' theory. This uses 'branes' [sic] – multi-dimensional topological structures akin to membranes – to generate the gravity that holds galaxies together but for which we cannot yet observe nearly enough matter to generate the forces needed.

Many astronomers are also physicists, and many physicists de facto cosmologists. All these disciplines explore ideas that address the question not only of how we came to be here but of why any stuff exists at all. There are limits to Earth-bound testing of theory, but fortunately the universe is a huge laboratory for experiments that our planet is too small or insufficiently energetic to accommodate. Astronomers are lucky enough to have an infinite supply of intriguing phenomena to look at.

(Susan) Jocelyn Bell Burnell (1943–), British, who as a graduate student at Cambridge supervised by the distinguished radio-astronomer Anthony Hewish, spotted an anomalously ordered trace only one inch long on a roll of graphic print-out that stretched to four hundred feet. She recognised its significance. This was the first discovery of the class of objects known as pulsars, rapidly rotating neutron stars. For their theoretical work on these objects both Hewish and Sir Martin Ryle won the Nobel Prize though many have felt that it was unfair not to award also Jocelyn Bell.

Niels Bohr (1885–1962), Danish physicist and Nobel laureate (1922), was one of the founders of quantum theory that changes our everyday perception of matter. At the quantum scale, classical physics no longer describes how things work; a terrible and complex ambiguity sets in. Bohr researched radiation and atomic structure, lending his name to one model – the Bohr Teardrop Model – of the nucleus. He was the grand old man of quantum physics.

Max Born (1882–1970), German theoretical physicist, was a pioneer quantum mechanic: Heisenberg, Pauli and Jordan Pascual were all his students. He did fundamental work on wave/particle duality and the probabilistic nature of the position of elementary particles. He was awarded the Nobel Prize for Physics in 1954.

Louis de Broglie (1892–1987), French Nobel Laureate, refined the theory of the wave/particle duality of matter at the quantum level. He confirmed this by experiment with the electron in 1927. Wave/particle duality lies at the very heart of quantum mechanics and remains difficult to understand or visualise for creatures like us who inhabit the macroscopic world of large objects that obey Newtonian rules.

Paul Dirac (1902–1984), English mathematical physicist and a patron saint of quantum mechanics, applied relativity to the quantum scale and modified the wave mechanics of Erwin Schrödinger with whom he shared the Nobel Prize for Physics in 1933. The mathematics are said to be so difficult that very few people even now understand Dirac's equations. He predicted the existence of an anti-particle to the negatively charged electron. The positron was not detected until years later by Anderson and Blackett.

Albert Einstein (1879–1955), The German–American physicist, was one of the world's most astonishing thinkers who transformed the classical (Newtonian) physics that had served well for a couple of centuries by his Theory of Relativity (the Special Theory 1905 and the General Theory 1916). He was awarded the Nobel Prize for Physics in 1921 for his work on the photoelectric effect. Einstein realised that we inhabit a very narrow range of conditions that makes our sense of how the world works very local. Because the speed of light (c) is constant (so that c+c= c, and not 2c), some very counter-intuitive things happen to space and time as c is approached. Einstein's insights confirmed the identity at the quantum level of mass and energy, giving rise to the famous formula $E=mc^2$. It was a revolution. When Hitler came to power in 1933, Einstein, a Jew and a pacifist, left Germany for the USA where he settled in Princeton at the Institute for Advanced Study where he spent much of the rest of his life working on unified field theory, the so-called Theory of Everything.

Enrico Fermi (1901–1954), emigrated from Italy to the USA. He won the Nobel Prize for Physics in 1938 and went straight on from Stockholm to America rather than return home with his Jewish wife to an increasingly anti-Semitic fascist regime. His work on radioactivity was vital for designing the world's first self-sustaining atomic reactor in Chicago in 1942. An exceptional experimental theorist, Fermi contributed to the Manhattan Project, the code name for the research project set up in 1942 to develop an atomic bomb His statistical approach to predicting the paths of elementary particles was enormously useful.

Richard Phillips Feynman (1918–1988), the precociously brilliant American physicist, worked on the Manhattan Project as a young man and then went into research and teaching. His collected essays *Surely You're Joking, Mr Feynman* are notable for their charm and vanity. With Julian Schwinger and Itiro Tomonago he won the Nobel Prize for Physics for his contribution to QED, quantum electrodynamics.

George Gamow (originally Georgy Gamov, 1904–68) Russian then naturalised American, was the brilliant physicist who worked out the detail of the Big Bang theory. He developed a quantum theory of radioactivity and in molecular biology he suggested that the patterns of DNA could be read as a code.

Alan Guth, Weisskopf Professor of Physics at MIT, is known as the father of Inflation, a theory that describes the rapid expansion of the universe in its early stages. It is an elegant explanation of why the universe is so smoothly isotropic in all directions. The minute ripples in the background microwave radiation (in the order of 30 millionths of a degree C) discovered by the COBE (Cosmic Background Explorer) satellite in 1989 are consistent with Inflation.

Stephen Hawking (1942–), Lucasian Professor of Mathematics at Cambridge (a job once held by Newton), is seeking a mathematical framework to embrace quantum mechanics and relativity. His work on relativity suggests that a singularity is a necessary start to the universe and he showed that black holes can radiate energy via the effects of virtual particles created at their boundaries. This is called Hawking radiation. His *A Brief History of Time* was an enormous bestseller though one which, despite the muscular clarity of the writing, many people found head-ache inducing. Hawking suffers from motor neurone disease, and his wheelchair and voice synthesizer have become something of an icon signifying huge, abstract intelligence.

Werner Karl Heisenberg (1901–1976), German physicist, was one of the founders of quantum mechanics. His famous Uncertainty Principle describes the impossibility of knowing both the energy (mass) and the direction (vector) of a particle. The two values are co-factors so as the precision of one increases, the other decreases. Heisenberg worked for Germany in WW2 and it is still unclear whether the German failure to produce an atomic bomb was the result of Heisenberg's miscalculation of the critical mass needed of fissile material or deliberate policy on his part. Michael Frayn's play, *Copenhagen*, explores this ambiguity through a series of meetings (that did take place) with Niels Bohr.

Fred Hoyle (1915–2001), English mathematician and astronomer, is most associated with the steady-state theory of the universe. In a spirit of satire he coined the term Big Bang (which has stuck) for the competing theory. Hoyle founded the world-famous Institute of Theoretical Astronomy at Cambridge where he did pioneering work on the nucleo-synthesis of heavy elements in the heart of stars. He and his colleague, astrobiologist Wickramasinghe, thought it was likely that life was seeded by organic molecules from space (the Panspermia theory), which was derided at the time though recent research has made it more respectable. Hoyle was also an occasional SF writer (*A for Andromeda* is his best known novel).

Edwin Powell Hubble (1889–1953), American, an erstwhile lawyer turned astronomer, transformed our sense of the scale of the universe. Using the then largest telescope in the world, the 100-inch reflector on Mt Wilson, he discovered that blurry patches of light were in fact distant galaxies. Analysis of the light from these galaxies, which is shifted towards the long, or red, end of the spectrum, suggested that they were receding. It was a profoundly shocking. The rate of recession of these unimaginably distant objects is called Hubble's Constant though the exact value – with its implications for the size and age of the universe – has been debated until very recently. The present consensus puts the universe at about 13.7 billion years old. The orbiting space telescope is named in Hubble's honour.

Georges Lemaître (1804–1966), a Belgian astrophysicist and Catholic priest, is often jokingly called the father of cosmology. He did research on cosmic rays and also the three body problem. In 1927 he suggested that the origins of the universe might lie in some infinitely dense event like the Big Bang.

Andrei Linde (1948–), born in Russia, spent time at CERN and is now at Stanford. Linde is one of the outstanding theoreticians in cosmology who refined the notion of the inflationary universe and calculated that the physics of the Big Bang allowed for the origins of many simultaneous universes – perhaps an infinite number – not all of which would have longevity. This is the Multiverse, an idea so utterly mind-boggling that the imagination retreats before it.

Bernard Lovell (1913–), British, is the doyen of British post-war radio astronomy. The 250ft steerable dish at Jodrell Bank in Cheshire was the best in the world for many years until the construction of very large arrays.

João Magueijo, British, is an iconoclastic young cosmologist at Imperial College, London, who is doing exhilarating work looking at theoretical models in which the speed of light is not constant but changed over time.

Jan Hendrik Oort (1900–92), a Dutch astronomer, noticed the clustering of cometary aphelia (points of maximum distance from the sun) around 10,000 AU from the sun. An AU is an astronomical unit, equal to the radius of the Earth's orbit (150 million kilometres). The Oort Cloud of comets marking the limit of the sun's influence in local space is named for him.

Wolfgang Ernst Pauli (1900–58), Austrian physicist, noticed that when a nucleus decays by emitting an electron, some energy seems to disappear. This was so disturbing that he posited a particle, the neutrino, with just the right characteristics to account for the observation. The neutrino was not detected until years later. Pauli gave his name to the famous exclusion principle which states that no two electrons can occupy the same quantum state. It is one of the foundations of quantum mechanics.

Max Planck (1858–1947), a German physicist, revolutionised science in 1900 by his realisation that there is a fundamental unit of energy, the quantum, which gives space/time its granularity on the atomic scale. His equation relating the energy of a photon to its frequency should be as famous as Einstein's $E=mc^2$, but somehow quantum mechanics are so strange and difficult that they did not capture the public's imagination in the same way as relativity. The term 'quantum leap' is widely misused as a synonym for large and significant. The change in the energy levels of an electron is microscopically tiny; the point of a quantum leap is that it is quantised – discrete and discontinuous.

Martin Rees (1942–) is Cambridge-based and Britain's Astronomer Royal. He is an important theorist about compact objects such as neutron stars or black holes and has invested much research in the problem of how complexity emerges from the iteration of simple rules. Martin Rees is also an excellent writer of popular science and a tireless advocate of the wonder of his subject

Carl Sagan (1934–96), American, was Professor of Astronomy at Cornell. He was associated with NASA and its planetary exploration probes and was one of the inspirers of the SETI (Search for Extraterrestrial Intelligence) program that uses radio astronomy and automated analytic techniques to search for extraterrestrial life. He was an assiduous populariser of astronomy and fronted a TV series called Cosmos.

Erwin Schrödinger (1887–1961), Austrian, is another founding member of the quantum mechanics' guild. His wave equation was a huge advance in our understanding. Now he is often remembered for his thought experiment about the cat in a box with a vial of poison gas which may be triggered to rupture if a radioactive source emits a particle. The point is that in quantum mechanics measurement of the state of a particle is like subjecting it to a process whereby you force it to adopt a value. Until you do that, the particle is said to be in a superposition of states. Schrödinger found this difficult to accept – hence the thought experiment in which an unequivocal macroscopic event, in this case the survival or otherwise of the unfortunate moggy (and what can be more binary than being dead or alive?), is contingent on a quantum event. The cat cannot be both dead and alive, he argued. In quantum mechanical terms the cat is in a superposition until you interrogate the system by opening the box.

Lee Smolin (1955–), American, now at the Perimeter Institute University of Waterloo, Toronto, is one of the foremost quantum cosmologists particularly interested in quantum gravity. He is one of the developers of the theory of quantum loop gravity.

Sir Joseph John Thomson (1856–1940), British, discovered the electron early in the century and won the Nobel Prize for Physics in 1906 for his work on the passage of electricity through a gas. He was an excellent mathematician who worked on James Clerk Maxwell's electromagnetic field theory.

Edward Witten (1951–), American, is at Princeton Institute of Advanced Study. He is a world expert on 'M' theory and is regarded by his peers as the man most likely to crack a Theory of Everything, unifying the binding forces of nature into one coherent account.

Hideki Yukawa (1907–1981), Japanese, won the Nobel prize for Physics in 1949. He is known for his theory of how the nuclear force holds the nucleus of an atom together. His ideas enabled him in 1935 to predict the existence of the meson, this particle discovered by Cecil Powell in 1949.

Fritz Zwicky (1898–1974), an astrophysicist born in Bulgaria to Swiss parents, was the authority on interstellar matter and produced the standard catalogue of compact galaxies. He predicted the existence of neutron stars.

Technologists who made the modern world

The criteria for inclusion in this category have to be rigorous as many volumes have been written on the subject. Technology and the history of science are inextricably linked, though the former has always led the latter; theoretical studies – certainly in earlier times – lagged far behind practical techniques. In this list – apart from Newton – you will find only those who actually made something, and then only the first to hit on ideas or principle.

The pace of innovation in clock-making, for example, was vertiginous with cathedral clocks displaying tremendous ingenuity within decades of their first appearance. Throughout the C17 and C18 the rate of improvement in time-keeping continued to be extraordinary, culminating in John Harrison's famous naval chronometer for which he won (half) the admiralty prize in 1765. But for all their brilliance, these developments were more in the way of technical enhancements. The focus here is on the first creator of a device that changed the picture radically – or if not the first creator, then the person who enabled the device to become widely available. For instance, the screw, a very old invention, was not used as a fastening device when it had to be cut by hand. The mechanical manufacture of the screw therefore earns it a mention (1569).

The explosion of invention, industry and technology in the last two centuries has been so overwhelming that it is uncontainable. For that reason the list stops at 1800.

c2.5 million years ago *Homo habilis*, precursor of modern man, uses simple stone tools, flakes of rock with little retouching. These tools are called the Oldowan toolkit after the Olduvai Gorge in Tanzania where the evidence was found.

c45,000 years ago Humans in Eurasia wear beads, bracelets and pendants. Stone blades are now bi-faced. Evidence of kilns for ceramic production.

c20,000 years ago Bone and antler needles used by people in what is now France and Spain, wood and stone tools, cats domesticated.

*c*15,000 years ago Early humans of the Magdalenian culture produce engravings on slate. Lascaux caves painted by early artists capable of symbolic thought. Dogs domesticated.

*c*4500 BCE The Egyptians smelt copper ore. Early agriculturalists grow maize, corn and rice.

*c*4000 BCE The ard, an early plough, used in Mesopotamia.

*c*3500 BCE The llama and alpaca are domesticated in Peru. Bronze made for first time. Hunters use bow and arrow as well as spears. Evidence of wine. Numbering systems and counting tokens found in the Middle East.

*c*3000 BCE Sumerians use clay tablets for writing.

*c*2500 BCE Sailing ships, silk in China, elephants domesticated in India, cotton grown, pins made of iron. Metal mirrors found in Egypt.

*c*1200 BC Ducts beneath the palace of King Arzawa in Anatolia (Turkey) suggest under-floor central heating. This was not rediscovered until 1,000 years later by the Romans.

*c*800 BC An Assyrian invents the pulley. Oars with rowlocks are used in boats. Querns (grinding stones), are turned with a crank allowing for continuous movement. The rotary potter's wheel is invented.

*c*600 BC Full scale written languages with signs for the consonants are spread by the Phoenicians and adapted by the Greeks and Etruscans. The Etruscan alphabet was taken up in modified form by the Romans and eventually became the dominant alphabet of Europe. Anaximander of Miletus invents the first sundial.

c 460 BC Hippocrates notices that a man in a lead mine develops stomach cramps, and puts medicine on an observational basis. Spartans invent locks.

c 350 BC Alexander the Great's military engineers devise the siege catapult for throwing large rocks.

c 250 BC Archimedes demonstrates the raising of water by means of a screw and formalises the principles of leverage.

c 200 BC Hipparchus, or possibly Apollonius of Perga, invents the astrolabe used for determining the elevation of the sun or other star above the horizon. An unknown engineer uses gears for the first time on an ox-powered water-wheel. Chinese develop a malleable form of cast iron. Concrete used by the Romans to build Palestina.

c150 BC The Chinese invent paper – though at first it is used for packing rather than writing.

c110 BC A Chinese farmer devises the collar harness for horses, the most efficient harness of its day and not used in the West until the Middle Ages.

c100 BC Some Dane makes roller bearings from wood and bronze to put on a cart – a proper wheel for transport at last.

Year 0 Vitruvius writes a book describing Roman architecture and technology and also discusses astronomy, acoustics and sundials. Gearing is used to reduce the speed of undershot water-wheels, a huge improvement in grain grinding. Roman engineers build roads, viaducts and aqueducts.

c30 Tu Shih invents the water-powered bellows for working cast iron.

c60 Hero of Alexandria invents the reaction turbine, a rotating steam-powered toy (the aeolipile) but there is no idea of putting it to practical use.

c70 According to Pliny the Elder the wine press was invented by the Greeks sometime in the previous century.

c80 Lou-en Heng demonstates an early form of the magnetic compass.

c100 Military engineers improve the catapult with torsion propulsion using a single arm. The Onager is named after a viciously kicking ass. The technology of killing each other has been under continuing and unrelenting improvement since the dawn of man.

c200 The Chinese develop porcelain.

c400 Hypatia improves the astrolabe and invents the hygrometer for measuring specific gravity.

c480 A Chinese or possibly Korean horseman invents the foot stirrup for mounting horses and stability.

c720 I-Xing, a Buddhist monk, and Lyang Lingdzan, a Chinese engineer, make the first proper clockwork with an escapement mechanism for use in astronomy.

c950 Gilbert of Aurillac, who become pope in 999, improves the escapement by the use of an oscillating, horizontal arm that controls the speed of a gear.

1035 A print shows a spinning wheel in use in China.

1044 Ceng Gong-Liang, Chinese, publishes no fewer than three recipes for gunpowder.

1105 The papal bull mentions windmills for the first time. The Abbot of Savigny is granted a concession to build windmills in the dioceses of Bayeux, Coutances, and Evreux. Military engineers devise the gravity-powered catapult using a long lever and a heavy counterweight. It is more reliable than torsion power that can be affected by humidity.

1180 Unknown Spaniards take up the art of paper-making from Morocco. Ibn al-Razzas publishes an influential treatise on the art of making ingenious machines.

1221 The Chinese make a gunpowder bomb that produces shrapnel, though the word is not used until late C18. A Frenchman, Jean de Garlande, lists several machines for making textiles.

1247 An unknown armourer deploys some type of firearm in the siege of Seville.

1272 Borghesano of Bologna invents a machine for spinning thread from silk. Remarkably, this remains a trade secret until 1538.

1286 Allesandro del Spina makes use of the invention of a friend, Salvino degli Armati, to make eyeglasses with convex lenses to correct near-sightedness.

1288 The Chinese manufacture a small cannon.

c1310 Iron masters discover how to draw wire by using a worker on a water-powered swing; At the peak of each swing the worker grabs the wire with tongs; during the backward swing the wire is drawn through a small hole in a plate, thinning it.

1370 Dutchmen construct the first canal lock at Vreeswijk. The arbalest, a steel crossbow tensioned with a crank or windlass and pulley, is invented. It fires a bolt that can penetrate armour. Some believe it to be a weapon that will end war.

1390 The Koreans demonstrate first use of metal type, but printing does not take off in Europe until Johann Gutenberg (c1396–1468) in Mainz, Germany, fifty years later.

1420 An unknown carpenter invents the brace and bit for drilling holes. First flintlock pistols in use.

1436 Venetian shipwrights introduce interchangeable parts for ships and build galleys on an assembly line. First representations of a drive belt being used to turn a grindstone.

1459 An unknown artisan invents a four-wheel passenger vehicle in Kocs, Hungary (hence the English 'coach') with strap suspension. Its design, with constant refinements, spreads across Europe.

1470 Louis XI orders the construction of the Mount Viso tunnel connecting the Dauphiné and the domain of Marquis de Saluces – the first civil engineering project of modern times.

1480 Leonardo da Vinci (1452–1519) describes – among other astonishing inventions – the first workable parachute. His design for a flying machine follows in 1492 and for mitre canal locks that can be folded back into recesses in the walls in 1497.

1530 The spinning wheel in general use in Europe is improved by Johann Jürgen who adds a twisting motion to the thread. Ralph Hog of Buxted, England, succeeds in making cannons out of cast iron.

1569 Jacques Besson in his *Theatre of Instruments and Machines*, largely based on the work of Francesco di Giorgio, describes many mechanisms of which the most important is his own design for a wood-turning lathe and a workable screw-cutting machine. Screws had been around since c300 BCE, but had been little used as they had to be made by hand.

1579 An unknown artificer invents the ribbon loom that can weave several pieces of narrow fabric at the same time.

1582 Dutchman Peter Morice installs a water turbine in London. It powers a pump that supplies the city with water from the Thames.

1589 The Reverend William Lee (15??–1610), an English clergyman, invents the first knitting machine and probably also the spring-beard needle, one of the two main types of knitting needle.

1590 Zacharias Janssen (1580–c1609), a Dutchman, invents the first compound microscope. Galileo develops the thermoscope, a primitive and rather inaccurate thermometer.

1608 Hans Lippershey (c1570–1619), a Dutchman, invents the telescope.

c1615 John Napier (1550–1617), a Scottish landowner, is credited with discovering logarithms and inventing Napier's Bones, an early form of calculator.

1620 Francis Bacon (1561–1626), English philosopher and Lord Chancellor to James I, devises a code that with two letters and five symbols can represent all the alphabet. He rejected *a priori* reasoning in favour of inductive inference, but his attempt to preserve a chicken by stuffing it with snow leads to his death from a chill. The ghost of the chicken is still said to haunt Highgate Hill in North London.

1621 Lord Dudley obtains a patent for making iron using coal rather than charcoal. The method is invented by his illegitimate son, Dud Dudley (*b* Worcestershire, England, 1599).

1631 Pierre Vernier (1580–1638), a Frenchman, invents a device, still in use today, for precise measurement. William Gascoigne (*b* Middleton, England) invents the micrometer which he places in the focus of a telescope to measure the angular distance between stars. In Newcastle, England, wooden rails for carts carrying coal are used for the first time.

1640s Blaise Pascal (1623–62), French, develops a mechanical calculator that can add and subtract. Evangelista Torricelli (1608–47) invents a barometer using mercury in a glass column sealed at the top. Otto von Guericke (1602–86), a German of Magdeburg, perfects an air pump and in his famous demonstrations shows that teams of horses are unable to pull apart a pair of evacuated hemispheres held together by atmospheric pressure. In 1660 he is the first to use a barometer to forecast the weather.

1662 Blaise Pascal proposes the introduction of a public transport system in Paris with fixed coach routes and low fares.

1664 Gaspar Schott, about whom little is known, invents a universal coupling.

1670 The great Dutch clockmaker, Christiaan Huygens, proposes a motor driven by explosions of gunpowder.

1673 Gottfried von Leibniz (1646–1716), the German philosopher and mathematician who independently (of Newton) discovered calculus, invents a machine that can multiply and divide as well as add and subtract. In 1694 his improved machine, based on the 'Stepped Reckoner', can store multiplicands and prefigures binary notation.

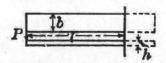

1682 Isaac Newton publishes *Principia Mathematica* establishing the three laws of motion and the law of universal gravitation. Although he is not credited with any technological device, this hugely influential book becomes the basis of theoretical mechanics and our understanding of the universe for over two hundred years.

1696 Thomas Savery patents 'the miner's friend', a steam engine for pumping water out of mines. Over the next century the steam engine will be improved by British engineers such as Thomas Newcomen, William Brown, James Watt, Matthew Boulton and Richard Trevithick. In 1801 Trevithick builds a full-scale steam-powered carriage which runs well for four days until he accidentally allows all the water in the boiler to evaporate and it burns out.

1701 Jethro Tull (1674–1741), English, invents the seed drill for planting seeds in rows.

1709 Gabriel Daniel Fahrenheit (*b* Poland 1686 – *d* Holland 1736) invents the sealed-tube alcohol thermometer, and the Fahrenheit scale whereon water freezes at 32° and boils at 212°.

1714 Dominique Anel (1679–1730), French, invents the fine-point syringe. Lady Mary Wortley Montagu (1689–1762) brings back from Turkey the practice of inoculating children against smallpox. Unfortunately this does not become standard practice until rediscovered by Edward Jenner (1749–1832), British physician, in 1796.

1716 Edmond Halley (1656 –1742) develops a diving bell with a system for refreshing the air.

1722 René Antoine Ferchault de Réaumur (1683–1757) discovers the role of carbon in the hardness of steel. Previously he has presented the French Academy of Sciences with a material woven out of glass fibre. His thermometer (1731) uses the Réaumur scale, whereon water boils at 80°R.

1725 Basile Bouchon, French, develops a semi-automatic loom. This is improved in 1728 by Jacques de Falcon whose loom is controlled by perforated cards fed into the machine manually.

1727 Johann H Schulze discovers that silver salts turn black when exposed to light. This was crucial for photography, an idea that waited to be developed until the work of William Henry Fox Talbot (1835) and Louis-Jacques Mandé Daguerre (1838).

1731 The Englishman John Hadley and American Thomas Godfrey independently invent the sextant for measuring the angle of the sun above the horizon. The use of a reflective surface for sighting the sun puts an end to old salts destroying their eyes and hence wearing eye-patches.

1733 John Kay (1704–64), an Englishman, invents the flying shuttle loom.

1735 Abraham Darby II (1711–63), English, introduces the use of coke in the manufacture of cast iron.

1739 Jacques Vaucanson, a French artificer who makes automata, appointed to improve the French silk industry. He not only suggests new working methods, but improves the automatic weaving machines and eliminates the need for a worker to feed in perforated cards. His machine is a precursor of Jacquard's automatic loom and leads to one of the first conflicts of the industrial revolution when silk workers go on strike in Lyons in 1744.

1742 English mathematician, Benjamin Robins (1707–51), puts ballistics on a scientific basis with his treatise, *New Principles of Gunnery*.

1746 Peter van Musschenbroek, Dutch, and Ewald Georg von Kleist, German, at about the same time discover how to store static electricity in a Leiden jar.

1748 John Wilkinson (1728–1808) in Bilston, England, develops a much more efficient blast furnace in his ironworks. John Canton (*b* Stroud, England 1718–1772) invents a method for making artificial magnets.

1754 An unknown English engineer designs the first iron-rolling mill in Fareham, England.

1758 Jedediah Strutt (*b* Derbyshire, England 1726–1797) invents the ribbing machine for making stockings.

1759 John Smeaton reintroduces underwater mortar in building the Eddystone lighthouse. It was first used by the Romans who found volcanic ash (pozzolana) the key ingredient.

1763 Joseph Oxley patents a method for getting rotary motion from a reciprocating steam engine. It is not very efficient, but an important principle, which will fool James Watt into thinking that he needs to patent alternative methods (1784).

1764 James Hargreaves (1720–1778), English, introduces the spinning jenny for making eight threads at once (later models handled 120). This is regarded by some as the true start of the Industrial Revolution.

1769 Richard Arkwright (*b* Preston, England 1732–1792) invents the water frame for spinning, so called because it was driven by water power. It works well, but is too expensive and complex for small-scale use and its invention heralds the introduction of large, centralised factories.

1771 Pierre Woulfe learns how to make picric acid. It's used as a yellow dye until a century later someone realises that it is also a high explosive.

1774 John Wilkinson's precision boring machine improves the manufacture of cylinders for steam engines and, of course, artillery.

1775 David Bushnell (1742–1824), American, invents the *American Turtle*, a one-man submarine using propeller power for horizontal and vertical movement. Two years later, he invents the torpedo.

1781 The Marquis de Jouffroy (1751–1832) tests the first steam-powered paddle boat on the Saône River.

1783 The Montgolfier Brothers (French), Joseph Michel (1740–1810) and Jacques Étienne (1745–99), demonstrate the hot-air balloon at Annonay, France.

1784 Joseph Bramah (1748–1814), English, invents a new lock and offers a prize of 200 guineas to anyone who can pick it. Ten years later he invents the hydraulic press multiplying force by changing the diameter of the cylinders. The lock-picking prize was not claimed until 1851 when A C Hobbs, an American locksmith, did it in 51 hours.

1787 James Watt invents the centrifugal governor for controlling steam engines. It makes them safer, and is an early and vital use of the principle of feedback.

1790 John Greenwood, an American, invents the dental drill; he had been George Washington's dentist. In Paris the Compte de Sivrac invents the *célerifère*, an improved adult version of the C18 toy, the hobby-horse. It is the precursor of the bicycle.

1793 Eli Whitney (1765 –1825), American, invents the cotton gin.

1797 Henry Maudslay (1771–1831), English, transforms machine tool manufacture by inventing the slide rest for lathes so that the operator does not have to hold the metal-cutting tool in his hands. In 1800 he perfects a lathe that enables the operator to make screws of any desired length and pitch. The modern industrial age is born.

Scientific eponyms

ampere or **amp** basic unit of electric current, named after the French physicist André Marie Ampère (1775–1836).

angstrom unit of length (now non-preferred) equal to 10^{-10} metres, used in measuring the wavelengths of electromagnetic radiations. It was named after the Swede Anders Jonas Ångström (1814–74), physicist, astronomer, and founder of the science of spectroscopy, through which the discovery was made of hydrogen in the sun.

Beaufort scale a means of finding out the speed of the wind, on a scale of nought to twelve, or calm through to hurricane force. Its inventor was the surveyor Sir Francis Beaufort (1774–1857), subsequently the Royal Navy's official hydrographer.

becquerel basic unit of radiation activity, named after the French discoverer of radioactivity, the physicist Antoine-Henri Becquerel (1852–1908).

Celsius scale for measuring temperature, where 0° is the freezing point and 100° the boiling point of water. The scale was named after a Swedish astronomer, Anders Celsius (1704–44) who was supposed to have invented it in 1742, but his scale in fact had 0° as the boiling point and 100° as the freezing point of water, and was 'inverted' by his colleague J P Christen (1683–1755) in 1743. The scale was known alternatively (and especially in English) as the centigrade scale, a term which was officially abandoned in 1948. Ambiguously, C is C whether it stand for Centigrade of Celsius.

curie unit of radiation measurement, named after the French chemist and physicist Marie Curie (1867–1934). It has since been replaced by the becquerel, which registers information in much smaller units.

Fahrenheit temperature scale, now replaced by the Celsius system, in which the freezing point of water is 32° and its boiling point is represented by 212°. Its inventor was the German scientist Gabriel Daniel Fahrenheit (1686–1736) who, by mixing salt and ice, registered 0 degrees as the lowest temperature he could achieve. He arbitrarily chose 32° as the freezing point of water, and 96° as the temperature of the human body (later determined as 98.4°). The fact that water boils at 212° was governed by the foregoing; not by choice.

faraday one of two units of measurement named after the English chemist and physicist Michael Faraday (1791–1867), whose work produced a range of outstanding discoveries. In electrolysis, a faraday registers the quantity of electricity being used; a farad is a unit of capacitance.

galvanise the term originally used to describe covering an iron or steel surface with a protective layer of zinc. It commemorates Luigi Galvani (1737–98), an Italian physician, as does the word 'galvanometer', *ie* an instrument for measuring small currents of electricity. It was Galvani who accidentally discovered the principle of current electricity when experimenting with frogs' legs towards the end of C18.

gauss in the centimetre-gram-second system of measurement, this is the unit of magnetic flux density. It is named after (Johann) Karl Friedrich Gauss (1777–1855), the German mathematician, astronomer and physicist credited with notable work on probability theory and number theory.

Geiger counter an instrument used to measure radiation; the joint work of the German scientists Hans Geiger (1882–1945) and Walter M Muller.

gilbert the unit of magnetomotive force employed in the centimetre-gram-second system of measurement. It is named after Queen Elizabeth I's physician, the physicist William Gilbert (1544–1603), sometimes described as the 'Father of Electricity' and author of the ground-breaking *De Magnete*.

henry the derived metric unit of electric inductance, named after Joseph Henry (1797–1878), the American physicist who is nowadays regarded as the founder in his own country of weather forecasting using scientifically derived information.

hertz at one cycle per second, the unit of frequency; it commemorates the German physicist Heinrich Rudolph Hertz (1857–94), the first scientist to detect the existence (1876) of electromagnetic radiation predicted in 1873 by James Clerk Maxwell the Scottish physicist (1831–79).

joule the metric unit of energy, named in honour of the English physicist James Prescott Joule (1818–1889). The theory of the conservation of energy derives from his researches.

kelvin a unit of thermodynamic temperature, *ie* the reading is proportional to the energy contained in a given volume of gas, registered on a scale that gives absolute zero as 0 K and 273.16 K is the point at which water freezes. Its name honours the Scottish physicist William Thomson, Lord Kelvin (1824–1907), whose achievements include the compass in its modern form. See also **Rankine**.

lambert in the centimetre-gram-second system of measurement, this is the unit of illumination. It is named after the German scientist Johann Heinrich Lambert (1728–77), whose fields of investigation included astronomy, physics, mathematics and philosophy.

Mach number this represents the ratio of the speed of an object to the speed of sound in the same medium. It commemorates researches into airflow by Ernst Mach (1838–1916), the Austrian philosopher and physicist.

maxwell unit of magnetic flux in the centimetre-gram-second system of measurement; named after James Clerk Maxwell (1831–79), the Scots physicist.

Mobius strip a continuous one-sided surface comprising a strip of material that has been twisted through 180 degrees and joined at the ends. It was the discovery of the German mathematician August Ferdinand Möbius (1780–1868).

mho the unit of conductance, the reciprocal of the ohm, *qv*.

newton the metric unit of force. It is named after the British physicist Sir Isaac Newton (1642–1727), known especially for his research into calculus, the theory of light, and the laws governing motion.

oersted the unit of magnetic field strength according to the centimetre-gram-second system of measurement. It is named after the Danish physicist Hans Christian Oersted (1777–1851), founder of the science of electromagnetism.

ohm the unit of electrical resistance, named after the German physicist Georg Simon Ohm (1787–1854).

orrery a device illustrating the relative motions of the planets and other bodies around the sun. It was invented c1700 by the mathematician George Graham (1673–1751); after a copy was constructed by John Rowley, an instrument-maker, the device was named after Rowley's patron, Charles Boyle, fourth Earl of Orrery.

pasteurise process of heating food or drink to kill bacteria; named after the French chemist Louis Pasteur (1822–95), 'the father of modern bacteriology'.

Rankine W J M Rankine (1820–72) gave his name to the Fahrenheit equivalent of the Kelvin temperature scale: Absolute zero = 0; water freezes at 459.69. Today, this is seldom considered.

Réaumur scale system of temperature measurement, choosing the freezing point of water as 0°, and 80° as its boiling point. It was originated by the French scientist René Antoine Ferchault de Réaumur (1783–1857).

Richter scale registers the magnitude of earthquakes; devised in 1935 by the American seismologist Charles Richter (1900–1985) together with the German Bruno Gutenberg (1889–1960), in whose honour this system of measurement is alternatively known as the Gutenberg–Richter scale.

röntgen unit of dose of ionising radiation, named after Wilhelm Konrad Röntgen (1845–1923), the German physicist. It was Röntgen's discovery of X-rays that led to him being awarded the first Nobel prize for physics, in 1901.

rutherford a unit of radioactivity, named after the New Zealander Ernest Rutherford (1871–1937) 'the father of nuclear physics' whose most celebrated discovery, in 1911, was that of the atomic nucleus.

siemens the unit of electrical conductance, named after the German Ernst Werner von Siemens (1816–92), electrical engineer and pioneer in telegraphy. Together with his three brothers he founded the huge industrial empire that bears their name.

tesla the unit of magnetic flux density, named after the Croatian-born American inventor and electrician Nikola Tesla (1857–1943).

vernier an additional scale appended to another instrument to help take measurements that are smaller than those given on the main device. It was developed from the nonius, an invention of the Portuguese mathematician Pedro Nunez (1492–1577), and described in 1631 by Pierre Vernier (1580–1637), the French mathematician after whom it is named.

volt the unit of electric potential, named after the Italian physicist Count Alessandro Giuseppe Anastasio Volta (1745–1827), inventor (1800) of the first electric battery, then known as the voltaic pile.

watt the unit of power, named after the Scots engineer James Watt (1736–1819), noted above all for his work on the steam engine. He is also known for having devised the term horsepower.

Some eponymous wheels from the age of the horse

Brougham Henry Peter Brougham, Baron Brougham and Vaux (1778–1868) was the designer, c 1850, of this closed four-wheeled carriage. Both the vehicle and its creator are pronounced 'broom'. Despite its aristocratic origin, it was widely used as public transport; its popular successor was the hansom cab (see below). Lord Brougham himself described it as 'a garden chair on wheels'.

Hansom cab The English architect Joseph Aloysius Hansom (1803–82) made a bad bargain when, in 1834, he accepted no more than £300 for the patent of his 'Safety Cab'. The various forms of this light covered two-wheeler, driven from a high seat at the back, became immensely popular – Benjamin Disraeli described them as 'the gondolas of London' – and earned their manufacturers large sums.

Phaeton The horse-drawn equivalent of a sports car; no wonder, then, that this light open carriage was named after the charioteering sun god. It was a two-seater, with a body as shallow as a cockleshell and the large rear wheels and lofty suspension raising the driver and passenger high above most other traffic.

Tilbury Not a place, but the name of the inventor of this swift, open, two-wheeled carriage. It enjoyed great popularity throughout the first half of the nineteenth century.

Victoria This light, low four-wheeler was named after the then British monarch (1837–1901), and described by one owner as 'the prettiest carriage a lady can possibly drive in'. It was something of a well-to-do person's family runabout, with a collapsible hood, an elevated box for the driver, and seats for two or more passengers.

People

Famous families

In families noted for more than one gifted member, no rule of nature insists that they share a particular talent: one sibling may be a celebrated painter, the other an immortal poet. Some forms of achievement seem better than others at enabling collaboration within families. Hence, perhaps, the quantity of painters who've worked together in this way; also the relatively large number of theatrical families.

Amis, Kingsley (1922–95), and his son **Martin** (1949–), novelists.

Attenborough, David (1926–), broadcaster and naturalist, and his brother **Richard** (1923–), actor.

Bach, Johann Sebastian (1685–1750), and his sons **Carl Philippe Emanuel** (1714–88), **Johann Christian** (1735–82), **Johann Christian Friedrich** (1732–95), and **Wilhelm Friedemann** (1710–84), composers. From the C16 to C18, more than fifty of J S Bach's relatives were musicians.

Bellini, Jacopo (c1400–1470/1), and his sons **Gentile** (c1429–1507) and **Giovanni** (c1430–1516), painters.

Bragg, Sir William Henry (1862–1942) and his son **Sir (William) Lawrence** (1890–1971), both physicists and Nobel Prizewinners.

Brueghel, Pieter I (c1525/30–69) ('Peasant' Brueghel), and his son **Pieter II** (c1564–1638) ('Hell' Brueghel), painters.

Brontë, Anne (1820–49), and her sisters **Charlotte** (1816–55) and **Emily** (1818–48), poets and novelists; early in their careers they used the pseudonyms Acton, Currer and Ellis Bell.

Carracci, Ludovico (1555–1619), painter; cousin of **Agostino** (1557–1602), engraver and **Annibale**.

Darwin, Erasmus (1731–1802), physician and natural scientist, and his grandson **Charles** (1809–82), discoverer of natural selection.

Day-Lewis, Cecil (1904–72), poet, and his son **Daniel** (1958–), actor.

Fonda, Henry (1905–82), his children **Jane** (1937–) and **Peter** (1939–), and grand-daughter **Bridget** (1964–), actors.

Freud, Sigmund (1856–1939), founder of psychoanalysis, his daughter Anna (1895–1982), psychologist, and grandson Lucian (1922–), painter.

Gabo, Naum (1890–1977), and his brother Antoine Pevsner (see below), painters.

Haldane, James Alexander (1768–1851), minister; his brother Robert (1764–1842), preacher; Robert's great-nephews Richard Burdon (1856–1928), Liberal party statesman; and John Scott (1860–1936), physiologist; and John Scott's son John Burdon Sanderson (1892–1964), biologist; and daughter Naomi Margaret (1897–1999), whose writings were published under her married name of Mitchison.

Holbein, Hans the Elder (c1465–1524), and his son Hans the Younger (1497/8–1543), painters.

Huxley, Thomas Henry (1825–95), biologist, and his grandsons Sir Andrew Fielding (1917–), physiologist and Nobel Prizewinner; Aldous Leonard (1894–1963), novelist; and Sir Julian Sorell (1887–1975) biologist and humanist.

James, Henry (1843–1916), novelist, and his brother William (1842–1910), philosopher and psychologist.

John, Augustus (1878–1961), and his sister Gwen (1876–1939), painters.

Kean, Edmund (1789–1833), and his son Charles (1809/11–1868), actors.

Kemble, Roger (1721–1802), theatrical manager; his sons Charles (1775–1854), John Philip (1757–1823) and Stephen (1758–1822), actors; and Charles' children Adelaide (1816–79), opera singer; Frances ('Fanny') (1809–93), actor; and John Mitchell (1807–57), Anglo–Saxon scholar.

Knox, Edmund George Valpy, pen-name 'Evoe' (1881–1971), humorist – and his brothers Alfred Dillwyn (1883–1943), codebreaker; Wilfred Lawrence (1886–1950) and Ronald Arbuthnott (1888–1957), theologians.

Limbourg, Pol, and his brothers Hennequin and Herman de (all dead by 1416, maybe aged about thirty); painters.

Lutyens, Edwin (1869–1944), architect, and his daughter Elizabeth (1906–83), composer.

Marx, Leonard (Chico) (1886–1961), and his brothers Adolph (Harpo) (1888–1964) and Julius (Groucho) (1890–1977), film comedians. Two other siblings originally included in their act were Milton (Gummo) (1897–1977) and Herbert (Zeppo) (1901–79).

Pevsner, Antoine (1886–1962), painter; brother of Naum Gabo.

Pisano, Andrea (c1220/5?–84), and his son Giovanni (c1245/50–after 1314), sculptors.

Redgrave, Michael (1908–85), his children Corin (1939–), Lynn (1943–) and Vanessa (1937–), and Vanessa's daughters Natasha and Joely Richardson (1963 and 1965), actors.

Renoir, Pierre Auguste (1844–1919), painter, and his son Jean (1894–1979), film and stage director.

Rossetti, Christina (1830–94), poet, and her brother Dante Gabriel (1828–82), painter and poet.

Scarlatti, Alessandro (1659–1725) and his son (Giuseppe) Domenico (1685–1757), composers.

Sitwell, Edith (1887–1965), poet, and her brothers Osbert (1892–1969), poet, novelist and autobiographer, and Sacheverell (1897–1988), poet.

Tiepolo, Giovanni Battista (1696–1770), and his sons Giovanni Domenico (1727–1804) and Lorenzo (1736–76), painters.

Trevelyan, Charles Edward (1807–86), administrator; his son George Otto (1838–1928), statesman; and George's sons Charles Philips (1870–1953), politician, George Macaulay (1876–1962), historian, and Robert Calverley (1872–1951), poet and playwright.

Trollope, Frances (1780–1863), and her son Anthony (1815–82), novelists.

Utrillo, Maurice (1883–1955), son of Suzanne Valadon (see below); painter.

Valadon, Suzanne (1865–1938), painter; mother of Maurice Utrillo.

Wilde, Jane Francisca Speranza (1829–96), poet, and her son Oscar Fingall O'Flahertie Wills (1854–1900), poet and playwright.

Yeats, Jack (1871–1957), painter, and his brother William Butler (1865–1939), poet.

Know your Mitfords ...

The seven children of Lord and Lady Redesdale – six daughters and a son – were raised in isolation on the family estates in the country. Thrown back upon their own resources, they invented private languages and in-jokes. In their very individual ways they were all rather eccentric and interesting, though not invariably likeable.

Nancy Freeman (1904–73) was the writer, author of such minor classics as *The Pursuit of Love* and *Love in a Cold Climate* which are witty and gently satirical. They were best-sellers in the immediately post-war period.

Pamela (1907–64) was the least rebellious of the sisters. She loved the country and was nicknamed 'woo' or 'the woman' by her siblings on the grounds that she was a bit boring. Nevertheless she looked after her sister Diana's children when Diana was in jail.

Tom (1909–45) loved music and became a lawyer. He was killed in Burma at the end of WW2.

Diana (1910–2003), the beauty, married Bryan Guinness, heir to the brewery fortune, and then caused a scandal by divorcing him and marrying Sir Oswald Mosley (1896–1980), leader of the British Union of Fascists. Both were imprisoned for treachery in WW2. Diana died in Paris at the age of 93, still an unrepentant fascist.

Unity Valkyrie (1914–48) tormented the family governesses; as a debutante she was known to take her pet rat to dances. Boisterous and prone to pranks, she met Hitler in the 30s and admired him hugely. However, when war came she was mortified and tried to shoot herself, remaining a semi-invalid until her death. It is noteworthy that Hitler assisted in her repatriation in 1940.

Jessica Lucy (1917–96) was a passionate communist who yearned to escape her upbringing. She met Edmond Romilly, Churchill's 'red' nephew, and they eloped to Spain together to fight the fascists. When he was killed in WW2, she was heartbroken and emigrated to the USA where she eventually remarried Robert Edward Treuhaft. Her darkly funny satire of the funeral industry, *The American Way of Death*, was justly famous.

Deborah Vivian (1920–) 'Debo' was hugely sentimental, and Nancy could make her cry by telling her poignant and soppy stories. Debo – or the Duchess – married the younger son of the Duke of Devonshire. When he inherited the title, they moved to Chatsworth where Deborah's mission became the restoration of that enormous house and estate.

Some famous mistresses

In the last century or so the mistress business has taken quite a knock. A C19 mistress might be a girl with adequate looks but no other aids to survival, kept in secret in some suburban villa. Alternatively, she might be a creature of sublime panache who, on Sunday afternoons, would parade around Hyde Park in her own carriage, with horses chosen to match her elaborate hair. Decades of sexual revolution have made both these species of womankind extinct. The parading *poule de luxe* has also been seen off by the fact that cruising in any kind of motor is no substitute for two matching pairs of dappled greys; for one thing, the more covetable the car, the worse your own chance of being upstaged.

This leaves small scope for potential disgrace, which is one indispensable essence of being a mistress. Nowadays it's down to more or less winsome purveyors of constitutional crisis or votes of no confidence to keep the flag of scandal flying; even the word 'mistress' is itself out of use. Through former ages, though, the term signified all sorts of liaison, carried on for every kind of reason.

Cleopatra (69–30 BCE), queen of Egypt, is represented in statuary and on coins as having the traditional profile of a witch, all nose and chin. Written comments, presumably disinterested, describe her nonetheless as physical perfection. Whatever the full range of motive for her choice of lovers, the fact that these tended to be a ruler of the known world does suggest a colonial politician making the best of things. Julius Caesar and Mark Anthony obliged by being her lovers; but Augustus passed, so ensuring her suicide.

Agrippina, mother of the tyrannical Roman emperor Nero (ruled 54–68 CE), had a dismal influence on her son, not least as his lover. Weary of being dominated by her, he at length arranged to have her murdered, though without initial success. One account of an attempt on her life recounts how Nero arranged for his mother to put to sea in a collapsible boat. When this vessel duly sank, Agrippina's maid put in a bid for survival by calling to nearby fishermen that she herself was the empress; they promptly killed her. Agrippina meanwhile kept quiet and swam to shore. Allegedly when she was at length assassinated, she instructed her killers to stab her first in the belly, as a punishment for bearing such a son.

Rosamond Clifford – 'Fair Rosamond' – was the mistress of the able and unprincipled Norman king Henry II (1133–89). Legend, dating from C14, claims that her death, in about 1176, was a murder brought about by Henry's queen, Eleanor of Aquitaine.

Mary Boleyn, like her sister Anne, was one of the several mistresses of Henry VIII of England (1509–47). Her fate, in being spared from marriage with the king, was less harsh than Anne's. Whereas Mary's sister achieved the ultimate distinction of being crowned queen, in a ceremony of great splendour, as the king's wife she paid for the loss of her husband's affections by being beheaded. As a mere mistress, Mary survived.

Shakespeare's **Dark Lady** has provoked a library's-worth of guesswork as to her identity. His sonnets, written between 1593 and 1600, whiff of sardonic enslavement in some of the verses written to or about her: 'My mistress' eyes are nothing like the sun.' Many scholars now identify her as Emilia Bassano, the strikingly beautiful wife of Alphonse Lanier, a court musician. Other candidates are the Countess of Pembroke, the brilliant sister of Sir Philip Sydney, or Luce Morgan, a local black prostitute.

Barbara Villiers, Duchess of Cleveland (1640–1709), bred four dukes – of Cleveland, Grafton and Northumberland – each fathered by Charles II: it cannot be said that as a lover the king was ungrateful. Barbara Villiers was famously shrewish and extravagant; her affairs too were notorious, featuring, among others, the future Duke of Marlborough and a professional strongman.

Louise de Keroualle, Duchess of Portsmouth (1649–1734), was likewise attracted to the plunder to be had as a mistress of Charles II; her possessions at his death included many fitments and furnishings of extraordinary splendour. As Duke of Richmond, Charles' son by the Breton-born and convent-bred 'Madame Carwell' was one of four illegitimate royal offspring whose descendants still hold a dukedom. Charles cannot be said to have had more mistresses than many other powerful men; they were merely better rewarded than most.

Nell Gwynne (*c*1650–87), having been born poor, survived a dodgy career selling oranges before going on to be an actress specialising in comedy and cross-dressing. By Charles II she had a son who became Duke of St Albans. Whatever may have moved some of her rivals to become the king's mistress, Nell was genuinely fond of Charles; after his death she rejected one would-be replacement, saying: 'Shall the dog lie where the deer once couched?'

The Elephant and the **Maypole** were the unkind names given by the public to two of the mistresses of George I. When he arrived in Britain from Hanover in 1714 to accept the crown, he was already equipped with one tall, thin mistress, Ehrengard Melusina von Schulenberg (the Maypole) and one short, fat one, Charlotte Sophia Kielmansegge (the Elephant). Not inhibited by being thought hypocritical, George I imprisoned his wife for adultery.

Madame de Pompadour, born Jeanne Antoinette Poisson (1721–64), was unusual among royal mistresses. Her role – though not with much success – extended far beyond any grandiose domestic life, into every part of French government policy during her years as mistress of Louis XV. In this semi-official position she kept the king's loyalty for life, partly by helping him avoid any official business. As a patron of the arts her legacy includes the royal ceramic factory at Sèvres and many portraits unparalleled in their power to suggest her as a creature of wit, fashion and unrepentant luxury.

Harriette Howard, Countess of Suffolk, was mistress to George II. Her first husband was separated from her and then died, but she kept the title. Her second husband also died. She was described as a reasonable and witty woman with a cultivated eye as a patron of the arts. George II helped her buy the land near the Thames on which she built Marble Hill House, a house both elegant and intimate.

Mrs Fitzherbert (1756–1837), born Maria Anne Smythe, was a young Catholic widow, one of several women to bring confusion to the public life of a Prince of Wales, in her case the subsequent George IV, whom she married in secret in 1785. In Britain at this time Roman Catholics still suffered from limited rights in law; moreover the marriage had taken place without the consent of the king, George III, whose relations with his eldest son were notoriously uneven. The union was declared invalid, resumed, and broken off again, in response to crises including Prince George's disastrous arranged marriage to the ill-chosen Caroline of Brunswick.

Emma, Lady Hamilton (c1765–1815), was the orphaned daughter of a blacksmith from Cheshire; while still in her teens she was rescued from a life of domestic service and sexual exploitation by the art connoisseur

Charles Greville, who made her his mistress and sought to give her an education. In this way she met the society painter George Romney, who immortalised her in dozens of portraits making the most of her grace, beauty and expressiveness: one admirer once told her: 'God Almighty must have been in a glorious mood when he made you!'

To meet his debts, however, Greville conveyed Emma into the keeping of his uncle, the diplomat and vulcanologist Sir William Hamilton, on the understanding that she would become Sir William's mistress. Emma was furious, and held out against Sir William until he agreed to marry her.

Perhaps the most celebrated phase of Emma's life was as the mistress of Horatio Nelson (1758–1805), to whom she bore a daughter in 1801. After Nelson's death her spendthrift existence dwindled into poverty, obesity and exile to Calais in flight from her creditors.

Harriette Wilson (1786–1855) enjoyed a career as one of C19 London's most successful courtesans; a fact she sought to exploit in middle age with the publication of her scandalous *Memoirs*. This was brought out in instalments, following much advance publicity and clearly aimed at blackmailing several of her prominent former clients, who included – when she was fifteen – the Earl of Craven; also the Marquis of Worcester, the Duke of Argyll, and the Duke of Wellington. It may be that the response was not as profitable as she had hoped: several ex-lovers shared the sentiment of the Iron Duke, who famously told her, so the story goes, 'Publish and be damned!'

Skittles is Victorian slang for a prostitute, but as a proper name it refers to the legendary courtesan Catherine Walters. She and her contemporaries such as Mabel Gray and Cora Pearl used to go riding in Rotten Row, Hyde Park, in their most fetchingly tight riding gear. Skittles was fearless and is said to have jumped her horse over Hyde Park railings. The young aristocrats also out riding were attracted by what was on offer; the Marquis of Hartington fell so completely for Skittles that he wanted to marry her, but his family sent him off to inspect the American Civil War instead.

Alice Keppel became the mistress of the Edward VII in 1898 when he was still the Prince of Wales; she shared his favours with Agnes Keyser, the daughter of an eminent stockbroker. Alice was the daughter of a retired Scottish admiral and MP and also the great-grandmother of Camilla Parker-Bowles.

Mrs Simpson is the name by which many people hostile to her role in the history of the British monarchy still refer to the Duchess of Windsor, wife of the former King Edward VIII. Bessie Wallis Warfield was born an American citizen in 1896; by the time of her marriage to Edward, in 1937, he had abdicated after less than a year as king. Their affair had been kept secret from the British public by a convincing press; nonetheless the intended marriage met with general disapproval. Edward had declared his determination to marry Wallis Simpson even though she was ineligible to be queen, mainly on account of her status as a divorcee. After his abdication he was made Duke of Windsor, and the couple lived the balance of their lives effectively in exile.

Christine Keeler unwillingly did more than most demi-mondaines of her time – more specifically 1963 – to sell newspapers hell-bent on muckraking. As a teenager with one foot in her own world of poverty and another at the junction of bohemianism and senior government, she inadvertently panicked the corridors of power and destroyed the career of the then War Minister, John Profumo. An adulterous affair featuring a Minister of the Crown wouldn't usually have such an effect; however, Keeler was not only bedding Profumo but also a Soviet naval attaché, Colonel Eugene Ivanov. From this, all sorts of threats, real or imaginary, could be derived. Keeler was hardly a mistress in any traditional sense and she was not looked after when the scandal finally died down.

Marilyn Monroe (1926–62) was the lovely blonde American actress, born Norma Jean Baker, who enchanted a generation of men with her husky voice and shimmering combination of sex appeal and wide-eyed surprise. She was married three times and bedded President John F Kennedy, and possibly also his brother, the Attorney General, Robert Kennedy. Conspiracy theories about her death (suicide or murder?) have sustained a library of books.

Monica Lewinsky was an unpaid intern in the White House during William Clinton's second term as president (1996–2000). She made the mistake of telling her experiences with Clinton to a 'friend', Linda Tripp, who made the maximum use of them to compromise Clinton. At first Clinton denied all, and men all over the world were thrilled to discover that the president of the United States seemed to think that oral sex did not count. The Lewinsky affair prompted allegations of a right-wing conspiracy bankrolled by Richard Mellon Scaife to remove Clinton. There was an investigation by an independent counsel (the Starr Report) that amounted to over 3,000 pages of prurience and cheesy detail. Despite the dirty-minded amusement this afforded other nations, the whole affair was damaging. The brightest US president for decades was distracted and put on the defensive.

Mrs Camilla Parker-Bowles (1947–) has been a life-long companion to the present Prince of Wales (1948–). They met in the early 70s and fell for each other. She was divorced from her army captain husband in 1995. Prince Charles was divorced from Lady Diana Spencer in 1996. Since then the relationship between the two has been in the public domain and has provided pundits the opportunity of speculating what Camilla's status will be when Charles inherits the throne.

Who's who in cockney rhyming slang?

Adam and Eve – believe. Always in full: 'Would you Adam and Eve it?!' to be uttered with cynical world-weariness when the tax man sends you an enormous demand just days after issuing a rebate. The answer is invariably 'Yes'. Still in common use.

The Artful Dodger – lodger. This is less used today as so few people have lodgers, though the practice has revived among the middle classes burdened with staggering mortgages resulting from the house price boom. The Artful Dodger was also the child thief working for Fagin in Charles Dickens's *Oliver Twist*.

Barnaby Rudge – the judge. Not in general use though the term is still heard in legal circles especially among defendants. Just the 'Barnaby' is favoured, presumably on the grounds that the Rudge would be too bleedin' obvious. Named for Charles Dickens's eponymous novel.

Brahms and Liszt – pissed (in British English sense of inebriated). These C19 composers even lent their names to a chain of now-vanished winebars. This expression is still in frequent use even though many Britons would struggle to spell Liszt accurately.

Bubble and Squeak – Greek. 'All yer Bubbles support the Gunners.' The London-based Greek Cypriots favour Arsenal Football club. Bubble and Squeak is a delicious left-over dish consisting mainly of potato and cabbage or other vegetable chopped up together and fried in fat hot enough to make it crispy.

China Plate – mate. 'Wotcher, me old china.' How are things, my old friend? Becoming unusual and often used in jest. Male friends were referred to as 'chinas'.

Cyril Lord – bald. "e's been completely cyril ever since I knowed 'im'. Cockney 'bald' rhymes with Lord, as it uses the untransliterable 'nasal w' sound for 'l'. Cyril Lord (1911–84) was a carpet manufacturer who specialised in bringing cheap, tufted, screen printed carpet to the masses '... Carpets you can afford from Cyril Lord'.

Fat and Wide – bride. 'Here comes the bride – short, fat and wide ...' as fits the oft-heard wedding march from Wagner's *Lohengrin*. This was a reference not to the unattractiveness of the bride, but her probable pregnancy. As the scholar, Gwyn Headley, points out this is not heard as often today because people get married because they want to, rather than feeling obliged by social convention.

George Raft – draft. Rare. 'Oi. Shut the winder, there's a helluva George in here.' Please close the window as it is draughty. The American actor, George Raft (1895–1980), was a star in the 1930s who specialised in playing immensely stylish gangsters.

Gregory Peck – cheque. 'Yer gregory's in the post.' (Eldred) Gregory Peck (1916–) was a good-looking American film actor who specialised in 'decent citizen' roles.

J Arthur Rank – bank (or other rhyming word). J(oseph) Arthur Rank, Baron (1888–1972), flour miller and film magnate, well known for the man with the big gong at the opening of his movies, of whom people are quick to point out that the gongmaster was the boxer Bombardier Billy Wells, and that he 'only got paid 50 quid for it'.

Joanna – a piano. This is not an eponym, but it makes sense if you remember that a Cockney Londoner would pronounce piano as 'pianner'. It is one of the few single-word examples of rhyming slang.

Rosie Lea – tea. Rosie Lea was a sultry fortune-teller of some fame, a tasseographer; one who often used wet tea leaves for divination. She lent her name to Britain's favourite hot drink. The term is still in use today – ' 'ere, fancy a cuppa rosie?' – but mainly among the older generation.

Ruby Murray – curry. A 'ruby' – the term is never used in full – is often the first dinner date offered to a girl in London, a city abounding in generally fine Indian restaurants. Ruby Murray (1935–96) was an Irish singer who had five records in the Top Twenty in 1955. Like much slang, it is used today by youngsters who have no idea who Ruby Murray was.

Sweeney Todd – the Flying Squad. The police are organised on a regional basis now and nearly all motorised, but there was a time when Scotland Yard ran an elite fast response team that drove to scenes of serious villainy in powerful cars. This was the famous Flying Squad that struck terror into the hearts of criminals. Sweeney Todd, the Demon Barber of Fleet Street, was a legend who started life as a Victorian 'Penny Dreadful' story and later became a musical. He was notorious for cutting customers' throats and tipping them into the basement with a special chair rigged over a trap-door.

Tea-Leaf – thief. A term in constant use, and always in full. 'Oi. That tea-leaf is taking a butcher's at your jam-jar!' Excuse me, a rather larcenous-looking individual is eyeing your automobile.

Tod Sloan – alone. 'Ullo, gorgeous, on yer tod?' You're an attractive woman, are you unaccompanied? Still in general currency, though few know its origins. Tod Sloan (1874–1933) was a jockey from Indiana who transformed horse-racing by riding with shortened stirrups. He was so often well in front of the rest of the field that Tod Sloan was 'always on his own'.

Trouble and Strife – wife. 'Sorry, me old mate. Gotta do a runner back to me Trouble or she'll have me bollocks off.' Apologies, old friend, I must return to my wife lest she be irritated by my absence. Headley remarks rather acerbically that this term is still in wide use as it so accurately reflects a common state of marital concord.

Twits, oafs, louts and lowlife

English has a huge vocabulary of insult that is constantly being renewed. Think of fairly recent terms of offence such as plonker, nerd, piss-artist, trailer-trash, couch-potato, wanker ... Here is just a sample of mainly historical and dialect words crying out for readmission to the modern lexicon.

Alcatote – a simpleton
Bawdstrot – a procuress
Beaunasty – a man who is dirty but elegantly dressed
Bezonian – a mean, low person
Borborymite – a user of filthy language

Caitiff – a base wretch
Chuff – a fat, coarse person
Clodpoll – a stupid person (also Clodpate)
Cockabaloo – a bullying, overbearing boss
Cudden – a born fool
Cuttle – a foul-mouthed defamer of others
Dandiprat – a prattling dandy; a worthless nothing.
Dogberry – an overly officious twit (from the constable in Shakespeare's
    Much Ado About Nothing)
Dotterel – a sucker
Drassock – a slovenly woman
Drumble – a lazy person
Dunderwhelp – both foolish and horrid
Franion – a man of loose morals
Fustilarian – a low scoundrel (from Shakespeare)
Gangrel – a dishonest vagrant
Gigg – a strumpet
Gormless – stupid and rather lacking in initiative
Gossoon – a large oaf (Irish)
Growtnoll – a blockhead
Gulchin – a young glutton
Hoddypeke – a cuckold
Jacksauce – a rude person
Jeeter – an ill-mannered slob
Kern – a peasant or bumpkin
Lickspittle – a sponge or parasite (also Lickspigot)
Lollard – a loafer (Dutch for mumble, originally a term of contempt for
    the followers of John Wyclif)
Looby – a hulking, indolent oaf
Losel – a sad, worthless person
Micher – a sneaky loiterer
Milksop – a weak or timid person
Mome – a blockhead
Moonling – a simpleton
Muckworm – a miser
Mullipuff – a twerp
Nipcheese – a cheapskate
Nobbler – a swindler
Nuthook – a sneak thief or burglar
Omadhaun – fool (Irish)
Pilgarlic – a self-pitying wretch

Ploot – a tart
Puckfist – a braggart
Quetcher – a constant talker; a bullshitter (from the Yiddish)
Rakehell – a debauched, drunken brawler
Rampallian – a sorry wretch (Shakespeare *Henry IV, Part II*)
Rumpot – a drunkard
Runnion – a paltry ne'er-do-well
Scelerat – a wicked person (French)
Scomm – a buffoon
Skellum – a villain
Smellsmock – a lecher
Taradiddler – a petty liar
Toady – a sycophant (originally Toadeater)
Troppop – a variant of trollop
Wheech – Scottish for nitwit
Xantippe – a shrewish woman (after Socrates's wife)